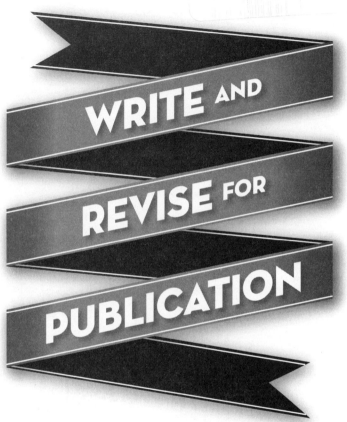

WRITE AND
REVISE FOR
PUBLICATION

WRITER'S DIGEST
BOOKS

WritersDigest.*com*
Cincinnati, Ohio

WRITE AND REVISE FOR PUBLICATION

A 6-MONTH PLAN FOR CRAFTING AN EXCEPTIONAL NOVEL AND OTHER WORKS OF FICTION

JACK SMITH

For more resources for writers, visit www.writersdigest.com.

17 16 15 14 13 5 4 3 2 1

Distributed in Canada by Fraser Direct
100 Armstrong Avenue
Georgetown, Ontario, Canada L7G 5S4
Tel: (905) 877-4411

Distributed in the U.K. and Europe by F&W Media International
Brunel House, Newton Abbot, Devon, TQ12 4PU, England
Tel: (+44) 1626-323200, Fax: (+44) 1626-323319
E-mail: postmaster@davidandcharles.co.uk

Distributed in Australia by Capricorn Link
P.O. Box 704, Windsor, NSW 2756 Australia
Tel: (02) 4577-3555

Edited by James Duncan
Cover designed by Claudean Wheeler
Interior designed by Bethany Rainbolt
Production coordinated by Debbie Thomas

DEDICATION

To my wife, Mary Jane Smith, and my four children: Penny, Nat, Nora, and David.

ACKNOWLEDGMENTS

Many thanks go to James Duncan, my editor at Writer's Digest Books, for great help on refining ideas in this book. And special thanks to my fellow writer and friend, Robert Garner McBrearty, for feedback at several stages of the process.

ABOUT THE AUTHOR

Jack Smith's novel *Hog to Hog* won the 2007 George Garrett Fiction Prize and was published by Texas Review Press in 2008. He has published stories in a number of literary magazines, including *Southern Review, North American Review, Texas Review, X-Connect, In Posse Review,* and *Night Train.* His reviews have appeared widely in such publications as *Ploughshares, Georgia Review, American Book Review, Prairie Schooner, Iowa Review, Mid-American Review, Pleiades, The Missouri Review,* and *Environment* magazine. He has contributed almost two dozen articles to *Novel & Short Story Writer's Market* and a dozen to *The Writer.* His coauthored nonfiction environmental book entitled *Killing Me Softly* was published by Monthly Review Press in 2002. Besides his writing, Smith coedits the *Green Hills Literary Lantern,* an online literary magazine published by Truman State University.

CONTENTS

INTRODUCTION

Good fiction calls for a method. This book won't teach you how to write genre fiction, such as science fiction, fantasy, or romance, but it will teach the principles of all good fiction writing, many of which can be transferred to any genre.

This book is predicated on the idea that the first draft must be a work of the imagination. Let the imagination have its way. Give it free rein as much as possible.

The first draft is worth a lot if it is truly a work of the imagination, but this doesn't mean it's a work of art—not yet.

Unless you're a natural, or you strike it lucky, the first draft of your story or novel will need a lot of work. Sometimes, if you have a burst of creative energy, the work will seem quite inspired, and when you quit for the day, you'll feel satisfied. And yet, if you're like me, when you take a second look, you will probably think otherwise. Suddenly the writing sounds amateurish, half-baked, and melodramatic. This discourages. You thought you had something fantastic, but look at *this*.

What to do? Dump it? Maybe do something else, like write *non*fiction?

This is a misunderstanding of the process. You should *expect* your first draft to require a lot of attention. Why wouldn't it? Fiction writing, after all, is a complex act—we are calling upon the powers of our creative resources, our imagination, and our intellect. We must create a whole world, one where characters seem real and compelling enough to make the reader want to keep reading, keep believing. This is difficult stuff, and you usually don't achieve perfection the first time around. And you shouldn't expect to either.

But you *will* get there if you take revision seriously—if you take a manuscript through a number of important stages. At any stage in the process, you're working toward your goal. You're not there yet, but you will be soon—if you just stay with it. You're on your way to producing good work—polished work ready to submit to a magazine, agent, or book publisher.

In this book I will recommend a two-stage approach, based on three-month intervals:

- **THE FIRST THREE MONTHS:** Produce your short story draft(s) or novel draft.
- **THE SECOND THREE MONTHS:** Revise and fine-tune your story draft(s) or novel draft, developing a submission-ready manuscript.

Stage One is the production stage. For a short story, the writing could be completed in a single or several sittings, but basically, you just get the story down without worrying about "getting it all right." Gun out as many first draft stories as you can in this three-month period. This will give you more options for revision later. For a novel, unless you need to do a lot of research, the first draft could be done in as little as thirty days, as with the National Novel Writing Month that's held each November, or it could take the entire three months. If you pound out a novel in thirty days, go over what you've written and supply missing material to fill in holes. Again, give your imagination free rein. This may take you the remaining sixty days of Stage One. But if you finish earlier, start revising.

Stage Two, revision, consists of a lot of rethinking and overhauling as you critically attend to the various elements of the craft. This means developing strong characterization, strong plotting, and strong scene development, among other things, including the ability to refine the language so it makes the characters live and breathe, grabbing the reader at both the emotional and intellectual level. While your critical abilities are certainly needed here, you must avoid killing the story, robbing it of its life. Therefore, your imaginative faculty is needed in both stages.

While this book covers both the production stage and the revision stage, it devotes more attention to the latter. Briefly, the first three chapters make up Stage One. In Chapter One, I offer a primer on the various elements and fictional techniques. In Chapter Two, I consider the resources for fiction writing and how these might help get one started. Chapter Three is devoted to drafting.

Stage Two consists of thirteen chapters that focus on revision techniques, fine-tuning, and submitting your polished work for publication. At times there may seem to be repetition of material, but each instance drives home the overall point of that specific chapter.

Once you've finished the process detailed in this book, you will have completed several stories or a novel—but don't try to do both. Writing a novel in six months is work enough—at least, writing a good novel is. And writing half a dozen good short stories is, too.

Think of writing and revising as a recursive process. As you change one thing in your story, you may find that you need to change something else. For instance, if you decide on a different antagonist, this may mean changing your plot in significant ways. If you change your prose style, you may begin to see your character differently. As you make one change, you will see several others to make. You will go back and forth from element to element, and because writing fiction is such a complex act, you will continue to make changes and adjustments and even add new material as you revise, and, of course, cut—always cut.

To help guide you in the process of drafting, revision, and fine-tuning, I've included Process Sheets at the end of each chapter. These sheets are meant to guide you in your revision with specific fictional elements in mind—the ones covered in the chapter. To practice the principles some more, I've also included exercises at the end of each chapter. These exercises pinpoint most of the writing techniques covered in the chapter.

For those who appreciate the craft, writing fiction is one of the great pleasures of life. It's also hard work, but it's work that pays off when you see a story coming together or a fine novel emerging, bit by bit, from all your labor of words.

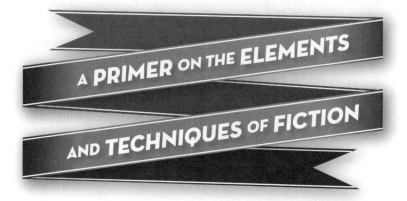

CHAPTER ONE

A PRIMER ON THE ELEMENTS AND TECHNIQUES OF FICTION

If you want to write fiction, read fiction. I cannot stress this enough. The fictional elements I cover in this chapter won't mean much to you unless you see them in action and reflect on how they work. If you haven't done a lot of fiction reading, start now. Read a little each day. Read critically and examine how writers practice their craft. How do they open and close stories? How do they develop characters and advance plot? How do they handle point of view? If you haven't been reading for craft, now is the time to start doing so.

You may already have a pretty good understanding of the elements of fiction—character, point of view, conflict, plot and structure, setting, style, and theme—but a review of each element may be beneficial to you before you produce your first draft. This chapter will cover the definitions, and more important, the complex nature of each element. We will only scratch the surface in this chapter, but your ultimate goal should be to handle each element successfully in a work of fiction—whether short story or novel.

ELEMENTS OF FICTION

Character

Character is one of the key elements that separate fiction from nonfiction. Think of it this way: If you're reading nonfiction, or at least expository, persuasive, or argumentative nonfiction, the author is speaking to you directly. He is informing you about certain matters of fact, explaining a theory, or trying to persuade you to accept certain ideas or beliefs. Even in the case of a nonfiction narrative, the author may frame this narrative with a point, which will be explained directly. Exceptions exist, of course, as in the case of more creative essays, which may be less direct, more elliptical, or more metaphorical; but a key difference between nonfiction and fiction—however direct or indirect a work of nonfiction might be—is that fiction centers on character.

Fiction shouldn't use character merely to illustrate an idea. Even with didactic fiction, one should be careful that this isn't *all* the character does—or is. The character needs to come alive. Seem real. Seem human.

If you're writing autobiographical fiction, this may seem easier to do, but not necessarily. As the author, you have to capture, in words, the felt life of the character, whether this character has its genesis in you or not. If you are writing about totally made-up characters, then you need what Keats called Negative Capability to enter into another consciousness—not an easy task, but one that every writer must learn. Creating characters is the staple of fiction writing—the heart and soul of it.

Character Vividly Rendered

As readers, we expect to feel the presence of characters, to be able to visualize them and get inside their minds. Writers make characters come alive through various means, through description, exposition, or—more often—through dramatic means, such as action and speech. A character becomes real to us when she is distinctive, not stereotypical—when we know her by her appearance, gesture, or manner of expression. When characters are unique in some way, we're hooked. We want to know more about them.

Character Motivation

Characters must act from believable motivations. I say "believable," not rational. People do things for different reasons. They say things they don't mean when they're angry or in a bad mood. They spend money they know they shouldn't spend because the background music in the bookstore is inspiring. They take chances on the highway because they feel exhilarated by the spring weather. They act based on emotion sometimes and reason at other times. We recognize their actions as typically human, but their actions are only believable within a given context. The character does this or that because these things have happened to her, and because the time is ripe. It makes sense. It adds up—or seems to, anyway. Of course, you won't find total agreement from readers on details like this, but the point is that characters can't just do anything you want them to do. They do what they're wired to do or driven to do.

Sometimes as readers we may think that a particular character wouldn't know this, wouldn't think this way, or wouldn't talk or act like this. This is a matter of plausibility and character consistency. Sometimes authors are tempted to jump in and engineer the character to think in a way compatible with the way the author thinks. This is one example of authorial intrusion, and it leads to characters that aren't real or believable.

Main Characters

Even though you may have more than one character, for convenience sake I'll deal with this matter in the singular. How do you make your main character, or protagonist, interesting and compelling? How do you keep your reader in your character's orbit from the first page to the end?

This is the question every writer is faced with, and there isn't one simple answer.

The answer you will most often hear is that the character needs to be one that readers can root for. In other words, you must create a "sympathetic character." Readers must care about this character and want things to turn out all right. They're interested in this character's outcome to the point where they feel they are confronting conflicts of various kinds right along with him. They can sympathize with what happens to him. They are drawn in—they care.

A second option: If readers don't exactly sympathize, they at least have empathy. They can imagine what it must be like to face such a crisis. They may not be completely sympathetic, but they can identify in some way. This character may not be like the reader in several particulars, nor is he facing the same struggles the reader is facing, but the reader can still relate because this character seems recognizably human and compelling in certain ways.

Third option? The character must at least be interesting, if not likeable. Consider this. Something stirs the reader's emotion to stay with this character through the story or—more of a challenge—the whole novel. Probably, though, most characters that are interesting have at least some human aspects that make readers capable of empathizing with them. And so if a character meets the bottom-line requirement of interesting, probably this character is fairly empathetic as well.

Main characters will be neither sympathetic nor empathetic if they are stereotypical. They must be multidimensional, or what E.M. Forster in his *Aspects of the Novel* refers to as *round* versus *flat*. They must be complex. If they're cardboard characters, readers probably won't be interested in them enough to care. Secondly, they must be *dynamic*, not *static*—terms commonly used for a character's ability to change. "The test of a round character," says Forster, "is whether it is capable of surprising us in a convincing way." Secondary characters are not as likely to change, but main characters must be capable of learning something new or gaining a better understanding of themselves and others.

Unless a story is a slice-of-life kind of story—one that shows us what the world looks like, what the daily fare is, for our protagonist—then readers will expect something to happen to change the character, in some way, by story's end. In *Writing in General and the Short Story in Particular,* Rust Hills says of the short story, "A character is capable of being moved, and is moved, no matter in how slight a way." The novel shares this same "quality of character-moved-by-plot." It may not be a major, life-changing discovery, as Hills suggests, but at least some new insight—something important enough to warrant the reader taking time to read this story. Because where's the *story* if the character doesn't change in some meaningful way—if the weight of all that conflict and experience doesn't have an iota of effect on this character?

Yes, it's possible for a main character to remain unchanged, but it's certainly the exception. Does Melville's Billy Budd change? No. In a story like this—one that emphasizes theme and idea—the character might not change, but the reader is expected to change. Most fiction is not like this. Writing a story or novel with an unchanging character is very hard to pull off—it goes against the presumption of most readers, who generally expect characters to come to some new understanding by story or novel's end.

Secondary Characters

Secondary characters are a different matter. For the most part, if you develop a secondary character too much, the material will seem extraneous. These characters, by definition, are less important in terms of the roles they play in the story or novel, but they do have roles, nonetheless. Each plays a part in terms of relevance to the main characters or overall plot or theme.

A secondary character might serve as a foil for the main character, helping the reader understand the main character. A secondary character can also act as an antagonist. Consider Pap Finn. Twain certainly didn't make Pap a protagonist. Despite the fact that he's a total comic riot, he's utterly despicable, and we would probably have difficulty reading an entire novel from his point of view. We see him through Huck's eyes—Huck's point of view.

Point of View

Point of view is the vantage point from which the story is told—the consciousness through which the character's experiences are filtered. We'll consider two principal aspects of point of view: The first has to do with the appropriate vantage point for the story; the second has to do with the narrative mode—that is, whether you choose to employ first-, second-, or third-person point of view.

Vantage Point

Deciding whose consciousness you will use to tell your story is an important consideration. Some vantage points are undoubtedly more interesting than others. Consider Huck Finn's perspective versus the Widow Douglas's or Miss Watson's. Huck is a young man trying to find his way in a puzzling, dangerous world—he's escaping from convention and from his alcoholic, abusive father. The Widow Douglas and Miss Watson are properly secondary characters in this novel because of their conventional ideas. In Miss Watson's case, these ideas are more pernicious and deserving of ridicule, and Twain delivers his comic upbraiding of her through Huck.

Consider the narrative technique in *The Great Gatsby*. While Jay Gatsby is a major character, the novel is nonetheless told from Nick Carraway's point of view, not Gatsby's. It's Nick's take on Gatsby that counts—we view Gatsby from the outside, filtered through Nick's consciousness.

What would the novel have been like from Gatsby's point of view? Could Gatsby have seen into himself the way Nick does? An important point needs to be made about Nick. Using the language of Janet Burroway, author of *Writing Fiction: A Guide to Narrative Craft*, Nick Carraway isn't just a "peripheral narrator" who's uninvolved in the story. Burroway emphasizes, seconding Rust Hills, that "by the end of the book it is Nick's life that has been changed by what he has observed."

Use peripheral narrators with caution. Make sure they have a stake in the story.

In the case of two protagonists, the question arises: Whose story is it? For instance, in Theodore Dreiser's *Sister Carrie*, written in the omniscient point of view, we enter fully into the consciousness of both Carrie Meeber and George Hurstwood. In this novel both characters' stories are equally important—their outcomes represent two sides of a coin. Carrie rises, becoming a successful actress; George falls, ending up on skid row. Together, the two reflect Dreiser's naturalism, which demonstrates how people's fates are determined by forces largely outside of their control. The point is that if you have two or more main characters, you need to decide which part they each play in the overall work—how important each is to the plot as well as to the theme.

First Person, Second, and Third

The first person is "in" today, quite fashionable. Not that this narrative mode wasn't used in the past—in fact, it was used by Daniel Defoe in two notable works of early fiction, *Robinson Crusoe* and *Moll Flanders*. Along with writing in the first person, it's also trendy today to use the present tense. What we have, then, is a first-person narrator talking to us about what is happening now—unless the narrator is flashing back. This gives the work a sense of immediacy it might not otherwise possess, especially because of the more stripped-down language of contemporary writing.

If first person allows us to enter, with immediacy, into the main character's life, second person grabs the reader and says: it's "you" doing this. You're going through this. Jay McInerney's novel *Bright Lights, Big City* uses this approach. One distinction needs to be made here. A first-person narrator may sometimes address the reader as "you," such as in J.D. Salinger's *The Catcher in the Rye*. When Holden Caulfield addresses the reader as you, Holden is confidentially sharing his life. Incidentally, not all first-person narrators are as self-reflexive as Holden; they act more as a window on the world which they experience and report on.

Third person provides more emotional distance from the character. In the limited omniscient form, you see things from the perspective of one character—your protagonist. If you want to describe your character's traits, qualities, or physical appearance, do so without authorial intrusion. Have your character know these things about himself, or in other words, make us feel like we're inside the character. You can enter fully into the character's consciousness. Depending on the story or novel, you may decide that you prefer the third person and choose this as an alternative to the first. Perhaps the first person seems to identify you too closely to the character—you feel the need for some emotional distance. The omniscient form is still used today, although most writers who use it tend to restrain themselves when it comes to authorial commentary or authorial knowledge beyond what the various characters know. If the writer sometimes does display authorial knowledge, for the most part he allows the characters, not himself, to hold the reins. The third-person omniscient, by its very nature, certainly puts the reins entirely in the author's control, and though this point of view can be used with great force—in Ian McEwan's *Atonement*, for instance—it does lend itself, in lesser hands, to authorial know-it-all. There's a certain philosophical reluctance out there today, and there has been for some time, regarding authorial omniscience: It was okay for the nineteenth century, the reasoning might go, but godlike omniscience and presence are not fitting for contemporary writers—or readers. Readers today tend to be more relativistic in their thinking, distrusting the final word from know-it-all authors.

Oftentimes in contemporary fiction the "author" is more or less effaced, and what we have instead is a multiple point of view approach, taking in the perspectives of several key characters. A good example of such a work is Kent Haruf's novel *Plainsong*.

I can't think of a better place to bring up a very important distinction: The author must not be confused with the "persona" the author creates to tell the story. The author could conceivably believe one thing, yet create a persona who believes the very opposite. We cannot equate the author with the novel's third-person persona. Nor can we do so with the first-person narrator. We certainly cannot equate Twain with Huck, nor Holden Caulfield of *The Catcher in the Rye* with J.D. Salinger. These works of fiction are separate from the authors who created them. They are worlds the authors have set in motion. This is always true in fiction—otherwise you would have nonfiction.

The third-person point of view takes still another form, and that is the dramatic, or objective form. This is the scenic treatment in which we learn about characters from what they say and do. No internal consciousness guides us. Once we get beyond the narrative portion of Shirley Jackson's "The Lottery," the point of view is dramatic: dialogue and action only. Whether or not you use this technique for an entire story, you may find it useful for scenes now and then. Look at Ernest Hemingway's and Raymond Carver's stories as good examples. Of course, dramatic sections of a novel can work quite well with this point of view.

Keep in mind that point of view may affect the voice of the narrative. Because of its intimacy, a first-person narrative may create a different kind of voice than would a third-person narrative, which will be more distant.

Conflict

Without conflict, there is no story. If everything is going well for a character—work, family, sense of personal dignity—readers will probably lose interest fast, unless something else engages them, such as a gripping prose style. But in such cases, the work will be seen as more of a character sketch than a story.

You're probably familiar with the standard types of conflict in a story: *man against man, man against nature,* and *man against himself*—the first two are external, the third is internal. Once you get past the obvious discriminatory language, these descriptions pretty much sum up the kinds of conflicts one might encounter in a story or novel. "Man against man" refers to a character against one person or against a group or whole society. "Man against nature" conflicts are often survival stories, in which the character battles against dangers such as the elements, wild creatures, or natural disasters. Internal conflicts in fiction are naturally related to external conflicts, whatever they might be. Most stories, unless they are utterly plot driven, involve internal conflict. If readers are to get interested in a character, this character better have some issues and not have everything packaged neatly and tidily, with the whole world's problems solved. Of course, if this character thinks he or she does, readers will assume some comeuppance is in order, as in the works of Flannery O'Connor. Remember the grandmother in "A Good Man Is Hard to Find"? Her self-satisfaction bubble is burst by the Misfit, who functions, in one sense, as O'Connor's nemesis figure.

Internal conflict is, in fact, the engine that drives character-driven stories. External conflicts of all kinds are internalized in characters. The stakes must be high enough in a story to make the reader care about what happens. The conflict cannot be utterly trivial but what most would consider fairly serious or important, at least to this character—or the reader will certainly not be engaged. This doesn't mean it has to be something as dire as general mayhem or death. An ordinary, day-to-day conflict can drive a story, and mundane conflicts can be quite important if they cause characters to reexamine their lives in believable ways.

Do realize that not every moment in a character's life is likely to be filled with conflict. Usually quiet times occur when characters reach certain equilibriums, and then, of course, rug pulling often follows.

In real life, certain behaviors affect some people more than they affect others. Some behaviors affect certain people at certain times. It's the same in fiction. It's not necessarily the case that an overheard remark will destroy a character's equanimity, though overhearing the words "wretched cur" certainly does Lord Jim in Joseph Conrad's novel. Jim is ripe for it, given that he overhears this derogatory epithet—ironically not meant for him—just after having abandoned his ship and now facing an official inquiry. And in Katherine Mansfield's short story "Miss Brill," the lonely, elderly woman who has concocted in her mind a place for herself in the world of others is hurt by an overheard remark, "stupid old thing," because it confirms her already low self-esteem. She's quite vulnerable.

The lesson is that you must think of conflict in terms of context—what is your character like? What pushes this character's buttons? What is your character's present life like? Knowing these details is crucial to understanding character motivation. Not everyone wants to be fully admitted to the high calling of Christminster, but Jude Fawley does, as Thomas Hardy well knows. Not everyone wants to live a life governed by the standards of romantic novels, but Gustave Flaubert's Madame Bovary does.

And so be a critical reader and watch for what matters to the main characters, and even secondary or minor characters. Conflict must come from the materials of character and circumstance. If the author engineers the conflict without considering these elements, the characters become pawns manipulated by an author who loves to make them squirm.

The big conflicts, as in real life, are what drive change. But don't ignore the little conflicts, because they accumulate sometimes, and even if they don't, they help us understand what makes a character tick and may also mirror the larger, more central conflict. Sometimes characters, and real-life people, hide their real feelings about the big conflicts; instead they pick at each other over the little conflicts. If you watch for these little conflicts in your reading—and your life experiences—you're more likely to watch for them in your writing as well.

Plot and Structure

In *Aspects of the Novel*, E.M. Forster distinguishes between story and plot. Story interests "cave-men," who simply want to know what happens next: "and then ... and then..." Plot, however, is more sophisticated because it demonstrates the cause-effect relationship between a story's events. This requires intelligence and memory, says Forster. How did this event lead to that event, and how did this whole series of events finally add up to this outcome? Plot is, of course, inseparable from character. Why does this character cause this event to happen? Why does this event happen to this character?

Structure is the way the work is organized. Is it presented chronologically? Does it begin in the present, flash back several chapters, and then return to the present?

Plot

A plot can be simple or complex—or let's call it "complicated." (I'm not drawing from Aristotle here for either term.) A simple plot doesn't mean the overall story or novel is simple. It may be a story with a lot of depth, dimension, and layers. It may be a complex psychological study, even if very little happens plotwise. The language itself may provide several metaphorical or symbolic levels. But for now—saving discussion of theme and idea for later—let's look at plot alone.

Shirley Jackson's "The Lottery" is very simple in plot. In the beginning of the story, townsfolk are busily gathering stones. They then gather to have a lottery. Ironically, the winner is the loser. The purpose becomes clear: A human must be sacrificed in order to appease the fertility gods and bring a good harvest. It takes only a few scenes to pull this off with quite a bit of impact. In some plot-driven short stories (I consider Jackson's story theme driven) you can imagine that a much more complicated series of actions might be needed, probably with several twists and turns to keep the reader on the edge of his chair.

Turning to longer works of fiction: A character-driven, as well as an idea-driven, plot can be quite simple or, at the opposite extreme, convoluted. Certainly the basic plotline of Henry James's novella *Daisy Miller* is rather simple: The innocent American Daisy Miller clashes, bit by bit, with the sophisticated Europeanized-American community in Rome. Faulkner's *Absalom, Absalom!*, however, is extremely complex, with numerous characters and intricate historical contexts. A plot is as complex as it needs to be. Faulkner's intricate vision of the South and slavery calls for a complicated plot. Watch out, though, for an unwieldy plot, one that takes on too much. If you see this happening, weed out strands that take the reader off course or blur the main focus.

A short story is much more limited in conflict, much more compressed. Most likely it won't have a subplot. A novel may have several subplots. Don't burden a short story with too much, and don't make short shrift of a novel. The overburdened short story will be unfocused, and the novel that takes on too little will come off as a bloated short story, ripe for pruning.

Structure

Structure is the organization of the various plot elements. The question is, how should the key scenes be spaced out? Where should flashback material, if you have it, be included? Ask yourself these questions: What impact do I want to create? How can

I arrange the various story parts so the structure of this story or novel helps me achieve the maximum impact?

If you've studied structure at all, you're probably familiar with the five-stage plot structure: The story begins with an existing equilibrium, then a complication and a rising action, a crisis and climax, a falling action, and a resolution. A second option is the three-act structure you find in screenwriting.

You may well be familiar with the epiphany story made famous by James Joyce in such a story as "Araby," in which a character comes, suddenly, to a transforming realization at the end. The often-anthologized John Updike story "A&P" provides such an epiphany. Sammy, the narrator, suddenly realizes at the end of the story "how hard the world was going to be to me from here on in."

A frequently used structure is one that alternates between two point-of-view characters—or even several in a novel. This may be accomplished in third person, as with T.C. Boyle's *When the Killing's Done*, or it might be told with multiple first-person narrators, as in the first three sections of Faulkner's *The Sound and the Fury*. But if you choose a multiple perspective, which character do you begin with? It may be a question of chronological time, clarity, or creating the right emphasis—getting the story off to the right start.

Take a look at the question of chronological time. Should you tell the story chronologically, or should you begin in the present, move back in time, and catch the reader up with backstory? The question becomes, how much should be handled by flashback and how much should be covered in scenes and brief memories in the present?

Be careful not to burden a short story with too many flashbacks; make sure they are essential. Why might they be essential? If the story is a very internal one, perhaps it calls for considerable memory and flashback. But tread carefully if this is so. You must spend a sufficient amount of time in the present as well.

In a novel you may be more at liberty to use flashbacks. Jean-Paul Sartre said of Faulkner that his characters were like people situated in a car looking backwards. Indeed so—they were haunted by the past. When thinking about backstory, consider how much is essential. Is it essential to character? To plot? Eliminate what's not essential.

The key thing to remember about structure is this: Like every other element in a story or novel, the structure must fit the character and plot. If the structure is scattershot, hampering characterization or impeding the plot, the reader will lose interest. If too many flashbacks might cause the reader to feel sidetracked, then avoid them. If, on the other hand, you have a scene where it is apparent that the author is pulling the puppets' strings to make them cover certain needed story material, a flashback might be a better choice.

Setting

Setting is time and place. A fictional work has a setting of some kind, whether stated or implied. In some works setting is quite important. What would Hawthorne's *The Scarlet Letter* be like without the descriptions he gives us of Puritan New England? The prison, the scaffold, the village, the deep forest—these are essential to telling Hawthorne's romance, dealing with the theocracy's judgment and sentencing of Hester Prynne. Here, carefully selected setting details capture a sense of place: the region itself, as well as the culture.

Works like Hawthorne's are, of course, not in the contemporary vein. Contemporary literature that focuses on setting is a bit unlikely—to put it mildly—to focus on an allegorical drama of sin and redemption. Today's writers of place, inheritors of nineteenth-century realism and naturalism, focus on the way setting affects the inhabitants of a given area: how it affects their psyches and their behavior. In *Plainsong* Kent Haruf evokes an unsettling sense of bleakness in an eastern Colorado setting. In *Winter's Bone*, Daniel Woodrell depicts the stark moral landscape of southwestern Missouri. Eric Miles Williamson's three novels—*East Bay Grease*, *Two-Up*, and *Welcome to Oakland*—each capture, with great force, the poverty and violence of Oakland, California.

Setting is, of course, important as a backdrop in historical novels. E.L. Doctorow, a master with a few brushstrokes, situates the reader in the Civil War in *The March*, in the turn of the twentieth century in *Ragtime*, and in the 1930s in *Loon Lake*. Setting provides an essential backdrop. Historical details common to the period help flesh out setting.

But beyond this backdrop, setting can also be symbolic. Think of Ken Kesey's *One Flew Over the Cuckoo's Nest*. In Kesey's clever hands, the psychiatric hospital setting stands for the larger world where the truly mad are not the strange and different, but those who reign over these people—those like Big Nurse Ratched.

If setting isn't crucial to the story as a backdrop or a symbol, then it may be enough simply to establish the whereabouts of the action—the apartment, public school, a lawyer's office, the swimming pool—and leave it at that. The thing to keep in mind is that you don't need to detail every sidewalk, every road or highway, every house and lawn. Describe what matters. If it matters to the character for some reason—perhaps it's a favorite haunt, which would suggest something about this character—furnish the key details. Be selective.

Style, Tone, and Mood

Style is the manner in which the story is told. While style can vary throughout a work, readers should be able to see an overall style. Some authors have an identifiable or signature style—Hawthorne, Twain, James, Hemingway, Carver, McCarthy.

Tone has to do with the apparent attitude of the narrator or persona toward the characters and the world they inhabit, but everything in the work contributes in some way to the overall tone.

Mood is the emotional feeling that is established in various places in the work, and, like tone, there may well be an overall mood to a story.

Style

To create a strong prose style, which is closely related to narrative voice, you must be sensitive to language. Developing a style means choosing the right words, organizing an effective sentence, and getting rid of the bloat (not to be confused with a style rich in detail). You can't necessarily get the right words from a dictionary, and certainly not a thesaurus—you have to read a lot. Read and mark passages that sound polished.

I would caution against thinking of style as "flow"—as in "it flows well"—unless you mean by this that the language is working. But if you confuse flow with smooth-flowing language, you might decide against staccato language or fractured syntax, both of which may be highly appropriate in certain cases where characters are nervous, frightened, or angry. And you might decide against a highly meditative passage that is slow, even sluggish, but accomplishes exactly what it's meant to accomplish by making the character sound sluggish. Style must go with story. It's not something discrete, and it doesn't work in isolation.

Style includes a host of properties, almost too numerous to mention, but I will introduce several here:

- **LEVEL OF DETAIL—SPARSE OR FULLY TEXTURED:** Hemingway (less is more) versus Faulkner (more is more). The stripped-down style is evident in such writers as Raymond Carver and Cormac McCarthy. The fully textured style still has its place, but most writers today tend to write somewhere in the middle. One thing to understand is that style can change radically from one part of a story or novel to another, depending on the needs of the story.

- **LEVEL OF DICTION—FORMAL, NEUTRAL, INFORMAL:** In terms of diction, sometimes a fully textured style goes with a more formal one. But if most writers today write somewhere between an utterly stripped-down style in the manner of McCarthy and a fully textured style like we find in Faulkner, most writers today also find a happy medium with diction. Formality pretty much died with James and Faulkner; neutral and informal diction endure.

- **DESCRIPTIVE DETAIL—DIRECT VERSUS INDIRECT METHOD:** Style can be specific and concrete—making us "see" characters and actions—or it can be handled through more dramatic means of voice and action so that we still get a good sense for the characters: hear them talk as well as visualize them.

- **PACING OR TEMPO:** Is the writing methodical, does it build increment by increment, or does it progress like a freight train, rushing toward some final moment of victory or defeat? Is it lyrical, melodic? Or is it staccato or jarring, making us feel jerked about much as the character is jerked about? Sometimes the tempo will change from one place in a story to another. Tempo results from a number of stylistic choices—among them syntax, sentence type (whether simple, compound, complex, or compound-complex), amount of detail furnished, and choice of diction.

- **TENSE:** The present tense is "in" and has been for some time. Literature used to be written in the past tense more often, but many writers find the present tense lends more immediacy. For the story or novel you are writing, judge how it sounds in present versus past tense—you can probably tell what will work best after a few pages.

- **OVERALL TONE:** Is it ironic, impassioned, wistful, light-hearted, or melancholy? Consider the difference between Thurber and Poe.

- **ACCESSIBILITY:** How hard is this story to read? How hard is this author to read? Twain is easy to read—at least on the surface. James isn't.
- **STYLE AND GENRE:** Romance novels don't sound like literary novels.

Tone and Mood

We often associate an author's prose style with the tone of his work—for instance, the ironic tones of Twain and Vonnegut. Tone is established by everything in a story: the characters, the setting, the plot, and certainly the style. As a general rule, you might think of tone as the narrator's apparent attitude toward the characters and the world created in this story or novel. A narrator might have an ironic stance toward this world, as in *Even Cowgirls Get the Blues*, by offbeat author Tom Robbins. The tone in this novel is certainly different from the tone in a much more somber work of fiction. A reportorial style would create a much different tone than a lyrical one. Different choices in diction, syntax, and other matters of style can certainly do a lot to create a desired tone, whether laid-back, meditative, or hauntingly tragic.

Mood is the emotional atmosphere that is conveyed at any given point in the story or novel. The mood will be shaped by the character's emotional state, whether happy, sad, exhausted, depressed, or frantic. James Dickey's *Deliverance* provides an excellent study of mood. Note how the first-person narrator's own moods create a mood for the scenes he describes. We feel his sense of foreboding, urgency, despair, relief. These emotions color the scenes. I wouldn't recommend writing like Poe today, but Poe's use of the word *melancholy* in the often-anthologized "The Fall of the House of Usher" certainly illustrates how single word choices reflect character emotion as well as create emotion in the reader.

Theme

Theme is the overriding idea of a work of fiction. Think of theme as more abstract than plot. Any number of plots might point to a given theme: success or failure in America, mercy or justice, art and life, love and hate, imagination or experience.

If your story has a basic coherence, which results from the characters and plot and from believable motivations, you undoubtedly have a theme of some kind: about humans, about the world at large, about the cosmos—something. It may be nihilistic, naturalistic, realistic, or existential. It may be muckraking. It may not be earthshaking at all: Maybe it's just a small sense of what the world can be like at given times, for given kinds of people. But it should be more abstract than the plot.

And incidentally, you will recall that I distinguished a simple plot from a more complicated one. Here, it's important to reemphasize that a simple plot doesn't mean a simplistic theme or idea—more can be happening underneath the surface than above it. A complex plot doesn't in itself mean a complex work in terms of range or depth of ideas. It might be convoluted in action, with many twists and turns, but short on idea, which tends to be the case with plot-driven novels.

In a short story, which is highly compressed, every plot development, character development, figurative language device, and scene is tightly connected to the story's theme or idea. This is less true of the novel. Study fiction closely to observe how all of these elements work together to create a unified whole. You should be able to make an overriding generalization about the work—where it's going, what it's "saying" (or suggesting), and what it's not saying.

But from a creative perspective, be very careful not to engineer theme in your short story or novel. Don't manipulate things. This method is employed in didactic fiction, and you will lose many readers. Keep your idea, but be more subtle about presenting it. You can certainly find ways to advance your theme—as long as it unfolds naturally.

Story ideas are born from character conflicts, beliefs, attitudes, assumptions—and the theme of the story is related to everything that emerges from the story's world. It's complex, and it must remain complex—the more difficult to state, the more ineffable, the better. That's life, and literature attempts—or at least the literary kind does—to deal with life, if not capture its essence. It may attempt to mirror it (realism); it may twist and distort it in the service of an idea (satire). But whatever literature does with life, it must not snuff out the human element in the pursuit of the abstract.

You should be able to state the theme of a work and leave out specific details, including character, action, and plot. In covering plot, I spoke of Shirley Jackson's "The Lottery." The theme of this story has to do with destructive customs and conventions and people's willingness to follow them—but it's also about other people questioning them.

PROSE MODES

Each of the basic prose techniques—narration, exposition, and description—is vitally important for writing fiction. Without them you're left with merely dialogue. It's possible to tell a story with dialogue only, but it's highly experimental. If that's all you can do, and you don't handle prose techniques well, you will miss out on what gives fiction much of its richness. Don't misunderstand the time-honored watchwords, "Show, don't tell." It's not that you shouldn't ever tell; you have to sometimes. But make your fiction as dramatic as possible, in a voice that pulls your reader in.

Narration

Narration is chronicling events, either over time (summary) or as they occur in a short time frame (scene). Let's look at both.

You may need some telescoping, or compressing of time, in a short story as well as in a novel. Not every event is of equal importance. If you are dealing with events that span a month, a year, or even several years, this will call for summary—which means using some narrative skills. It means employing language that interests the reader, a selection of events that relate clearly to the actions and scenes that follow, and the appropriate brevity. Even in the best hands, a summary can go on too long. Read your work for this—and watch out for it especially in a short story. When do you get bored? Summary works when the character is interesting, the events compelling, the style energetic—and of course, when the summary is needed. No matter how good the summary is, if the story could do without it, lop it off.

The narrative mode is not only for summary; it's also for scene, for real-time, up-close dramatic presentation of action. This doesn't have to be the stuff of thrillers or action movies. It can simply be a scene with your character doing something important—important enough to dramatize. To decide if it's important, you must ask certain key questions: What does the scene reveal about the character? How does it advance the plot? How does it contribute to the overall theme of the story or novel? If a scene *is* called for, you need to make it interesting and compelling. This means lively sentences and a strong prose style.

Exposition

Exposition—by this I mean *expository prose*—is one of the most difficult prose forms to write. Exposition means "explanation," and what can be more hazardous to dramatic writing than having to explain? But exposition can be useful if you charm the reader with just the right word—the *mot juste*—and, as odd as this may sound, if you use it to build the dramatic power of your characters. After all, expository prose is a tool that fiction writers constantly use, and use well, as even a cursory look at the great authors from the present and past will show you.

Facts about a character's life, beliefs, thoughts, attitudes, and feelings—these are all the province of exposition—but if you include such things, you have to keep it interesting. And as with any story material, decide what to keep and what to pitch. Not every fact about a character's life is important enough to mention, nor is every belief or attitude you've imagined including. What's important is what ultimately fits into the story and drives it. Do know this: Exposition doesn't need to come off as mere authorial telling. Strong expository passages can make the reader feel as if she is *inside* your character, experiencing the rich depths of this character's inner life. With good expository prose, readers forget the presence of the author.

Still, it's true that writing strong expository prose is quite a challenge. Masters may be able to handle it, but in lesser hands it may come off as the author standing outside the character filling in the reader with relevant facts and information. This is what gives exposition a bad name. The standard alternative is the scenic method: In scenes rich with dialogue, protagonists can reveal important information about themselves—their worries, doubts, fears, beliefs, attitudes, thoughts, feelings, and the like—as long as the motivation to introduce this information seems credible. Or, other characters can serve an expository function by commenting on your protagonist.

Description

Description can be abstract or concrete, general or specific. Writers are told to be concrete and specific, and to ground the story in the five senses: sight, sound, touch, taste, and smell. Yes, this seems obvious, but general and abstract kinds of description have their place as well. You may want your protagonist to classify or peg another character as a certain kind of person— perhaps a curious mix of the innocent and menacing. A well-turned phrase may become quite powerful—and memorable. Still, concreteness may serve you better if you want your readers to come away with striking images that live on in their memories. Consider the big fish eaten away by sharks in Hemingway's *The Old Man and the Sea*. That image certainly remains with many readers.

Vivid description, like good narration and exposition, requires that *mot juste*. Don't depend on adjectives, adverbs, or flowery language to carry the load, and avoid purple (ornate) prose at all times. Remember, you want your reader to see it, hear it, feel it, taste it, smell it. Much of the ability to write concrete description comes from reading good fiction, and a lot comes from rewriting and fine-tuning. If a passage or description sounds dull to you, you can bet it will sound dull to readers. Avoid hackneyed comparisons, clichés, and trite expressions. Whether you have this ability naturally or not, strive to describe people, places, and things in an absolutely fresh and insightful way.

At this point I *must* raise an important question: To what extent must you depend on description—that is, *concrete* description? As I will show later, some writers are able to make us "see" characters by dramatizing their actions and speech intonations. And, by an author's carefully chosen specific (if not concrete) details, we can even picture settings.

So which methods work better? You will have to answer that based on the needs of your own characters and your reading of quality fiction.

SCENE WRITING WITH DIALOGUE

What is a story without scenes? If the story begins with summary, the reader is waiting for the scene, for the "One time…" or "One day…" tip-off. Scenes ground us in the drama of the story. Without scenic treatment the reader isn't as likely to be engaged. Hearing characters talk can pull the reader right in—if the dialogue is good.

Dialogue is what makes scenes live, and if you want to write dialogue, you must have an ear for it. Read a lot of dialogue. For now, I won't get into the grammatical particulars: direct versus indirect dialogue, double versus single quotation marks around character speech, the use of dashes to set off speech, and the absence of any such features. These are matters of style and we will take them up in Chapter Thirteen. But more generally, what makes good dialogue?

First, understand that dialogue in fiction isn't by any stretch real, but it needs to sound real—that is, it must have an air of reality. If your characters sound like they are giving prepared speeches, the reader will most likely put aside your story, unless something about your character warrants this. People in real life don't converse in prepared speeches. Heed this: If prose style is often informal in contemporary fiction, dialogue is even more so.

Make your dialogue vibrant. A character's spoken words should reflect her personality, attitudes, and bearing, and it should be filled with the typical hesitations, interruptions, and differences in tone and volume. Make dialogue subtle. People in real life don't say everything that's on their minds. Listen to people talk. You can learn a lot about dialogue by listening, but even so, remember that dialogue is always artifice: It must seem real, but it can't be real. Real speech, recorded in a story, would likely bore us to death. Art shouldn't.

Be careful about handling dialect or ethnic or regional speech patterns unless you've done your homework. Chris Cleave does a convincing job in *Little Bee*.

OPENINGS AND ENDINGS

Fiction can begin in several different ways: with exposition, description, summary, or scene—with or without dialogue. In an opening, your goal is to get the reader's attention, but also to create the right emphasis for the story. Story endings must give readers a sense of closure and yet keep them, to some extent, wanting more—so they go back and rethink what they've read.

Openings

If you're submitting a novel to an agent, it's probably wise to begin with a scene. Commercial presses tend to like books that get off to a fast start, and a scene is more likely to accomplish this than summary or description, and probably more than exposition, unless it's particularly lively. But putting aside the matter of publication for a moment, what can be accomplished with each type of opening? And are there any drawbacks?

A scenic opening can certainly give the story some dramatic impact. It has a lot of potential to create reader interest. But it can also present a problem. Let's say you need to bring in some backstory. Let's also say you cannot address this backstory and its various particulars by using brief memories or present time frame scenes; instead, the only choice you have is flashback. The question is, how effective would it be to follow up an opening scene with a summary of past events? This may work better in a novel than in a short story—especially in a very short story. It may be better to begin with summary, though this is a risk, too. Even if it's quite lively and rich, summary doesn't give as great a sense of live, in-the-moment action.

Why begin with description? Perhaps the setting is especially important, or perhaps a specific character's appearance, personality, traits, or gestures are particularly intriguing when viewed from an interesting narrative perspective. This might get a story off to a compelling start.

Exposition? It's especially risky—unless you can begin with character thoughts, feelings, or beliefs that are provocative. But exposition that is stylistically brilliant will also pull readers in.

Endings

With literary fiction, endings need to be open to interpretation. If you use exposition, tease your reader a little—leave something to the reader's imagination. A tidy summary will kill your story. If you end with an image, make it suggestive. What does this image suggest in terms of the character and action of this story? What idea does it convey?

Is it possible to end with a scene? Yes, of course, and many stories do. A scene always hooks readers as long as it's full of dramatic power. It must, in a way, satisfy but not satiate.

Think of it this way: Openings must grab your reader's attention. Endings must in some way follow naturally from the story and give the reader a sense of closure without actually closing things. Like life, nothing is ever quite finished in fiction. And if it is, the ending is too facile and cheapens the story.

FIGURATIVE LANGUAGE DEVICES

Figurative language includes such devices as symbol, metaphor, irony, paradox, understatement, and overstatement. Figurative language is sometimes a feature of style, but it also creates meaning. I want to emphasize that you can't insert figurative language at random; instead, you must realize that clusters of meaning develop from such figurative devices, and you must consider the logic of what you're doing—in the revision stage, that is. How do these clusters of meaning relate to everything else in the story: character, plot, setting, and theme?

Symbolism and Allegory

If something literal in your story—some particular object, something in nature, a character, a character's actions, a place— suggests a larger meaning, this is symbolic. Symbols can be cultural (like a wedding ring), universal (like water), or contextual (taking their meaning from the contexts of the story itself). The fissure in the House of Usher of Poe's story means something different to Roderick Usher than it would mean to the average person. A symbol can radiate a number of different meanings, and readers may not always agree on these meanings. Of course, they may have a more fundamental disagreement on what is symbolic to begin with.

Is the river in *The Adventures of Huckleberry Finn* more than literal? Is the whale in Melville's *Moby-Dick* more than literal? Yes, surely, in both cases—and it's because of the way each is presented that it takes on a larger meaning. In Twain's novel, the river becomes a symbol of freedom—but it's a freedom that could soon end, as Huck and Jim head south into the very heart of slavery. In Melville's tale, Ahab invests the whale with all the evil in the world. In both novels, we cannot, however, assign just one meaning to these literal things. They might suggest several different meanings the more we think about them in the context of the novels.

Allegory, however, suggests a one-to-one correspondence. In Hawthorne's "Young Goodman Brown," Brown's journey into the wilderness is much less a literal than a figurative one—a journey into the nature of evil, where the so-called good are unmasked for what they really are: as sinful as the rest of us.

Through both allegory and symbolism you can layer your story so it taps into universal truths about the human condition. But again, let me emphasize that you can't force this. The fissure in the House of Usher doesn't feel forced. In that Gothic setting, and with the haunted mind of Roderick Usher, the preternatural, if not supernatural, existence of that fissure seems pretty compelling.

In more realistic stories, place can also be symbolic. The psychiatric ward in *One Flew Over the Cuckoo's Nest* comes to stand for the world. It's a kind of microcosm. This happens convincingly after considerable dramatic development relating the Outside to the everyday workings of the insane asylum.

The lesson, then, is to not import symbolism or allegory—if you use the latter at all—externally. Let them bloom on their own.

Metaphor and Simile

Though metaphor is often used interchangeably with symbolism, there is technically a difference between the two. Remember that with symbolism, a literal or actual thing, person, or place—call it X—stands for something *more* than X at some level of idea: Call it Y. In the case of metaphor, you are saying X *is* Y. With a simile, X is *like* Y.

Is Gregor Samsa in Kafka's *Metamorphosis* actually an insect, or is Kafka suggesting that his life is insectlike? It's hard to read this story as anything but metaphor, whereas in Frost's poem "Mending Wall," you can't help but believe that Frost's narrator, along with his Neanderthal neighbor, is mending an actual stone wall; there is a wall there to be mended, and this wall has symbolic meaning—namely, how we often wall ourselves off, or alienate ourselves, from others. Yet we can make too much of this distinction. Often, what is symbolic is referred to as metaphorical.

Here's the point: Because language has so many possibilities for layers and shades of meaning, you have the resources to make your fiction rich on several levels. But don't try too hard to be literary. Building these layers must happen naturally, or they won't work at all.

Metaphor and Simile Clusters

I've been speaking of symbol and metaphor in terms of how certain ones point at ideas and themes. But not every symbol or metaphor carries such a heavy weight. Writers often use metaphors and similes to help readers see characters and places in a certain light, in certain contexts. As you read, watch for how metaphors and similes coalesce to create clusters of meaning. And in your own writing, be sure that you don't send your reader contradictory signals. You will address this sort of thing more in rewriting. As you're writing your first draft, don't worry about it. You may create some interesting metaphors when the creative juices are really flowing—if you just let it happen. And then, when you tighten in the rewrite stage, you can decide if the various metaphors and similes you've used are in harmony with each other.

Irony and Paradox

Irony is the discrepancy between what we expect and what we get—there's built-in contradiction. Paradox, on the other hand, is seeming contradiction—a result that defies logic.

Stories that have levels and complexities that aren't simply surfaces but involve depths—making readers ask questions and puzzle out meanings—often include irony and/or paradox. Stories that involve skepticism about people, society, and the world at large seem to thrive on irony and paradox. Irony delivers a punch simply due to the tension between expectation and result. Paradox works similarly.

Three forms of irony are verbal, situational, and dramatic. Verbal irony is a discrepancy between what you say and what you mean. It's close to sarcasm. It is certainly a useful tool in character conflict. Situational irony is the discrepancy between what you expect to happen and what actually happens. If you win the lottery you expect your life to get better. But, no, it takes a sudden turn for the worse, as in "Riches," by Richard Bausch. Cosmic irony is situational irony at the cosmic level. We expect the universe to care about our hard struggles; we expect nature to care (the pathetic fallacy), but Stephen Crane, in "The Open Boat," a classic work of American literary naturalism, paints nature as indifferent to our fate.

Dramatic irony is the staple of satirical fiction. The character believes one thing, and the reader knows something else to be true. Pap Finn may believe his own outrageous rant in his "Call this a govment" speech, but perceptive readers won't give it any credibility. If a first-person narrator fails to judge correctly but the reader knows the score, then we have dramatic irony. And thus we have dramatic irony in Huck's belief that he will go to hell for not turning in Jim. An unreliable I-narrator can provide for dramatic irony; however, when the irony is too much at the expense of the I-narrator (this isn't the case with Huck) it's hard to create a sympathetic character. Perhaps one can create an empathetic character this way, or at least an interesting one. This is the case with Tim O'Brien's *Tomcat in Love*, a satire of the first order that turns the hose on the protagonist but nonetheless makes him compellingly human.

Paradox is closely related to irony. Consider this paradoxical advice in Conrad's *Lord Jim*: "The way is to the destructive element submit yourself, and with the exertions of your hands and feet in the water make the deep, deep sea keep you up." It's paradoxical to "submit yourself" to "the destructive element." Paradox captures the ostensibly contradictory—that which is not contradictory at some different or deeper level.

Situational irony, as well as paradox, can work in part of a story, or as a pattern of the story as a whole. Watch how authors use these devices. Again, don't force anything, but if you are sensitive to the element of contradiction in life as well as in literature, you may thicken up your fiction, giving it more levels—more density of idea.

Understatement and Overstatement

These two devices also create levels in speech or dialogue and liven it up. Understatement grossly underplays the importance of an issue or situation. Before confronting a bloody carnage, the deputy of Sheriff Bell in *No Country for Old Men* asks what he thinks they'll find. Bell answers with characteristic understatement: "I don't know ... But I can't say as I'm much lookin' forward to it."

Overstatement works in the opposite direction, by greatly exaggerating. Holden Caulfield is an inveterate user of overstatement. This might make sense for him: He is young, idealistic, and feels overwhelmed by life—he can't deal with all the phonies in this world. His overstatements are both telling and humorous, and add depth to his character. Both understatement and overstatement are devices you might find useful in creating interesting characters.

SOME FINAL REMARKS

This is a rundown of the key elements of fiction. In Stage Two of the book, we will consider each of these elements and how they provide principal techniques in rethinking your first drafts. But first, we need to consider how to begin the drafting—where do you start?

PROCESS SHEET #1

Unlike most process sheets in this book, this one will deal with your reading only.

1. Read three short stories. Take notes. Comment on how the elements are working in each story.
2. Comment on the ideas in each story and how the fictional techniques develop these ideas.
3. Think about your own techniques. How do they compare with the techniques used in these stories?
4. Write down the ideas in these stories and list as many related ideas as you can—ideas you might take up in a story or novel.

EXERCISE 1

Comment on characterization in one of the three stories you read. Was this a round, dynamic character? What makes this character round? In what way or ways did this character change?

EXERCISE 2

Comment on plot in one of the three stories you read. How did this plot work? Describe it—the way events advanced from one point to another. What were the main scenes?

EXERCISE 3

Comment on setting in one of the three stories you read. How much setting was described? What purpose did the description serve?

CHAPTER TWO

PREPARING TO WRITE

Do you need to prepare in any way before you write? If you have a story pretty well in mind, you are probably ready to write. But if you need story ideas to get started, you can draw upon or make use of several resources: a journal you've kept, freewriting, brainstorming, reading and reflection—or a combination of approaches. And, to aid in learning technique, many self-help writing books like this one are on the market.

JOURNAL

Not all writers keep a journal, and I'm not suggesting that everyone should do so. A journal takes time away from your creative writing. You may end up expending energy on journal keeping instead of fiction, and you may never end up using the material you write in your journal. Having said that, a journal can be a great resource for story ideas—at both the drafting and revision stages—and the writing you do in a journal is nonstructured writing. Journals encourage freewriting, brainstorming, and imagining. Any idea, observation, or question can later be used to help develop characters, flesh out plots, or add realism to a scene.

If you've kept a journal, look it over carefully for potentially useful material. I suggest concentrating, at least initially, on the following fictional elements: character, conflict, setting, plot, and idea. Whenever you discover details related to these elements, note them in some way for future reference (e.g., highlight the text or add tabs to the pages). As you mine your journal, you may want to write down interesting combinations of details and add new ones. In other words, take time to flesh out what you find of value. What intrigues you? Work with that. Go for the passages that exude energy, the ones that spark the imagination.

Character

Mine your journal for all of your notes about character. We can think of a character as having an interior as well as an exterior. Let's consider both.

Character Interior

Throughout your journal, you may come across any number of details that relate to the interior characteristics of real or imagined people. These can include character traits, sensibilities, motives, thoughts and feelings, attitudes, assumptions, goals and aspirations, and a host of other things true of humans and their emotional and intellectual lives. Check your journal for:

- **TRAITS:** Did you note descriptive words such as *honest, forthright, dishonest, devious, hardworking, slothful, intense, laid-back, energetic, sluggish, imaginative, dull-witted*? Read your journal to see if you've included these kinds of details. Which ones might you use as starting points for interesting character creation?
- **SENSIBILITIES:** Look for any evidence of a character being open or receptive to a particular kind of pursuit, subject area, or activity: music, art, technology, travel. Look for any details that pertain to beauty or ugliness, to flights

of fancy, to endless routine. What is ugly to one person is beautiful to another. What is challenging to one person is horrifically boring to another. Details that capture basic sensibilities can really define a character. Sensibilities get close to who a person is, so if you've recorded this kind of material, you'll profit from tapping it well for your story or novel.

- **MOTIVES:** Comb your journal for any indications of motives drawn from your experiences, imagination, reading of fiction, the media, or wherever you picked up details that help explain what drives people to do what they do. You may have noted how someone acted solely for money, or for fame, or for altruistic reasons. Or for a sense of well-being, perhaps to make up for some wrong committed in the past or to give someone needy a leg up. Ferret out all of these. Motives drive actions. And in fiction, this usually means conflict.

- **THOUGHTS, FEELINGS, AND CONCERNS:** It's difficult to separate feelings and thoughts. What is emotional and what is rational? These concepts overlap. But if you've expressed your own feelings and thoughts about a given matter in your journal, or if you've written about a character's feelings and thoughts, these might be quite useful in a creative piece. They might be feelings and concerns about the many stresses of living in this world: getting everything done, trying to stay afloat economically, trying to keep one's kids out of danger and trouble. Who doesn't have such thoughts, feelings, and concerns? You can see how useful these might be in a story. This is the stuff of realism and of plot.

- **ATTITUDES:** Character attitudes greatly contribute to reader interest. Unless it's an utterly plot-driven story, readers like to know a character's take on the world. Look for attitudes that are particularly provocative. Let's say your journal entry reads something like this: "My character will have the attitude that no one, absolutely no one, is to be trusted. Everyone out there is out for number one." This attitude is likely one that will spark conflict.

- **ASSUMPTIONS:** Look for places in your journal where you've recorded things that people, or imagined characters, assume. What kinds of things do we assume about the world? That people like or dislike us, that a particular kind of work will be interesting, that certain people are against us, that certain people have ulterior motives, that what we absorb from the media is factually true or isn't, that we are mostly good, that other people are mostly good. Assumptions are unsupported by hard evidence. Read through your journal for possible reflections on assumptions. Who in this world doesn't live according to some assumptions? Mere assumptions are sometimes the bedrock of great fiction—of stories based on the appearance/reality theme. Youthful innocence often makes a lot of assumptions about the world; such assumptions end up being wrong and lead to painful results. We call this the rite of passage story—the story from innocence to experience.

- **GOALS AND ASPIRATIONS:** Somewhere in your journal, perhaps in several places, you may have written about your own goals, others' goals, or imagined characters' goals. Reader interest is naturally stirred by goals that characters set for themselves, or that others (parents, spouses, teachers) set for them, however rightly or wrongly. Look for these. Don't separate such goals from other details that you may have linked to them as you wrote: motives, thoughts and feelings, attitudes, and assumptions. After all, goals don't exist in isolation. As you look over your journal for such goals, you may think of more goals to write about. See if you can connect goals with other character aspects of one kind or another. Goals are often critical to the creation of interesting protagonists. With goals naturally come rug pullings. True in life, true in fiction.

External

Now we come to the observable—i.e., the characteristics we take in through the five senses. External character details include physical appearance, mannerisms, peculiarities of speech, and actions.

- **PHYSICAL APPEARANCE:** If you've kept a journal for very long, you've undoubtedly described a character. You may have described this character generally ("tough," "weak," "harmless looking"), or specifically ("6' 2", 180 pounds"), or concretely ("leather-neck, biceps the size of most men's thighs"). If in one place in your journal you have general characteristics and in another place you have specific or concrete details that could conceivably go with these general characteristics, you may want to make the connections. You might take time to add details and explore the relationship between the general and the specific—in this way you will visualize characters that might end up peopling your fiction.
- **MANNERISMS:** Very likely, you have noted such characteristics as tics, interesting or distinctive facial expressions, or tendencies to compress the lips, shrug the shoulders, bite nails, or interrupt others. You may find isolated notations about these, or they may be connected with other details, such as emotional states, concerns, or attitudes. Useful stuff here! Such details individualize characters, and in fiction we want distinctive persons, not mere types.
- **PECULIARITIES OF SPEECH:** This could include stuttering, clearing the throat, pauses at significant times, hurried speech, slurring, or long spells of silence. Perhaps in your

experiences simply listening to conversations, you've noted these kinds of peculiarities. If so, they may be useful
for individualizing a character. What, after all, would Billy
Budd be like without his stutter? Or for that matter, Billy
Bibbit of *One Flew Over the Cuckoo's Nest*?

- **ACTIONS:** You may have noted examples of devious behavior: lying, cheating on one's spouse, and shaky business practices. Or you may have recorded noble behaviors: saving someone's life, giving a rescue animal a
home, honoring a loved one's memory. It's likely that
some of your entries may be linked to internal characteristics: motives, feelings, concerns, attitudes, beliefs,
and values. Such actions, with accompanying motivations, can be useful in creating dramatic movement in
your story or novel.

Synthesizing: Pulling It All Together

Now it's time to make as many associations as you can between
the various, perhaps numerous, entries you've made in your journal regarding the multifaceted nature of character. What goes together? What possibilities do you see as you match interior and
exterior qualities—sensibility, say, with certain observable mannerisms? Play with these things, noting interesting combinations.
Can you see a character beginning to form?

Conflict

Fiction thrives on friction and fire. Go over your journal and seek
out the following kinds of conflict:

- **COMPETING INTERESTS:** Characters often collide when
they both want the same thing. Perhaps your entries reveal how ruthless a character is or how willing or unwilling he is to compromise, how willing or unwilling
to fight. Maybe your journal entry reads something like
this: "He is extremely invested in the pursuit of his own

goals, and he refuses to back off no matter how much trouble he encounters." Or: "She makes too many compromises, she feels, and she attributes this to a hesitancy to engage in conflict." These entries invite further exploration. What are the goals? What's the nature of the opposition? What's the nature of the compromise? If and when you encounter entries like this in your journal, dig a little deeper. You might discover great material for character conflict.

- **PERSONALITY CONFLICTS:** Look for details related to how personality itself often leads to conflicts. Let's say you've written about antagonism between an extrovert and an introvert—how one can't relate to the other, how the extrovert expects the introvert to come out of his shell. And maybe you have a line like this from the introvert's point of view: "Give me a break if I don't want a public self." You can see how this kind of clash—perhaps between friends or spouses—could yield some interesting real-life conflict.

- **COMPETING VALUES:** Characters collide because they possess different values. Maybe you've written about how some people value their jobs and careers more than their families. Maybe some of your entries deal with a clash of values over such issues as war, poverty, or the environment. Differences in values can make for substantive conflicts. Sometimes people are quite invested in their values—whether or not they've carefully examined the underpinnings for these values. Characters who haven't done so sufficiently can certainly make interesting dynamic characters—as their values come into conflict with others' values, they may grow in self-knowledge. Perhaps some journal entries provide the makings of an interesting character arc.

Synthesizing

It's very likely that when you look for journal entries related to conflict, you will find, as with other kinds of entries, some isolated details—perhaps a notation from the news about two people who both wanted X, a quarrel broke out, and there was a killing. But you may find several entries that explain character conflicts in terms of character goals, attitudes, values, or assumptions about the world. These multidimensional entries are quite valuable, as I've suggested. In other cases, where only conflict issues are apparent—with no delving into character—look for relevant connections you might make with journal entries on character. Imagine, for instance, a conflict entry reads something like: "A character goes after the neighbor's dog, that little beast that's constantly tromping on his flower beds and urinating on his roses." Let's say you have an entry on character that could go well with this conflict/action passage that reads something like: "A character thinks that his space is his space, and others will have to respect that or pay the penalty." Maybe when you were combining character details, you placed along with this attitude what was once an isolated physical appearance detail: "He's a small guy, but very well built. He's no one you would want to mess with." You could put all three of these details together—the conflict/action, the attitude, and the physical appearance—and a really interesting character begins to develop.

Setting

A typical activity in journal keeping is noting interesting details about place and storing them for future use. In some cases, perhaps you've written only one-liners. In others, you may have written an expanded description that might run half a page or more. As with character, these lines or passages could be general, specific, or concrete. You may have connected setting with other elements, perhaps character—situating this character in a given context. A lover of nature? One who feels alienated in an urban environment? Look for entries on the following kinds of places:

- **NATURAL:** Descriptions of natural settings might include accounts of the countryside: pastures, cropland, woods, rivers, mountains. These might be quite useful not only to situate your characters but also to create mood and, in some cases, could be used symbolically.

- **DWELLINGS:** You may find cause to describe your character's gated mansion, house, mobile home, apartment, hotel room, or some other dwelling where she lives or is temporarily located—perhaps just a room in someone's house. If the latter, perhaps it's on the dark side ... consider how crowded and depressing Raskolnikov's room is in *Crime and Punishment*. Or perhaps you discover a journal entry more on the lighter side: "Her house was full of surprises. Everything seemed to be rigged up like a practical joke." This would bear some probing for plot as well as theme.

- **WORK PLACES:** You may have extensive commentary on places of work, especially your own work place. Some work settings can certainly create considerable interest, and much of this interest is stimulated by the physical details of the setting itself. The iron foundries in "Life in the Iron Mills" by Rebecca Harding Davis are a good example. As is the meat-packing plant in Upton Sinclair's *The Jungle*. Work-place setting details can certainly be useful in creating characters whose lives center around work. Consider how important work-place setting is in the popular TV series *Mad Men*.

- **INSTITUTIONS, PUBLIC AND PRIVATE:** This can include hospitals, prisons, university campuses, and government offices. Of course, these are all work places as well, so decide on their best uses. Are you interested in developing a character whose work life is at an institution of some kind, or are you interested in a character whose life is affected by a government entity? In both instances, setting could be pretty important. If you've recorded details related to institutions of some kind, explore different possible uses, imagining a character and a possible story line as well.

Plot

As writers, we are constantly coming up with plots for stories—something we get from the newspaper or television, or something overheard in a conversation. What plots have you identified in your journal? Imagine a character that would make this plot work well. Or choose from the characters you may have already discovered. Explore this plot. Can you plan it out a little? How would it begin? How would it turn out? What would be the major causes?

Abstract and General Ideas

Look for abstract ideas you've written about—thoughts about the nature of people, the nature of society, romantic relationships, gender differences, war, natural disasters, the nature of success and failure. Maybe you'll think of more as you note the ideas you've captured in journal entries. When you're getting into your story drafts, some of these ideas might emerge in a character's thoughts or dialogue. They will be grist for the mill in terms of theme.

Connecting Journal Entries

The combinations and permutations of your journal entries could be manifold, and if so, they will likely invigorate your imagination. Play around with numerous possibilities by connecting items in different ways. Maybe a story will take shape in your mind. The more it does, the closer you will be to completing a general plan for your story or novel. But, as I suggested at the outset, it's possible that your journal won't yield useful information—at least not for a story or novel you'd like to write at this point. If that is the case, save your journal for later—maybe you'll discover a use for it when you work on another story or novel. For now, don't worry. There are other avenues for generating ideas and material: namely, freewriting and brainstorming.

But before I go into the details of these methods, I want to emphasize that you can use journal details for both drafting and revision. Once you have a draft to work with and you're in revision mode, look over your journal and plug in details at various places in the story or novel as you see fit. You can do this by inserting boldface notations in the text itself or by making use of the comment function in Track Changes, assuming you work in Microsoft Word. Or, if you prefer to work on hardcopy, mark on your manuscript in pencil or pen.

FREEWRITING

If you have not kept a journal, try freewriting to come up with story ideas and details. There are two kinds of freewriting: unstructured and structured.

Unstructured Freewriting

If you have nothing in mind—no character, no plot, no subject—a totally unstructured freewriting exercise can be especially productive. Writing is discovery, and freewriting promotes discovery through writing. Set a timer for ten minutes or longer and write nonstop for that amount of time. Keep the pencil or pen scribbling or computer keyboard clicking away. Some would suggest that if you can't think of what to write, then write something like this: "I can't think of anything to say." Keep writing that over and over. Don't stop! No matter what. Keep writing, regardless of how nonsensical it gets.

That's unstructured freewriting. And I suppose that if you keep writing, "I can't think of anything to say," over and over, eventually you'll tire of this and ask *why can't I?* And then let the answer take you to a subject, which will then lead to another subject, and so on. Try this sometime, if you haven't already. Or you might cheat a little and look around and see an object—a tree, anything—and start writing about it.

Structured Freewriting

If you have a subject—just an idea or two about a character, conflict, or setting—that intrigues you, you can use freewriting to help you come up with ideas pertaining to that subject. Let your imagination run. Free-associate, letting one thought or detail lead to another. The result will be scrambled, but that's fine. You're generating ideas and information—that's all. Don't stop to organize! To give you some structure to work with, I'm going to suggest that you freewrite with the following in mind:

Starting With Character

If you start with a character, perhaps a character you can visualize and have some sense of, let your imagination explore various aspects of this character. Write about what this character looks like, the character's makeup or physical traits, the character's past, what this character does for a living, whether the character is single or married, has children or doesn't, has friends or doesn't, what this character wants out of life, whether this character is pleased with his or her life. As you write, you will think of other things to explore. If you end up writing about another character and not the one you started with, that's perfectly okay. It's where your imagination took you.

Starting With Conflict

If you have a conflict in mind, consider what's happening—and why. What's the nature of the conflict? Is it internal? External? Both? Where is this conflict likely to go? What kinds of scenes can you imagine? Who will gain ground? Who will lose ground? What's the crisis situation—where does everything come to a head? How will this conflict be resolved? Explore these questions without stopping to think about them. If you stop and reflect, you're likely to constrict your imagination's free flow.

Starting With a Setting

If you begin with setting, is it isolated and quiet, or is it busy? Is it comfortable or uncomfortable? Is it boring or exciting? Safe? Dangerous? Who goes there? Why? What are they like? What's the daily routine like at this setting? What do people say about this place?

Starting With an Idea

Literature usually deals with ideas, whether explicitly or implicitly. Sometimes writers begin with ideas and want to explore them in a story or novel. The danger is in reducing your characters to pawns to illustrate your ideas. But don't worry about this as you're freewriting. Follow up on your ideas. What is intriguing about this idea? Who has it? Is it important in some way? Why is it important? Who's affected by this kind of thinking? Where do you see expressions of this idea in the everyday world? Or do you?

Synthesizing

Go over your freewriting and put together as many details as you can. See if you can develop a character, a conflict, a setting, and an idea that might drive a story. If your material for the different elements is pretty diverse, then concentrate on one fictional element—perhaps character—and do some more freewriting to see what you can discover about this character. Which conflicts will she deal with? Who will her antagonists be? Is setting important? In other words, dig deeper into what you have and see what it yields, how it shapes up.

BRAINSTORMING

Brainstorming is very much like freewriting, except it's done by creating lists instead of by writing sentences and paragraphs. (If a combination of these works best for you, why not try it?)

As with freewriting, you can brainstorm your way to a topic, or brainstorm a topic. You may want to begin with the same areas I suggested for freewriting—character, conflict, setting, and idea—using some or all of the prompts I supplied. Go over the lists you generate, synthesize, looking for patterns, add more details, and watch as a topic begins to take shape.

You can brainstorm independently, or with family, friends, or writing colleagues. It's a toss-up as to whether you should do this independently or with others. Brainstorming independently means you have no help, and others often have great ideas and insights that you would never come up with on your own. But brainstorming with others might lead you to kill a potentially good story idea if others show lack of enthusiasm or downright discouragement. Still, that's feedback too, so give it its due. Stick to the story idea if you believe in it. Others are a resource, but you have to decide how you'll react to their feedback.

READING AND REFLECTION

Read both fiction and nonfiction. Read fiction for techniques and ideas—not to use those specific ideas or even techniques, but so you can learn more about the craft of fiction, about how the pros handle the genre, and how there are no specific rules to follow. Read nonfiction for ideas. Read widely: history, current events, philosophy, psychology, science. The more you read, the more you will be aware of the world around you and the more you will be able to bring to your fiction.

Reading for Technique

Read stories more than once, and mark them up or take notes. Study the ways authors handle openings and endings, character, conflict, plot, setting, and scene, and how they energize the language, making us want to read on. Notice how the texture of the language creates character, setting, story movement, and idea. A story's style alone won't make a story, but it is indispensable to a story's craft. You will work on this in the revision stage, so store up an appreciation for language and steep yourself in the good language of compelling fiction.

Reading for Ideas

Study how authors bring out ideas in their stories and novels. Do they make authorial pronouncements? Do characters discuss these ideas? Are these ideas suggested through actions and events, or by the setting? How important are the ideas to the author? How do authors avoid mounting a soapbox? How obvious are these ideas? If they are obvious, do they seem preachy?

SELF-HELP WRITING BOOKS

There are many, many self-help books on writing, and always more coming down the pike. The value is to learn about process, technique, and resources, but also about the nature of fiction itself. What is fiction? A lie, according to scholars in the eighteenth century, so Defoe took great pains to give his work a semblance of truth. Fiction gets at the truth of the human heart, said Hawthorne. Fiction is moral, said John Gardner.

You may not need a particular theoretical framework for the fictional act, but I do think it is good to connect technique with idea—to see that the act of fiction is an act of creating a world that suggests something—that's larger than its literal self. Fiction is an art form that has many dimensions: aesthetic, philosophical, moral, and so on. To learn technique, I certainly don't think you need to read a shelf full of writing books before you begin writing, but I do think if you make them part of your reading regimen you will get a better idea of what you're doing, just as a craftsman who studies technique gets a better idea of his craft. Study the craft by reading fiction and reading about fiction.

PROCESS SHEET #2

Lay out your strategy for generating ideas for your stories or novel. Complete this process sheet for each story for which you generate potential ideas.

1. Choose one or more of the following for pre-writing: A. Journal entries, B. Freewriting, or C. Brainstorming.
   A. If you choose journal entries, play around with possibilities for your entries for character (both interior and exterior details), plot details, and ideas you've generated. Try to put these details in some workable order—something that will help you get started on a story.
   B. If you choose freewriting, try to shape any details you have accumulated that might get you started on a story. Add more as these spark thought.
   C. If you choose brainstorming, shape any notes you've taken during brainstorming sessions. If these organized notes spur further thought, add to your list.
2. Take an hour or so to write down what you've recalled from your reading, whether fiction or nonfiction. What ideas have you picked up that might work well in a story or novel? What ideas for characters have you picked up, if any?
3. If you've gathered some ideas on craft from reading stories or novels, or have read any books on the craft, write down some key things you've learned.

EXERCISE 1

Keep a journal for a week. Write down interesting ideas
for stories, interesting people you've encountered, intriguing settings, imagined thoughts, overheard conversations. Shape these details and thoughts for a future story.
Go over what you've written. Is there anything you need
to add? Fill in holes as well as you can.

EXERCISE 2

Try either unstructured or structured freewriting. If you
use unstructured freewriting, follow it up with structured
freewriting on a topic of interest that emerged in your
unstructured session. If no topic of interest emerged,
choose one now. Let your imagination go, and see what
you can produce using structured freewriting. Try to
shape your materials into a story or novel idea. Read over
what you've done and add more details if you see places
to embellish.

EXERCISE 3

Try brainstorming by yourself, with another person, or
with a few writers you know. Pick a topic that interests
you—one you think might be good for a story. Write down
the ideas, or record them on tape. See if this session
produces anything you might be able to use for a story. If
it does, write up a tentative story idea.

EXERCISE 4

Take notes on your fiction and nonfiction reading for one week. Be attentive to places, ideas, and characters and the way they tick. What useful insights have you learned from your reading? Sum up. Is there anything here for a story?

CHAPTER THREE

DRAFTING

Before you begin drafting your story or novel, be sure to review Chapter One to brush up on the elements of fiction, especially if you've been a nonfiction writer up to this point. Also look over any preliminary work you may have done: journal entries, freewriting, and brainstorming. Now it's time to make a plan—or refine a plan you may have already come up with.

THE INITIAL PLAN

It is certainly possible to write a first draft of a story or even a novel without any plan at all, without generating a single thing from journal entries, freewriting, or brainstorming. You can simply freewrite your way into a story: Wait for characters to pop up, watch for conflicts to emerge, observe the story line as it unfolds before you, and take it all down. But the risk of doing this, especially with a huge project like a novel, is that you will produce a story that goes every which way, with no focus at all. This will require much more drafting during the revision process. If that works for you, then by all means do it. Otherwise, consider adopting one of two different plans—a general one or a more detailed one.

But I do want to emphasize: Writing from a plan doesn't mean simply connecting the dots. The imagination must have plenty of room to play.

A General Plan in Mind

Think of a general plan as a map showing the principal streets, roads, or highways of your story. Much remains to be filled in and to discover, and that's the role of the imagination. This basic plan will work for a short story or novel. The latter simply calls for a broader canvas that includes subplots and more secondary characters. Here are some points to consider as you develop your plan:

- **WHAT YOUR MAIN CHARACTER IS LIKE:** Have a general sense of your character's personality, traits, ambitions, goals, and aspirations. What does your character do for a living? Do you have more than one main character? If you have more than one, how do they differ in their traits, goals, etc.?
- **POINT OF VIEW:** What makes your character an interesting vantage point for this story or novel? Which point of view seems right for this story—first or third? Why do you feel this way?
- **GENERAL PLOT:** If you have one main character, how will the plot turn out? If you have two, how will it resolve— more in favor of one than the other? If so, why?
- **SUBPLOT:** If you're writing a novel, will you have any subplots? What will your subplots be? How will they relate to the main plot?
- **SETTING:** Where do your characters live? A rural or urban environment? Is the setting important or symbolic in some way?

This general plan does not have to be completely intact for you to begin. You can start with a plan that isn't as fully developed and let your imagination kick in to help you discover a possible direction as you write. If at any point you feel your story or novel seems to be going nowhere, or everywhere, read over what you've written up to this point, do some more planning, and then get back to writing. Do keep in mind that whatever plan you create is tentative and subject to change—not just in the revision stage but also in the drafting stage. And if your imagination is fully fired up, it *will* most likely change.

Detailed Plan

With the detailed plan, the general road map becomes stronger in focus. You move in for a closer look. The question is, how much do you want to micromanage a story or novel in advance of writing it?

In an extreme case, the detailed plan covers practically everything that you can imagine at the outset: a complete portrait of your character, most conflicts that arise, most of the action, the overall plotline and novel subplots, the spots for summary and scene, the various setting details, how the story will open, how it will close, good symbols and effective metaphors and similes, and the story ideas that will relate to all the foregoing. Some scenes might even be planned out with lines of dialogue added.

This may sound really attractive because the work seems close to finished—all that's left to do is connect the dots. But if you engage in too much planning, you will probably rob your fiction of its imaginative power. A detailed plan that isn't *overly* detailed might look something like this:

- **WHAT YOUR MAIN CHARACTER IS LIKE:** In addition to a general sense of your character, you would want to know what specific things will happen to this character at various stages in the story: how key conflicts arise and are resolved or not resolved in relation to the character's overall arc. If you have two main characters, do the two arcs intersect at some point? Does one character rise, the other fall? Do they compromise? You'll want to be able to trace the trajectory of each character from section to section in a short story or from chapter to chapter in a novel.

- **SECONDARY CHARACTER(S):** In addition to knowing the basic functions of the main characters, you will plan out secondary characters as well, assuming you have more than one. This will be a much larger project for a novel. You'll show how, at each stage of the main characters' stories, the secondary characters enter in—if they do. What effects do they have? How do they help drive the plot?

- **POINT OF VIEW:** In addition to choosing the right vantage point and the right narrative point of view (first, second, or third) for the story or novel, you will decide on the character's voice and the style needed to create this voice. If you have two characters, considered together, will these two voices create the overall tone you want this story to have?

- **GENERAL PLOT:** You will create a skeletal plot outline, identifying the key movements of the story for your character or characters and how they all add up to the final scene. In the case of a novel, it makes sense to write brief chapter outlines or summaries.

- **SUBPLOT:** Plan out each subplot of your novel the same way you did for the general plot, deciding how subplots relate to the main plot. Perhaps they are parallel or even contrastive.

- **SETTING:** Identify each key setting. Does setting act as a structuring device? How does setting relate to character? To mood and tone? To the story's overall theme?

With all this, you have a pretty extensive guide to write from—perhaps too extensive, but not if you remain open to change at any time. You certainly should have the confidence to get started. Think of this plan as a collection of great starting points for further discovery. It's not all here—yet. There are plenty of pockets to fill.

DRAFTING

Before we get into drafting from a plan, I want to urge you not to "fix" as you draft. Granted, fixing as you write is a valid approach, but I'm suggesting an alternative method in this book: Draft now and wait to fix later.

I do want to make two exceptions, especially for the novel. If you realize after you've written a few pages that your point of view seems off—something just doesn't sound right—then restart and try a different point of view. The mechanical changes of *I* to either *he* or *she* are certainly daunting enough in a novel, but changing point of view may well call for substantive revision—not just mechanical substitution. There's more at hand than that, as I will show in Chapter Six.

The other exception I will make up front is the question of tense. It's quite tiresome to have to change the tense of an entire novel, so if after a few pages you see that present tense doesn't sound right, shift to the past—or the other way around.

Other than these two exceptions made early in the drafting process, keep a steady forward momentum as you draft. You will have plenty of time to fix things later.

Now, how do you go about drafting from a plan? You let the plan, whether general or detailed, guide you in a particular direction. Meanwhile, you let your imagination have its own way.

Giving Your Imagination Free Rein

In the drafting stage, it's important that your imagination have dominion over everything you've planned for the story. Let's consider character. A character in literature is a complex creature. To seem real, it must spring forth from the materials of the story and emerge with a life of its own. If you want characters to have the spark of life, don't trap them in a given mold. Don't control them like a puppeteer. Things you thought might happen, based on your conception of your character, might not happen after all because you misunderstood your character. Perhaps this character doesn't respond the way you had imagined or planned. Because even if a character is your own creation, the imagination takes over and sees other possibilities at the intuitive level—contrary to what straight reason had planned. Characters with vitality are like dogs on leashes; they want to do their own thing. And you must let them.

The same can be said for conflict and plot. You have in mind a general idea regarding what's going to happen in your story or novel, but if you find yourself shifting to different conflicts— perhaps more interesting or more surprising—don't hold back. And don't engineer the way the conflicts in your story are resolved. A forced ending will *feel* forced, to you as well as to the reader. If a completely different ending insists to be written, indulge it. Maybe in the revision stage you will see how improbable such an ending is, but meanwhile let it have its own way.

Avoid engineering dialogue. Don't force your characters to speak in a certain way—as either educated or uneducated, or with a certain regional or ethnic accent. Don't write long, labored sentences to reflect the speech of an educated person unless such dialogue comes naturally to this character. Let the language happen—you hear it and record it.

The point is: Don't force things, but don't hold back either— my two watchwords on letting creativity have its way. You may end up with a story or novel quite unlike the one you had initially planned, but it may also be a much better work of fiction. Maybe the one you planned is flawed in some way. Maybe the characters you conceived in the passion of creation refuse to be straitjacketed to fit your outline; they're more complex than that. Don't trash the outline, though; it may have some use in the revision stage— or even later. There are always more works of fiction to be written.

Taking Risks

You can do more than let creativity have its way. You can go out on a limb. You can spin improbable details about your character, improbable conflicts and plot developments, improbable scenes and language. Improbable ideas. Maybe some of this would come anyway when you open yourself up to the imagination, but I'm speaking here of charging the imagination with new fire: making things up that challenge fact, truth, ordinary beliefs, and reason itself. I don't mean forcing aspects of the story—I mean letting yourself really go, breaking all barriers.

What does "novel" mean, after all? It means "new." Fiction itself must be new, and not tired, trite, or hackneyed. So let your mind wander now and then from the general direction and see what happens. You can always chop away during the revision stage—mercilessly, if need be. But meanwhile, do the unexpected and take risks.

Some Cautions

Truth is not necessarily your friend in the production stage. Truth can intervene and hold up a stop sign. *That is off. That isn't the case.* Or: *That would never happen.* But fiction is about a different sort of truth. Truth in fiction is the truth related to a particular context; it can be bent or adjusted to support a unique story or idea, unless we're speaking of straight realism, where we expect the reader to match up the reality in the short story or novel pretty squarely with the observed reality of the everyday world around us.

Fiction and Fact

One area of caution, then, is the question of fact. If, in a realistic novel you say the biggest mall in the country is in St. Louis, readers will raise their eyebrows. The largest mall in the country is not actually in St. Louis, but it *could* be in St. Louis, and if you're not writing strict realism, you can take the liberty of putting it there—as long as it doesn't jerk your reader out of the story. If you're writing historical fiction, you must be careful to give a sense for the time, the place, and the historical persons, but you clearly have room for the imagination to roam. Fiction isn't about verifiable facts, nor is fiction social science, and its truth has to be judged by different standards.

Notions of the Improbable

Some readers may have a mental list of certain improbable human behaviors, regardless of the contexts of the story. Don't cave in, thinking you cannot include a given behavior just because some peevish reader out there might think people don't act in this way, have never done this, or never would. In your story, they do. At least in the production stage they do. Go with it.

The element of improbability always comes up in fiction. What we mustn't do as writers, or as readers, is judge a character's action in isolation. We must see it in the context of character and circumstance. With some characters, and in some circumstances, it might be quite convincing that a character would quit a job within a few months of retirement. It's hard to believe, sure, but believable for *this* character in *this* situation. Even so, this is a matter to be addressed in revision—to test out the action to see if it does, in fact, work. For now, in the production stage, don't imagine that anything is out of the question. People do all kinds of things. When you're in the midst of drafting, you don't want to be held back—at all—by limited or conventional notions of human behavior.

Ism's

Your imagination can really be stifled in the drafting stage if you listen to your mind's charges of racism, sexism, and speciesism. Write it as it comes; rethink it when you get to the revision stage. You'll have to decide later whether or not a woman who is represented as empty-headed or a man who is represented as muscles-only is sexist. Or whether a person of color comes off as stereotypical for a given ethnicity. Or whether a deer hunter is a speciesist. If you self-monitor and trim early on, you will limit what your imagination can come up with and perhaps damage the potential power of the work. Please understand that I'm not suggesting in the least that it's okay to produce a racist, sexist, or speciesist story or novel. I'm simply saying that you need to save these matters for the revision stage, where you will take a critical eye to everything.

Personal Revelation

The fear of revealing facts about yourself can really block imagination. While fiction is different from memoir, you might still worry that revealing certain autobiographical facts will come back to haunt you. But again, save this concern for later, when you can take a more objective look at your work. Then, if you see fit, you can use your scalpel to cut out anything that might offend others or make you feel uncomfortable. Perhaps you will decide to veil the information in some way. Or perhaps you will keep it as is, regardless of the costs.

Writing for the Market

Keep in mind that if you continuously tell yourself that this piece of fiction is just not marketable, you will maim your story. And besides, maybe it *is* publishable. The important point for the production stage of your piece is that you mustn't scotch the wheels of your creativity. Concerns over marketability could dig into every aspect of your story: You may worry about characters who won't be of interest to readers, plotlines that are overworked, or politics that are going to offend certain readers. Put aside such concerns for now. Wait until the writing is finished, and then shop the manuscript around. If it's not publishable, revisit and revise—if you so choose. But don't stifle your work in its earliest stage—the first draft's life depends on your unrestrained creativity.

Writing Time

A short story can run anywhere from ten to twenty-five pages, double-spaced, 12-point. If it's much shorter than ten, it's flash fiction; if it's much longer, it's a long story; and if it's very much longer, it's a novella.

Writing a standard-length short story is certainly an invest-ment of time, but a novel is a much greater investment. Which-ever form you are writing, try to find time to write. Your schedule may not permit a set time, and that's okay. Work in time for your writing whenever you can, and aim for steady progress.

Short Story

When writing a short story, either gun it out in one sitting, or pace yourself over several writing sessions. The benefit of a one-sitting story is that you don't lose momentum. It's all written in that flash fire of creation: the character, the conflicts, the scenes, and the setting. To change the metaphor, the cake is baked. Of course, it may actually be half-baked, but for now that's okay be-cause you've put something together that feels complete, even if it's not. And who knows what the imagination has stirred up? In that one-sitting story, you sometimes find your voice.

But can you actually write that much in a single setting? An entire short story will run, as I've said, from ten to twenty-five pages. To type a standard-length story (notice I wrote *type*, not *write*) of about twelve pages takes between one and three hours. If you're really on a roll, really reeling in the material, you can pro-duce this much work in a single sitting, though you'll be pretty exhausted. But yes, it can be done.

If you can't find time for a single-sitting first draft, or if you'd prefer to take more time to let the story evolve, a longer course might be best for you. The upside to this approach is the leisurely pace, which might work better for your creative temperament. It might also work best for your time schedule, which may already be full with work, family, and other responsibilities. You might think of it this way: If you write one story a week, you will have twelve story drafts in three months. That's good production in-deed. Now you have a dozen drafts waiting to be revised. In the revision stage, you can choose which, if not all, of the stories are worthy of revision.

But what if you are simply tired of first drafts and want to go on to revision before the first three months are up? If you do this, I would recommend that you have at least a half dozen drafts to work with.

Novel

How much time must you devote to a novel? You can spend a few months on a novel, or ten to twenty years if you are very busy, get sidetracked, or write an especially long novel. If you write a novel between 250 and 300 pages in length, you should be able to craft a first draft in one to three months, which is the premise of this book.

A one-month program, modeled on the National Novel Writing Month plan, is as hurried and intense as the single-setting plan for the short story—but it takes thirty days. Over the thirty days, you crank out seven to ten pages a day to develop a novel of two hundred to three hundred pages (the NaNoWriMo plan calls for 50,000 words, or around two hundred pages). If you have an outline that is somewhat detailed—with at least sectional, if not chapter, descriptions—it will keep you on track, and you can produce your daily quota probably in two to three hours—or maybe four hours if you run out of steam, get sidetracked by life's other demands, or question the direction of your outline. If you slow down or the pace seems too onerous, you can always add an extra month to make a two-month plan. If you finish the novel in one to two months, read your manuscript and fill in where needed. If you're satisfied that you have a relatively complete draft, take a breather (a few days) before going on to the revision stage.

The three-month plan is more leisurely but still demanding. You will need to write three pages a day—much less than the one-month or two-month plan, but still a commitment. It's easy to be distracted or called away by the demands of other responsibilities, and if you're serious about drafting a novel in three months, that will mean making up for lost time by writing perhaps four instead of three pages a day or even doubling your efforts.

There is value to writing the first draft of a novel in three months or less. It is more present in your mind; the material that makes up your piece is less diffuse. It's easier to return to it, and to go on. If you write a novel over the course of years, you get further away from the characters. You have to reacquaint yourself with their struggles, and you forget some details. You can still forget things in a three-month time frame, so it's a good idea to keep notes in a writing log on where you are in your plan and reminders about characters and major aspects of your plot.

If you finish your novel in ninety days, let it simmer for a few days (that little breather I spoke of) before starting the revision stage.

SUMMING UP

When you begin a story or novel, if you do not have a direction in mind, you can draw on prewriting such as journal entries, freewriting, and brainstorming. From there you can develop a plan, if you so choose, either general or detailed, based on your preliminary work. Once you start drafting, be sure not to stifle your imagination or force things to fit your plan. Let the story unfold before you. You will probably depart now and then from the outline, but that's okay. What's important is to create a story with a lot of imaginative power.

For all novelists, I strongly suggest keeping your entire novel in one file. It's pretty inconvenient to have to remember what happened in which chapter and to have to open several files to hunt down details of one kind or another. One file makes electronic retrieval easier as well. Scroll up and down or use the Find function. When you revise, one change may lead to several others, and it's nice to use the Find function to quickly navigate your manuscript.

Save your drafts under file names that are easily recalled. Save files in more than one place—on your hard drive and on a flash drive, for instance. E-mail them to yourself. Hard copies are also a good backup plan.

PROCESS SHEET #3

1. Write a general plan for your story or novel. Include a summary of character, tentative plot, and overall idea.
2. Write down a more detailed plan for your story or novel.
3. Draft your story or novel. The draft of the story may take you one to several days. The draft of the novel should take you one to three months. As you write, keep the brakes off your imagination. Let it go where it wants to. It's okay to stop now and then so you can reason things out a little, but the more you give your imagination free rein, the more exciting your work will be. Encourage your imagination. Go a little wild at times.

EXERCISE 1

From what you gathered and shaped in either Exercise 1, Exercise 2, or Exercise 3 in Chapter Two (or from all three, if they relate), write a general plan for a story.

EXERCISE 2

From what you gathered and shaped in Exercise 1, Exercise 2, or Exercise 3 in Chapter Two (or from all three, if they relate), write a more detailed plan than what you've written in Exercise 1 above.

CHAPTER FOUR

REVISION STRATEGIES

If it's important to have a plan for drafting your story or novel, it's certainly important to have a plan for revision. In the previous chapter, I stressed the necessity of giving your imagination free rein in the first draft. Yet what you produced in that draft will certainly not be finished work—most likely it will be inspired but uneven. Solid revision transforms unfinished work by giving it levels or depths it didn't have before, smoothing it out, and producing a polished product. The chapters that follow discuss the areas you will need to consider very carefully as you revise. But before dealing with specific revision steps, I think it's important to consider some general revision strategies. What is revision all about, and how do you go about it?

ORDER OF REVISION

I want to emphasize that as you revise, you don't need to follow the order of the chapters in this book, and you might find it helpful, even necessary, to handle more than one story aspect at a time. For instance, as you work on character, you may also need to change the plot because the character, as you now conceive her, wouldn't be likely to do what you had first imagined. Or, as you work on style, you see that changing certain metaphors will change the way the reader thinks about your character or your character's world. Everything is interconnected in some way, directly or indirectly. So when you revise, think about the work as a puzzle in which every piece has its place.

THE NATURE OF REVISION

Revision is overhaul—partial or total. Revision is about tearing down walls and ripping up floorboards. It's not about changing light fixtures to make the place look a little more presentable or spiffy. Real revision digs below the surface of the work to seek out possible depths that might give the story or novel complex meanings and to further explore and refine these deep structures. (Incidentally, I'm not using "deep structure" with any specialized theoretical vocabulary in mind.)

Work with lasting value calls for some interpretation on your reader's part; it poses questions—questions that have no easy answers. The point of revision is to make your story or novel as complex and integrated in all its parts as possible, and yet to keep it as lively as possible—to keep intact its imaginative power. This, of course, is no easy task, but it's well worth the effort. When you revise, you should do five basic things:

1. Make Sure Your Work Is Complete

Is anything missing? This question leads to questions like these:

- Is your protagonist's overall arc convincing, or does it require more development?
- Does the end of the story come too quickly?
- Do some scenes need more development?
- Do some subplots in your novel need more fleshing out?
- Could more be done with secondary characters?
- Could some themes in your story or novel be given more attention?

It may take several readings of your draft to be sure it's complete. An outline, especially a detailed one, will probably serve you well here as a blueprint. Yet the question of completeness may also come down to a nonrational or intuitive sense that this story or novel "feels done." It's not too short, nor is it overlong. What's the right amount? When fiction is working, it's working because it bears the fullness of life. The course has been run. The distance covered. We're at the finish line. Or, to change the metaphor: We want no more—the meal's over—we're satisfied. But that ending ... what to do? There's, of course, plenty of room for creativity in terms of the final closure. Remember the close of the last episode of *The Sopranos*—how it ends, abruptly, in darkness? You will have to decide on the right ending for your work. I deal with that subject in Chapter Twelve.

2. Develop a More Complex Work

Range and Depth of Character

Protagonists, as I pointed out in Chapter One, should be "round," not "flat," and "dynamic," not "static." This means they are complex and have range as well as depth. But what is the benchmark of complexity or depth? How can you know where to draw the line between round and flat, dynamic and static? Certainly this is an important question to consider as you revise your manuscript. I will take this question up in general terms here and will tackle characterization in more detail in the next chapter.

A complex character resists easy summation. You can list her personality attributes, attitudes, beliefs, typical behaviors, and quirks, but something about her surpasses all of these things. Like people in real life, a complex character isn't predictable or cookie-cutter and may even have contradictory impulses. She is not a stereotype. This doesn't mean that you set out to create characters so contradictory that no explanation is possible. However, it's important as you revise to look for ways to develop more complexity in your character and to let your imagination take a second run to keep her from being pigeonholed.

Strong character conflict is crucial to creating a character with depth. An untested character is merely a sketch or portrait. When a character faces a conflict that truly matters, one in which the stakes are high enough that failure or success will affect his life in a fairly significant way, he becomes interesting to the reader. His motivations for action or nonaction must be believable and convincing. With depth comes energy and vitality, and both are essential to good fiction.

A word about secondary characters: They don't need a lot of depth, but they must nonetheless ring true. Populating your story or novel with secondary characters that are mere stereotypes or props will maim your main characters. After all, main characters play off secondary characters. Secondary characters must contribute to the energy of the main characters in some way. An exception might be a farcical, one-dimensional secondary character who becomes an interesting foil for your main character. But as a general rule, keep this in mind: If secondary characters are plain dull without an underlying benefit—say, a comic effect—their contact and dialogue with the main character could affect this character in a negative way.

Range and Depth of Ideas

Any number of human issues come up in fiction: the condition of being human, the challenges to human happiness, and the compromises people make. All of these are important issues. As you revise, avoid clichéd treatments of such issues, obvious conventions, and the hackneyed. Your first draft—unless your imagination has truly been charged and has led to some real surprises—will include some clichés. The whole draft, alas, might be one big cliché—but don't be alarmed. Clichés can be freshened up. Now is the time to rethink, re-experience, tackle the draft with new energy, and uncap something new. Read the story over carefully, and give your imagination another chance to have at it.

What is a cliché? A cliché may be a phrase (he *ran like the wind*) or an occurrence or idea. If you have heard it before, if it seems like the same old thing, it's a cliché. If your character learns that life is precious and that we should live each day as if it's our last, your plot is clichéd and your story idea is clichéd. If the father in your story is an alcoholic who abuses his wife and children, you are once again traversing well-tilled soil. And yet, a refreshing treatment could redeem your story if you see new qualities in the father that aren't the typical qualities we've seen and heard before. To escape clichés, you must peer more deeply into your characters and their issues, going for as much complexity as you can. Again, this means deep-structure revision.

3. Work on Overall Focus

A literary work must have sharp focus, though how this focus is achieved certainly varies from work to work. Issues of focus naturally arise in the handling of plot and structure or the order of story parts. Plot-wise, does the story include extraneous material that sidetracks the reader? Structure-wise, are the story parts organized to achieve the desired effect? Or does the work feel scattershot? Be prepared as you revise your story or novel to determine what is needed, what isn't, and where it should go structurally to create the best effect.

Basic Plot

A plot can lack clear focus if too many conflicts are included. If the plot is overcomplicated, the reader might miss the main conflicts. As you revise your manuscript, look for places to keep the key conflicts in the forefront of your reader's attention. If the cause-effect relation between the various conflicts isn't clear—if the story doesn't advance clearly from A to B to C—the reader may become confused and the work will seem diffuse.

I don't mean to say you should aim to make the work overly obvious. You can keep the reader guessing, but by the end of a short story, the reader should be able to separate the main conflicts from the minor ones—and by the end of a novel, the reader should be able to separate the main plot from the subplot or subplots.

Also, don't clutter your work. Imagine if Flannery O'Connor wrote several pages about Pitty Sing, the grandmother's cat, in "A Good Man Is Hard to Find." Wouldn't that throw the reader off? Imagine a substantial portion of "The Open Boat" given over to the narrator's life prior to the present time frame of the story. The story would surely lose essential unity—and force. The key is to find the heart of your story and dump what doesn't pertain. Ask yourself this: Does this material belong, or does it take the work off course? This is, of course, a judgment call.

Structure

Certainly you will need to decide on the order of story parts: summary, flashback, scene, exposition, and description. Which should go first, second, third, and so on? Do as much as you can to avoid a scattered effect. Sometimes flashbacks cause readers to lose focus, especially if the flashback is too long. A long summary or long expository section can have the same effect if the momentum of the story is lost because the key conflict is delayed. Make note of such issues as you revise. Determine the key conflict and decide on the best way to organize your story to achieve the greatest impact.

4. Work on Appropriateness and Effectiveness

The issue of appropriateness comes up in regard to both point of view and style. Does this point of view deliver the right effect: an interesting plot and ideas, a compelling effect on the reader? Is the style appropriate for your protagonist, for this story? Does it enhance or does it detract?

Rethinking Point of View

When considering or reconsidering point of view, you must address two separate issues. One issue is the vantage point of the story: Is this character the right lens or filter for this story? Or should the story be told from a different character's point of view?

A second issue has to do with narrative mode. Should your story be told in first person, second, or third? To rethink point of view, you must also consider what each narrative point of view can deliver. A brief review of Chapter One may help here. First person gives immediacy and intimacy, especially with I-narrators who are particularly self-reflexive. The third-person limited establishes more narrative distance from the character, and the third-person omniscient establishes even more distance.

Deciding on the right vantage point and the right narrative mode is important to any substantive revision. Even if you feel pretty confident about point of view, you should reconsider both aspects as you set out to revise your manuscript.

If you decide to revise point of view, you will certainly have some work ahead of you, especially with a novel. As I indicated in Chapter Three, it's not merely a matter of changing *I* to *he* or *she*. If you move from an I-narrator to a third-person limited POV, you now have much more narrative distance in your story. The intimate "I" is no longer speaking directly to us. Instead, the story has an authorial voice: a persona created by you, the author.

Such a revision means rethinking the emotional feel of the character. It can be very transformative and can give the story a completely different sound. If you have more than one protagonist and you shift from multiple first-person narrators to omniscient, or from omniscient to multiple first-person narrators, the revision will likely be even more extensive—and again, the sound of the work will undoubtedly change.

Rethinking Style

Style is the manner of expression, and it's closely connected to voice. A first draft will undoubtedly require considerable attention to style. Consider whether the dialogue needs to be more hurried and clipped in places, or perhaps the prose should be more lyrical and impassioned. Maybe the exposition seems too formal for this particular character and setting. These are matters of style, and attending to them can sometimes mean a major overhaul.

How do you determine what is appropriate? It comes down to questions about the character, plot, and key ideas of the story. Does your story's style seem fitting? Is it at odds with the narrative in any way? Is the tone off? To find the right style you must be willing to experiment with language. What feels right? What feels wrong? Should your style be informal and stripped of most detail? Or should it be formal in diction and rich with detail? Your narrative point of view may become a stylistic consideration as well. As you work on style, you will have to fit prose style with narrative point of view. The two will work hand in hand to create a certain voice. Together, they will affect the tone of the work.

5. Make Your Story a Lively Work of the Imagination

By lively, I mean inspired. The work may be quite sober or heart-rending, but it remains a lively work because the imagination energizes it at every level. If this is the case in your first draft, you should be highly thankful; maybe you're great at first drafts because you just let things happen and don't block your imagination with too much naysaying. It's possible that as you rework your manuscript with reason as your guide, you will lose some of that imaginative power. If you feel this is happening, you must return to first draft activities, keeping in mind that you must do everything to avoid turning the story or novel into something that is "perfect" but as dead as dust.

And how do you do that? On the one hand, you recognize the value of your novel plan, synopsis, or outline, but, on the other hand, you understand that art isn't bound by the rules of reason or logic. It has a sort of logic to it, sure, but art surpasses logic. There is that spirit in it, that breath of human life—that being infused in the very interstices of the story or novel—that resists a verbal summing up. This is what you go for—that pulse of life. And when the reader cannot feel that, the work is dead. The work may be competently written. It may answer to the dictates of a sound syllogism, but who cares? Is it breathing? Are the characters? Are the words? Are the ideas?

My advice is to:

- Dig more deeply into the felt life of the characters and the world they inhabit. Feel them and picture them.
- Find your voice in the material. This isn't easy, but take a section of your work where the voice sounds like you are in control of the material—where you have an air of authority. Find that same voice, a voice you want to listen to.
- Read a great novel or story, one that has that breath of human life, and try to discover how the author does it. It's important to read the whole work because you want to find out how this voice is *sustained* from section to section.

FEEDBACK

Once you have your basic story down and have done some polishing, it's a good idea to get feedback from other writers. You can make it clear that you still need to improve certain things and do some fine-tuning, but that you'd like some help on the major elements: the characters, the plot, the basic thrust of the story—whether these seem too stale or clichéd. You can ask if the opening draws readers in. You can also get interim feedback on your prose style and your handling of dialogue—in selected places—just to see what readers are thinking.

Feedback is important, but it's best to get feedback from several people, not just one or two, and also to make sure it comes from writers and not only family and friends—preferably writers who have published, who know their craft well.

What do you do, though, when responses vary? Thank those who gave responses, consider all the feedback carefully, and set aside these varied responses for later consideration. When making such decisions, you must ultimately go with your own instincts and understanding of the craft. You can't please everybody, and you shouldn't. Some readers won't get what you're trying to do. Others will be put off by attitudes inherent in the work and won't focus enough on the craft itself. Some readers simply won't be the right readers for this story. But the main thing is to profit by hearing the ideas of others and making use of what you can.

FINE-TUNING

Fine-tuning is not the same as revising, but I will touch on it here because it follows naturally on the heels of revision. The act of fine-tuning includes anything from correcting spelling mistakes to improving wording, sentence construction, and basic grammar. Fine-tuning is cleaning up the manuscript to make sure the work reads as well as it can. Sometimes when you fine-tune, you slide back into revision again. That's okay. For instance, if you begin to tinker with metaphors and similes, you might be back to revision because, as I've noted, changing metaphors may well change character, or even character action.

THE IMPORTANCE OF READING

As I noted in Chapters One and Two, reading is vitally important to good writing. As you revise, you need to continue your reading, noting how authors handle the various elements of fiction. In the chapters ahead, I will provide numerous examples from stories and novels, and you may want to read deeper into the novels or story collections that I cite. In doing so, you will see the language at work and will get a sense of the whole story versus the short excerpts I've chosen from them.

MISCELLANEOUS MATTERS

Consider working with electronic copy instead of hardcopy. Electronic copy is more affordable and also less time-consuming to work with. If you opt for hard copy, once you've made your changes, you will still need to enter them into your computer. Having said that, working with hard copy sometimes reveals issues in the writing that you may miss on the computer screen. Sometimes I've found, for instance, that I catch awkward sentence constructions, misspelled words, or flabby prose more easily on the typed page—it's hard to say why. Perhaps you've had a similar experience.

Whichever method you choose, if you're not ready to make changes yet, leave yourself notes for later. If you work with hard copy, write revision notes on your manuscript. If you work with electronic copy, leave notes in the text itself or use the comment function in Track Changes.

Saving drafts in a clear way is crucial. I've found it convenient to save drafts with dates. Then I know, without question, which is the most recent draft.

CONCLUDING REMARKS

First drafts are paint splashed on the wall. Revision is the actual act of painting, the smoothing out. It's unusual for a first draft to need little revision. It happens occasionally if you "find your voice." If it's all there, you'll feel it in your bones, the muse will be with you, and you may turn out a great draft in one sitting.

More likely, significant overhauling, with the aforementioned revision strategies in mind, is necessary.

If you're writing short stories, read through them and decide on the ones most ready for revision. Put the others aside—but definitely don't pitch them. They might strike you as great material later. During the revision phase, don't take on new writing projects. You will be lucky to revise three to six short stories well. As you will see in the upcoming chapters, turning out a short story that works on many levels is a very involved and extensive process.

If you're revising your novel, it will take all your time. Again, don't take on new work. A two-hundred- to three-hundred-page novel takes time to read and more time to revise. You might pace yourself at ten pages a day, and in one month or less—depending on the length—you'll have one revised draft. Or better yet, if you can complete twenty pages a day, you'll have two drafts in a month. That's six drafts of your novel in three months.

Looking ahead to marketing your work, for a novel you will need to develop a short synopsis, plus a "logline" (a script writing term), or one-sentence description of your book. As you revise, it's good to anticipate this because it's a way to judge the novel's overall coherence. Can you sum up your novel in a short paragraph? In one sentence? Of course, as a creative work it may be impossible to describe it adequately in a simple prose summary, but nonetheless you must attempt to get at its essence as well as you can in a paragraph synopsis. What better time to do this than when you are really close to the work—revising it, getting into its inner workings?

Revision isn't easy, but it's the nuts and bolts of writing a finished work. In some ways, producing a first draft is harder than revising—at least as far as our reluctance to begin. We must, after all, create a whole world *ex nihilo*—that is, out of nothing. And when you revise you have something to work with, and that feels good. Just don't get discouraged. A mediocre draft has the potential to turn into a great piece of fiction—the question is whether you're willing to devote all the hard work it takes.

PROCESS SHEET #4

As you've seen in previous chapters, I provide a Process Sheet at the end of each chapter. For the upcoming revision chapters, each question will be meant to provoke thought about the fictional element covered in that chapter. For now, I'd like you to do a preliminary self-check on your draft—just a way of thinking about revision issues for later. Don't let your answers alarm you—this is but the first step in the revision process.

1. If you have started writing your story or novel, what are some clues to roundness in your major character or characters?
2. What are some clues that you are hinting at ideas and themes in this work?
3. Where does your draft seem to be going at this point?
4. Does the point of view you've chosen seem appropriate?
5. Does the style seem fitting?

EXERCISE 1

From your general plan or detailed plan from Exercises 1 or 2 in Chapter Three, write two to three pages of a story. Make sure you have at least one short scene with dialogue. Does the character you've created seem round? Why or why not?

EXERCISE 2

Working with the story passage from Exercise 1, where might this story be going? In at least a paragraph, state what you think the direction seems to be.

EXERCISE 3

Working with the story passage from Exercise 1, does the point of view you've chosen seem appropriate? Why (or why not)? State your opinion in a paragraph or so.

EXERCISE 4

Working with the story passage from Exercise 1, does the style seem fitting? Why (or why not)? Explain in a paragraph or so.

CHAPTER FIVE

REVISING FOR STRONG CHARACTER

Let's start with the one element that is absolutely crucial to a solid story: believable, convincing characters. Even if the impetus for your story is an idea and not a character, the characters you create must be more than mere pawns to carry this idea out. Fiction isn't a treatise on idea or perceived truth. It's an experience that your reader must be able to enjoy imaginatively, by entering the lives of very real characters. Your fiction can certainly be rich with ideas, but *characters* attract most readers to fiction—strong characters. By "strong," I don't mean heroes or heroines. I mean characters that are richly developed— complex characters.

In this chapter we will look closely at key revision issues for characterization with an emphasis on main characters, but with some attention to secondary characters as well. We won't explore how to create strong antagonists in this chapter—that discussion belongs to Chapter Seven, where we look at the various nuances of building conflict.

Don't let your studies end with this chapter. Be sure to read pieces of fiction with an eye toward characterization. Study my examples, but seek out more of your own.

RETHINKING CHARACTERIZATION

Your main character must be a strong character—one who captures the reader's attention. Strong characters are complex; they exhibit range as well as depth. And because of this range and *depth*, we find them compelling. They are also called "round" characters. Like human beings, round characters are multifaceted: in their overall make-up, their motivations, and their actions. They are believable to readers because they possess the fullness of life and all of its wellsprings and depths. But how do you achieve such characterization? The following section of the book addresses the techniques you need for solid character revision. Beginning with roundness...

The Round Character

Creating a *Fully Human* Character

A character's overall make-up includes physical appearance, personality, attributes, habits, quirks, mannerisms, speech intonation, and typical behaviors—pretty much everything that makes a fictional character. A character without any of the above is merely a series of actions and a disembodied voice with nothing distinctive about it—hardly a character at all.

But even a draft without a shred of characterization could be substantially improved by adding details to help the reader visualize this character: his or her physical appearance, maybe a few gestures, or a distinctive tone of voice. How much more is needed? You must add whatever it takes to make this character a living, breathing human, so alive to the reader that she could step right out of the pages of the story or novel.

Consider this character description by a first-person narrator from Saul Bellow's short story "Zetland: By a Character Witness":

> Max Zetland himself had a white face, white-jowled,
> a sarcastic bear, but acceptably pleasant, entering

the merchandising palace on Wabash Avenue, neat in his office, smart on the telephone, fluent except for a slight Russian difficulty with initial aitches, releasing a mellow grumble when he spoke, his mind factual, tabular, prices and contracts memorized. He held in the smoke of his cigarettes as he stood by his desk. The smoke drifted narrowly from his nose. With a lowered face, he looked about.

This descriptive passage certainly covers a broad range: physical appearance, personality, behavior, and ability. And in this range, we discover a human being, not a stock character. On the heels of this general portrait, the character's distinctive personality is revealed in his smoking of the cigarette and his final gesture.

Or consider how human—and comic—Vladimir Nabokov makes Professor Timofey Pnin:

Ideally bald, sun-tanned, and clean-shaven, he began rather impressively with that great brown dome of his, tortoise-shell glasses (masking an infantile absence of eyebrows), apish upper lip, thick neck, and strong-man torso in a tightish tweed coat, but ended, somewhat disappointingly, in a pair of spindly legs (now flannelled and crossed) and frail-looking, almost feminine feet.

These portraits make these characters very real, though what is immediately apparent is how detailed they are. This is a matter of style, and we will explore it more fully in Chapter Thirteen. For now, suffice it to say that not all writers depict their characters—whether protagonists or secondary characters—with such profuse detail. Some are much more sparing in their use of such direct methods as description and exposition. They select representative details and rely more on the dramatic method of scene.

A good example of the dramatic method is Cormac McCarthy's postapocalyptic *The Road*. McCarthy provides no concrete description of his protagonist. His protagonist's personal attributes—his bravery and commitment in the face of terrible odds—come through not by authorial commentary but by action and speech only. Note the minimalistic style in this short excerpt:

> This was not a safe place. They could be seen from the road now it was day. The boy turned in the blankets. Then he opened his eyes. Hi, Papa, he said.
> I'm right here.
> I know.

More is suggested than stated. But clearly we feel the father's protective role in assuring his son he's right there.

So as you revise consider these two methods of characterization:

- **OPTION 1: The direct method:** You ratchet up description and exposition to capture your protagonist's appearance and distinctive qualities or attributes. Two things to consider: 1) If your point of view is third person, be as careful as you can not to *intrude* as author—keeping the reader as much as possible inside your character. 2) Be sure that your character's actions match up with, and don't seem at odds with, any descriptive passages about this character—or any expository passages covering character attributes.
- **OPTION 2: The indirect or dramatic method:** You rely almost exclusively on scene; readers depend on the details of action and speech to visualize your protagonist. Expository passages do not directly mention key character attributes; instead, you impart them via character thought.

You may decide to combine parts of each method. Describe your character physically but do not explicitly name personal attributes. Or don't describe your character physically but do explicitly name personal attributes. It's best to try these things out, and then decide.

Now that we've looked at two useful methods of characterization, let's look for specific ways to make your character fully human. As you revise, give your character:

- More than one primary goal, behavior, or attitude
- Several interests—practical, romantic, intellectual, etc.
- Some inner conflicts—about goals, about self, about others
- A personal quirk, odd gesture, or noteworthy habit
- Distinctive speech patterns or qualities

In other words, individualize your character—but don't overdo it. The character must be multidimensional but not global in dimensions. If you pile on too many inner conflicts, the story will lose focus. If your character possesses too many distinctive traits or quirks, he may seem over the top. If this is what you intend—if you're writing farce or satire, for instance—that's a different matter. But generally speaking, more is not necessarily better. Develop range and depth, but be selective.

Look for contradictions that can be explained at one level. For instance, John Harvey Kellogg of T.C. Boyle's *The Road to Wellville* reads as a truly complex human: He has an altruistic vision for his flock at the Battle Creek Sanitarium, yet many of his methods, shortsighted and extreme, contradict his impulses for good. Kellogg's grandiose dream of health at his turn-of-the-century clinic accounts for his contradictory nature. Boyle, in spite of his savage satirical thrusts, has created a fully believable, convincing human being.

Believable Motivations

As you revise for character motivation, keep in mind three things, each of which has to do with predictability. Strong characters with range and depth are not predictable—at least not generally.

First, characters, like real people, are not governed by the laws of logic. Boyle's Kellogg is an instructive example. We feel in the presence of a true-to-life character when the character's motivations are complex and even contradictory—but nonetheless believable because they are contradictory. Humans, after all, have contradictory impulses. We have two sides: the emotional and the rational. We are driven by both egoistic and altruistic concerns. Conflicts between these needs are inevitable. When you revise, make sure that you look for the possibility of contradictory motives in your character—contradictions that can be explained or understood in some way.

Second, remember my caution in Chapter Three regarding notions of improbability: Some readers might not believe your character would do what she, in fact, does. Make sure to build the context fully enough so your reader will believe that this character would do *this thing* at *this particular time*, even if it goes against conventional wisdom. Who can say what a character might actually do, given the right motivations or the right circumstances?

Third, like real people, characters might not be clear themselves as to why they do certain things. As complex human beings, we often try to figure out our own motives. If we analyze our past actions, they might make some sense; yet, we can't fully account for why we did what we did. Were our motives mixed? In human motivations, there are always gray areas—areas not defined by reason or logic—and that's what makes round characters more interesting than flat, predictable ones.

Having ended on the above note, I don't mean to suggest that it's all up for grabs as to what a character will or will not do. Several factors and influences help to explain character motivation, however ambiguous such motivation might at times be. Think about each of the following as you revise:

- **CHARACTER'S PERSONALITY AND TEMPERAMENT:** Depending on the conflict (for example, speaking in public), an introvert may react one way, an extrovert another. We can't be sure, of course. People surprise us, and characters should surprise us, too. But personality is certainly a contributing factor in character motivation. So is temperament. A person who is easily riled may react differently than a person who is slow to anger. A person who is easily frustrated may react differently than one who takes things in stride. Can you connect your character's motivations to his personality or temperament in some way?

- **ANTAGONISTS:** Antagonists of every stamp—personal, societal, natural—are an important factor in character motivation. Is your character affected enough by this antagonist to react in the way you have shown? Do the antagonist's beliefs or actions affect your character in convincing ways?

    This raises, at least in part, the question of character make-up. Different people react differently to different events. Recall my example in Chapter One regarding Miss Brill, an elderly woman who was hurt by an overheard remark.Some people are vulnerable to certain statements made by particular antagonists. Others would not be. As readers we should see connections between a character's basic make-up and her reaction to an antagonist. A complex character may or may not react in predictable ways toward antagonists. Whatever the outcome, we should see a deeply human engagement between opposing parties, and the protagonist's personality, attitudes, and personal attributes should be evident in some way—if not crystal clear.

- **CHARACTER'S PAST:** A character's past can affect how she acts in the present and can help clarify certain choices. But be careful not to oversimplify cause-effect relations. Did this past event really cause your character to do what she did? Cause and effect is, of course, a complicated matter, and it's easy to make hasty conclusions. But if you've made this past event, as well as your character's psychological reactions, compelling enough, the reader may suspend disbelief. Look for opportunities to link backstory, if you provide it, to character motivation in a believable, convincing way.

- **CHARACTER'S ACTIONS THEMSELVES:** It may seem paradoxical to say that actions can both reflect character (motivations) and affect or *develop* character. But actions have effects, not only on others but also on the person who performs these actions. Ask virtue theorists. Once one acts, one's character may change in some way. Minor crimes, if they are committed often enough, can certainly change a person. More serious crimes can certainly affect one's thinking about oneself, others, and the world as a whole. If one commits murder, isn't it credible to say that this person may never be quite the same person again? In a complex character, we see how actions aren't simply rooted in given motivations—they're more complex than that. Characters given to edgy behaviors have a way of spiraling out of control as one action leads, almost lockstep, to the next.

As you revise for character motivation, make convincing ties between your characters—their complex make-up, what influences them, affects them, and so on—and their resulting behaviors and actions. But *convincing* doesn't mean utterly logical—so allow for surprises. Don't nail everything down like the answer to a math problem; leaving your reader with some questions is a good thing to do.

Speech That's Real

To make your characters real, you must make your dialogue convincing. Perhaps your character is complex and real in all the ways we've discussed so far. But if he speaks in calculated phrases, he won't seem human or real.

We will explore dialogue in much more detail in Chapter Ten, but for now, let's look at the issue more generally. How do you revise your dialogue so that it creates strong characters? Consider the following:

- **MAKE SURE YOUR DIALOGUE DOESN'T SOUND LIKE A PREPARED SPEECH:** Unless your character speaks this way—perhaps to comic effect—the character will be very flat. How does "real" speech sound? Dialogue is artifice, as all art is, and yet it must have interesting speech rhythms that hook us and make us feel like we're in the presence of a real human being.

- **BE CAREFUL WITH DIALECT:** If you try to capture an accent, whether it's regional or ethnic, you will probably need to do some fieldwork. Otherwise you risk the character coming off as both unbelievable and hackneyed. A true-to-life character imparts a distinct air of reality. Well-researched and accurate dialects, accents, and colloquialisms will help achieve this realism.

- **MAKE SURE YOUR DIALOGUE ISN'T CANNED:** If the dialogue seems typical of what everyone says all the time about this subject or conflict, your character won't seem very unique—or complex.

- **REVEAL CHARACTER ATTITUDES:** Look for ways to let dialogue illuminate character traits and motivations. And think about this as well: Sometimes what is not said is more revealing than what is said.

Dynamic Versus Static

A round character is one who changes, while a flat character isn't likely to change—this may mean a change in behavior or a change in vision, or both. Oftentimes, it's a new way of seeing things. Sometimes, it's almost imperceptible, and yet we know this character will never be quite the same.

If you will recall, I asked about the point of a story in which the character doesn't change. If the character is a certain way at the beginning and at the end is exactly the same way, what has really happened? Is the reader expected to come to a new realization, as in *Billy Budd*? Let's consider this novella more fully. Billy Budd doesn't change at all, unless one argues that Billy's act of striking Claggart reflects change. But striking Claggart was not intentional; it was more visceral, like a leg kicking out after the knee has been struck. Billy Budd remains purely good, a sacrificial lamb; Claggart is the snake in the Garden. Both Billy and Claggart are one-dimensional characters. This fiction is much more allegorical than realistic.

In contrast, consider Charlotte Perkins Gilman's "The Yellow Wallpaper," where the protagonist does change. She descends increasingly into madness due to the oppressive regimen her husband inflicts upon her in response to a diagnosis of so-called hysteria. He encloses her in the house, discourages any mental effort, and casts her into utter dependency and isolation. Thus the seeds of her madness are planted and ripen in the story. She changes, bit by bit, before our eyes. The story is the impact this regimen has on her sanity.

In another oft-anthologized short story, Kate Chopin's "The Story of an Hour," the protagonist gains new vision, new insight. At first, she grieves when she learns of her husband's death, but then she realizes, upon further reflection, that she is in fact now free. But when her husband appears, quite alive and well, she drops dead. Is it because of her heart condition, or because she cannot tolerate living with her husband now that she has entertained the idea of being liberated from him? Surely, the latter. Chopin makes both sudden realizations—that she is free, and that she's not after all—quite compelling.

It isn't necessary for characters to change significantly. If they change too much, the reader will wonder how it happened. Even in dire circumstances, people may learn something new about themselves and others, but it's unlikely that their entire outlook on the world or personality will change. It's not easy to gain a completely new vision overnight or to change old habits. Ask yourself, is your reader likely to buy that your protagonist suddenly becomes an absolutely new somebody in the course of ten to twenty pages, perhaps spanning a few weeks or even a year? You must make the transformation convincing and real. As extreme as it might seem, we accept the transformation of Gilman's protagonist because of her intolerable situation and because Gilman meticulously dramatizes the woman's descent, by degrees, into madness. We accept Chopin's protagonist's sudden realization—symbolized by her sudden death—because the marriage had little substance to begin with. When characters are granted new insight, this realization must be earned. Also, it can't be over some utterly trivial event. The stakes must be high enough that the reader cares.

Here's a revision checklist to consider for the dynamic character. Look for the seeds of this change in:

- Your character's overall make-up
- Your character's past, if relevant
- Other characters, including antagonists
- Major incidents and how they have affected your character in terms of emotions, behavior, and so forth

As you head into revision, allow me to harp on it again: Don't attempt to work out character change with mathematical certainty. That your character would come to this new insight, whatever it is, should be believable. But if it's a little vague or obscure, that air of mystery will be interesting to your reader and probably more satisfying than a totally obvious ending—or worse yet, a tidy explanation.

THE COMPELLING CHARACTER

A round/dynamic character grabs our attention and holds onto it. We care about this character's actions. If we don't entirely sympathize, we at least empathize. We find the character engaging—compelling.

If the character is sympathetic, then this is a real plus, but be careful. Is this sympathy based on sloppy sentimentality? Stories about teenagers dying in car wrecks or children dying of cancer, though tragic and horrible in real life, tend to be thin in fiction because they quickly turn sappy. They involve *bathos* instead of *pathos*. With the former, the desired emotional response is not genuinely earned, while in the latter, it is because of the intellectual component within the story.

The central event in Tim Johnston's title story in his Katherine Anne Porter Prize-winning collection, *Irish Girl*, is a car accident and the death of a teenage boy. Johnston deals with the tragic aftermath, but the story takes on more than this. Johnston's focus is on the parochial and confining nature of a Midwestern town from which teenagers try to escape. The story moves beyond the predictable sad tale of teenage death to address this larger cultural issue. The narrator, the younger brother of the dead boy, thinks back to an occasion when his cool older brother was speaking of his girlfriend, the so-called Irish Girl. Captured in his brother's eyes the narrator saw "…the blue light, the wild secret rush when William said the words 'Irish girl.'"

This passage, taken in context, gives the story an emotional and intellectual dimension beyond the tragic accident itself. It's about youthful spontaneity versus adult restraint: wayward youth's need to break free from the constraints of dull conformity to parental rules and societal conventions. This is something we can think about intellectually. This transforms the story beyond the simple bromide that it's so sad when young people die so needlessly—which is indisputably true, but it's a truth that depends on an emotional appeal only. Johnston makes his characters sympathetic and compelling, but he doesn't do so by manipulating us emotionally.

Putting aside the question of bathos, let's consider the larger question: What is it about your character that will make your reader sympathetic? We may or may not sympathize with Henry Fleming in *The Red Badge of Courage* when he enlists to go off to fight in the Civil War; he wants to earn honor, and he is quite naïve in terms of what he's about to undergo. But if we don't sympathize with his reasons for joining up, we probably do sympathize with his profound psychological distress in confronting grisly war death. And if we don't sympathize with his running off, we can at least empathize with his choice and find something compellingly human in his need to do so, and in his need to rationalize doing so.

It's when readers can neither sympathize nor empathize that characters need real attention. If readers can find no human qualities within your characters with which they can relate, you must find ways to impart these qualities. This takes us back to the question of a complex character—a complex character will certainly be empathetic, if not sympathetic.

Yet, what about those characters who commit despicable acts? What about murderers? What about Raskolnikov, the protagonist of Dostoyevsky's *Crime and Punishment*? Raskolnikov is certainly a character with depth, and we might be able to empathize with his troubled soul, if not sympathize with his actions. We don't have to approve of what he does, yet on one level, what he does, though monstrous, can be understood in human terms. It's undoubtedly the author's deep psychological study of his crime and punishment that keeps us interested. The treatment is dramatically intense and realized fully in human terms; we want to discover more and more about this character because we find him compelling.

Largely, then, roundness, sufficiency of motivation, and adequate dramatic treatment produce compelling characters. Be attentive to the following in your creation of a compelling character:

- **MAKE SURE YOUR MAIN CHARACTER IS COMPLEX.** Very likely if your character is complex, he will be empathetic; if not sympathetic, he will at least be interesting.
- **CHOOSE PATHOS** over bathos.
- **KNOW THIS:** Even if the ideas in your story or novel are compelling, if the character is a turnoff, the reader will likely put your work down.

SECONDARY CHARACTERS

Thus far, I have discussed only main characters, or protagonists. Main characters must be developed with range and depth, but secondary characters are a different matter. Secondary characters that are developed too much overshadow main characters. The possibility of doing so is always a risk. Sometimes we might feel that our secondary characters are actually more interesting than our protagonists. And that's fine, as long as the main character engages the reader and is quite compelling. The opposite—when the protagonist is not engaging or compelling—is certainly a problem.

The same fictional techniques apply to creating secondary characters as to main characters, except secondary characters are far less complex. But you certainly do not want one-dimensional secondary characters unless they play really minor roles—or perhaps serve some comic role as I mentioned in Chapter Four. Give them a few dimensions. Those with a somewhat important part in the plot deserve some range and depth—as much as they need to fulfill their respective roles in the story. The greater the role, the more sides of that character need to be seen. But add just enough to support their secondary part in the story.

AUTOBIOGRAPHICAL FICTION

Many writers draw largely from their own experiences, and some draw almost exclusively from personal experience. They may find support in the old catchphrase, "Write what you know." This is fine as long as you keep your fictional character separate from you, the author. You are not this character. Even if you *are* alike in some or even many respects, this character is not you. You must realize that this character is a fictional creation. If you don't, you will tend to confuse fiction with fact. This will lead to more than one bad result:

- **YOU WILL ROB YOUR CHARACTER OF ITS VITALITY:** You will try to make your character fit you, the author—your traits, your attitudes, your mannerisms—but your character needs a life of her own. She may be a bit like you, but make sure you give her plenty of room to grow—to be unlike you.
- **YOU WILL ROB THE STORY OF ITS IMAGINATIVE POWER:** Your character wants to go in a certain direction, and you hold him back—note my comment in Chapter Three on restraining your characters. Your character must have his own energy and be empowered by your imagination—not by "true" life events or the way things "actually" happened.
- **YOU WILL LIMIT YOUR SETTING:** If you stick to the facts too much, you will avoid taking certain, perhaps important, risks; for example, setting your story in a city if you're from a small town, or a small town if you're from a city. Setting your story away from your own origins or present location might free up your imagination more. If you feel you've limited yourself in this regard, it may be good to rethink or change the setting, though it may take some research and a field trip or two. It's possible to energize your story by simply changing settings, unless you find they are too integral to your present story line to change without great disruption. Even so, you should feel free to change details about the setting you've chosen. What's "true" about the setting is what's true for the characters, not you as author.

PROCESS SHEET #5

1. Do you use concrete description to capture key features of your main character? If so, what are they? Who provides the description—the author or another character? Do you see any need to use more concrete description to capture key features of your character? Where might you use it?

2. Do you use exposition (or expository prose) to capture key features of your main character? If so, what are they? Do you see any need to use more exposition to capture key features of your character? Where might you use it?

3. Which of the two—prose techniques (description and exposition) or dramatic revelation (scene)—do you rely on to reveal the nature of your main character? Do you rely too much on prose techniques? Would it be better to rely more on dramatic revelation? Where might you do this?

4. What basic features of your main character help explain his motivations? Do you see any new ways to link personality and temperament of your main character to his motivations? Where might you do this?

5. Which events, if any, from your main character's past help explain her motivations? Do you see any ways to link your main character's past with her motivations? Where might you do this?

6. What are your main character's chief antagonists? How do these antagonists motivate your main character to do what he does? Are there ways to show more fully how antagonists' actions, attitudes, remarks, and the like, account for your main character's motivations? Where might you make ties or connections?

7. Do you find places where your main character's speech or dialogue seems more like prepared speech than lively dialogue? Make note of these places and plan on fixing them later when we get to Chapter Thirteen, on style (see my section on speeding up dialogue).

8. Do you find places where your character's speech or dialogue sounds canned? Which places? What plans do you have to liven up the dialogue so it's not so predictable?

9. What does your main character's speech or dialogue reveal about her key features, personality, and so on? What changes, if any, do you propose to make your dialogue reveal more about your character?

10. Is your main character round or flat? Explain. If she's flat, what plans do you have to make her more complex?

11. Is your main character static or dynamic? Explain. If he's static, what plans do you have to make him a dynamic character?

12. Is your main character compelling? If so, in what ways? If you find problems here, what plans do you have to make your character empathetic, if not totally sympathetic?

13. What is your take on your secondary characters? Are they one-dimensional or stereotypical? If so, what plans do you have to make them less so?

14. Have you written this story based on your own life? If so, are there places where you've depended too much on the facts of your own life, your background, experience, and beliefs, and on actual places and events? If so, what plans do you have to transform your story into more of a work of the imagination and less an autobiographical nonfiction piece?

EXERCISE 1

Write a sketch of a character about 200 words long. Describe this character fully: appearance, traits, gestures, and so on. Read over your work. Does the sketch create a person? Now put this person into a short scene. Again, read your work. Does the character in action seem like the one you've described? If not, make additions or deletions to be sure he is.

EXERCISE 2

Write a few pages about a character engaged in some kind of conflict. Have this character react in a scene, using dialogue and action. Do not identify the character's motivations through exposition. What are this character's apparent motivations? How can you tell? If the piece needs more work to make the motivation apparent, work on it until it's clear.

EXERCISE 3

Write a short scene with two characters who are arguing. Choose one as your main character. What ideas and attitudes are expressed? Are they canned? If so, try to make them more original.

EXERCISE 4

Write a short autobiographical piece, sticking to actual events. Use this to imagine a character different from you in a few respects. Change the setting. Change one thing that happens.

CHAPTER SIX

RETHINKING POINT OF VIEW

Point of view, as I've explained before, is the vantage point from which the story is told—the lens, or consciousness, we see the action through. A second aspect is the choice of narrative mode: first, second, or third person. Both aspects become matters of appropriateness. In Chapter Four I posed the question: Is this the right consciousness for your story? In other words, will this character's point of view be interesting or compelling? Is this the right mode? Should I use first person instead of third, or third instead of first?

If you will recall, I urged you in the drafting stage to do a test run of your point of view because changing the point of view of a finished piece requires considerable work, especially with a novel. But even if you did the test run, you may still decide during revision that you're not happy with the point of view you've chosen. You might realize that you'd like to write the story from a different character's consciousness, a more interesting vantage point. Or you might decide to view your main character from the outside, from another character's perspective. Or you might choose a different narrative mode. Of course, you may be satisfied with your point of view just as it is.

This chapter will serve you if you need to make a complete overhaul or if you simply need to tweak some areas so the point of view is handled with more skill. We'll begin with the complete overhaul of narrative vantage point.

LENS OR VANTAGE POINT FOR YOUR STORY

Whose story is this? Consider the various characters that play a part in this story. Whose perspective is the most interesting, the most engaging, both emotionally and intellectually? Think of it this way:

- Whose perspective would give us a better understanding of the human condition, the human experience, human nature, human psychology?
- Whose perspective would tell us the most about the nature of human relationships? Of some social or cultural practice?

Put your current point of view under a microscope. Would it be better to choose a different character as the vantage point?

If you pursue the revision of vantage point, keep in mind that you might be filtering your story through the mind of a character with a different personality, a different take on the world, and a different set of expectations. Whichever vantage point you switch to, you could run into one or more of the following issues: character's experience of the world, maturity of thinking, gender attitudes, and class consciousness or bias. The story material itself would surely change, probably substantially, as you recast the point of view with a different character. What would happen if the vantage point or narrative perspective in *Huck Finn* were changed from Huck to Jim? What if *The Great Gatsby* were filtered through the narrative perspective of Jay Gatsby instead of Nick Carraway?

If you're questioning your narrative perspective—or perhaps you're considering two narrative perspectives instead of one—

you should decide on the best possible vantage point, or vantage points, from which to tell this story. Besides the general character issues I named above, plus more—personality, traits, sensibility, and so forth—you will have to consider the following character-specific issues related to your new character or characters:

- **STAKE IN THE MATTER AT HAND:** Will it be the same as your present character's? What gives this character a stake in the matter?
- **KNOWLEDGE OF CERTAIN CHARACTERS, ACTIONS, AND CONFLICTS:** Will this character be as likely to know as much about these matters as your present character? Is this character an insider or an outsider?
- **ABILITY TO CHANGE:** What will it take to make this character change? Does this character have as much potential to change, or less, than your present point-of-view character?
- **ISSUE OF SYMPATHY/EMPATHY:** Will this character elicit a strong emotional response from the reader? Why? What will make us care about this character?

It's possible that in redoing the vantage point from which your story is told, you will end up working with a character who has a lot more going for him. He may have a greater stake in the action, he may be more likely to change, and he may elicit more sympathy from the reader. Be open to overhauling your short story or novel in this way if you think your present point-of-view character isn't strong enough.

NARRATIVE POV

Whichever point of view you chose in writing your first draft, you probably did so instinctively. It sounded right to say "I" or "he" or "she." How did you decide what sounded right? It may have been an entirely emotive reaction and hard to account for. You might not intend to change the point of view, but maybe you can do something to handle it better than it is presently handled. A key question for revision, though, is whether this is the best narrative mode to use—and if not, what you must do, or deal with, to change it.

To answer both questions, you must examine the complex nature of point of view and how it is closely connected to characterization.

First Person

The first person provides a sense of immediacy that is certainly lacking with the more distanced third-person point of view. What would it be like if Huck Finn or Holden Caulfield were represented as "he" instead of "I"? Written in the third person, these two characters wouldn't have the same feel, and we might not connect as intimately with them or with their experiences. These two I-narrators pull us in. Holden even speaks directly to us, the reader:

> If you really want to hear about it, the first thing you'll probably want to know is where I was born, and what my lousy childhood was like, and how my parents were occupied and all before they had me, and all that David Copperfield kind of crap, but I don't feel like going into it, if you want to know the truth.

This voice certainly gets our attention. But with the first-person narrator, more is at hand—for instance, character description. How is this to be handled with an I-narrator? Certainly an I-narrator can create a self-portrait by supplying many character details—general as well as specific. The extent to which an I-narrator will engage in self-portrayal, though, depends on the nature of the character. If the character is self-absorbed or self-dramatizing like Holden Caulfield, perhaps he will be more likely to provide a lot of personal commentary. When this happens, the focus is placed squarely on character. This isn't to say that the narrator who doesn't provide loads of personal commentary can't also be strong. That character may reveal things about herself by more indirect or dramatic means.

If you have an I-narrator, you need to decide how best to handle character description. Is your character the self-absorbed type? If so, consider having this character engage, now and then, in a fairly detailed self-commentary. But if your character is not self-absorbed, you can still reveal this character through dialogue and action. On the other hand, if your character, not typically self-absorbed, becomes self-absorbed over a serious problem, you might try the more direct method of self-portrayal through description and exposition. How much you supply depends on how given to self-analysis the I-narrator is at this point in the story.

Third Person

The third-person narrative mode includes the omniscient, or authorial, which allows the author to comment on the world of the character, and the characters themselves, and enter the minds of any of the characters in the story or novel. Many writers today choose instead multiple points of view, where the author is more or less effaced. When only one character's consciousness is needed, the limited omniscient form serves that need. With the dramatic or objective point of view, also third person, we do not have access to character thought, but only action and speech. Each of these narrative modes provides different access to character, and thus your choice of narrative mode will affect characterization.

Omniscient

Generally speaking, authorial omniscience, with a godlike narrator who knows everything about everyone, is not suitable to the contemporary age that resists objective and absolute truths—that is much more relativistic in its thinking. It's a rare author today who displays full omniscience, standing outside the work and providing commentary. Milan Kundera, whose work is openly philosophical and political, engages, at length, in extensive authorial commentary. Russell Banks does so at times in *Continental Drift*. But unless you're as skillful or as compelling as Kundera or Banks, I wouldn't advise this.

Today's fiction tends more and more to the effaced author. We see this in the use of multiple points of view, for instance in Kent Haruf's *Plainsong*, though the author is still somewhat present on occasion. Here's a passage from Victoria Roubideaux's point of view:

> The evening wasn't cold yet when the girl left the café. But the air was turning sharp, with a fall feeling of loneliness coming. Something unaccountable pending in the air.
>
> She went out of the downtown, crossing the tracks and on toward home in the growing dark. The big globes had already shuddered on at the street corners, their blue lights shining now in flat pools on the sidewalks and pavement, and at the front of the houses the porch lights had come on, lifted above the closed doors. She turned into the meager street passing the low houses and arrived at her own. The house appeared unnaturally dark and silent.

Notice "the girl"—how this establishes a little distance. An authorial point of view can be quite subtle. The omniscient author stands back, at a short distance, say, and then moves into the character's consciousness. And this is what we see in the rest of the passage: how the action is filtered through the girl's mind. The author is mostly absent, except as narrator. We don't see or feel an authorial presence other than this.

If the trend today is to efface the author as much as possible, perhaps it does have one distinct advantage for writers learning their craft: It's easier to avoid authorial intrusion. You can tell the story through the characters themselves, with the author serving only as a narrative voice.

But perhaps you've chosen the omniscient point of view. If so, it's important to read your work over carefully to make sure that you, as author, are not controlling the story too much—not standing in the way of the characters' dramatic performance. *In A Wild Surge of Guilty Passion*, Ron Hansen uses the omniscient point of view and even looks ahead at times to provide information beyond the characters' present knowledge. And yet Hansen doesn't tell too much, never interferes with his characters' dramatically lived experience. His authorial presence is thus *not intrusive*. An author who exerts substantial omniscience runs the risk of intrusion, and while authors like Kundera, Banks, and Hansen know how to avoid it, in lesser hands, full authorial omniscience tends to sound like an explicator drily summing up plot and character.

If this is the case in your work, strip out authorial commentary and replace it with strong scenes. Make sure that character observations and thoughts are internalized—or kept within the minds of your character—and keep the all-knowing author away. You don't need to entirely efface the author—which is a difficult task to begin with, and not necessarily desirable—but eliminate intrusive authorial telling.

Limited Omniscient

The limited omniscient, in which the author limits omniscience to one character, is much less problematic. You're not capable of hovering over the entire fictive world and making cosmic pronouncements. Basically, what you can do is get inside your protagonist and reveal his thoughts. Avoid overt authorial description of physical appearance and authorial commentary on character traits, qualities, attitudes, assumptions, concerns, and the like (unless you have a really compelling voice). Instead, efface the narrator as much as possible and internalize these details in your character's mind. That is, make the *character* know these things, not the author. And don't forget that some points you want to make about your character can be handled using the indirect method—through scene.

Notice the point of view in Robert Garner McBrearty's "The Bike":

> Henderson heard the automatic garage door opening and he came out to greet Janet. Her new job selling real estate meant longer evenings away, and her late arrivals didn't fit in with his vision of things—a cheery little supper, and over the meal an exchange of work stories revealing small amounts of triumph and disappointment. But since she'd started the real estate job, by the time she arrived home, they were both tired.

We're in Henderson's mind here, as we will be throughout this story—thus the limited point of view. The author is pretty well effaced, serving the function of narration only.

It's certainly possible to limit consciousness to one character and still exert some authorial knowledge outside of this consciousness—as we see in Dennis Must's "Queen Esther":

> Perhaps the most interesting bureau drawer in Ben's mother's room was her unmentionables drawer. Most of the items looked fragile, the same shade of pink, coral and dusty rose, stacked in three rows like silk scarves. Further, once the compartment was drawn open, a sweet aroma wafted out of a calico sachet bag.

The opening "Perhaps" sounds, at first, to be authorial, but we can also read this "perhaps" as Ben's judgment, too. But the author does exert omniscience now and then, outside of Ben's knowing:

> The social was being held in a rambling Queen Anne Victorian with a grand wrap-around porch in a rural community called Harmony. . . .
>
> The Bible class, at first stunned, gradually effected a smattering of nervous laughter.

In this story where churchgoing people ritualistically shed their churchy demeanors, we're mostly in Ben's consciousness, but it's also important to be able to bring in things that Ben, as an adolescent, might not be aware of or fully appreciate. Authorial knowledge provides a larger, adult context in which to illuminate Ben's youthful innocence. Must's skillful handling of point of view keeps the shift subtle, nonintrusive.

Dramatic or Objective

The dramatic or objective point of view is the scenic method, and in some short stories, it is used to a great extent, for instance, in Hemingway's "Hills Like White Elephants," which reads almost like a play. It's not likely that you would use this point of view entirely for a novel, though. Instead, you can use it to great effect in sections of a novel. With the dramatic point of view, readers are not inside a character at all. They learn what characters think and feel from their actions and speech alone.

Here's an example—a scene drawn from Leonard Gardner's *Fat City*:

> On the dusty floor of the closet was a clean square where the carton of Earl's clothes had been.
>
> "Is Earl out of the bucket?"
>
> "Huh?"
>
> "Was Earl here?"
>
> "Earl?"

"Did Earl come in here today?" Tully demanded, hanging up his jacket.

"Yeah."

"Why didn't you say so?"

"He was just here long enough to get his stuff."

"Is that any reason for not telling me?"

Notice that no one's thoughts are represented here. Sometimes it's best to just let characters talk. If characters' thoughts are included, the writing might become cluttered and lose impact, distracting readers from what they can see and hear. But certainly in some cases, characters' reflections and thoughts are essential to driving the scene. So make your judgment scene by scene.

As you revise your manuscript, be open: Look for the right places to create impact with scenes based on the dramatic or objective point of view. Characters can really come alive in the heat or turmoil of words and actions, and in this way give scenes a real punch.

Second Person

I save this point of view for last. It is certainly an unusual point of view, but now and then it can be quite effective. Consider its effect in Jay McInerney's *Bright Lights, Big City*:

> You are not the kind of guy who would be at a place like this at this time of the morning. But here you are, and you cannot say that the terrain is entirely unfamiliar, although the details are fuzzy. You are at a nightclub talking to a girl with a shaved head. The club is either Heartbreak or the Lizard Lounge. All might come clear if you could just slip into the bathroom and do a little more Bolivian Marching Powder.

The whole novel is written from this point of view, and it effectively places us, the reader, in the position of the protagonist, so we see things from his perspective. We are the character. This might work in a short story—or possibly a section of a novel if you want to be experimental—but it's really hard to pull it off in a whole novel. However, because McInerney's character is intriguing and his style is hard hitting, he somehow does.

A suggestion for short story revision: If your story draft doesn't work very well with the first-person point of view, try this one. It can certainly energize a story.

CHANGING NARRATIVE POV

Let's now consider what is involved in transforming a work from one narrative point of view to another. Decide first the overall feel you want for the work. Do you want it to be upbeat, impassioned, or meditative? Do you want an edgy sense of calamity in the making? Do you want irony? Of course, any of the narrative modes might work well with any of these desired tones. But if you shift from third to first:

- **THERE WILL BE LESS DISTANCE AND MORE IMMEDIACY.** Let's say you've aimed at something impassioned and semitragic. Somehow third person didn't work very well to achieve the right emotional engagement. First person seems better, but while your reportorial prose style seemed right in the third person, it seems way off in the first. You may need to go for a different style—perhaps less formal, perhaps a different pacing or tempo. Style may not always be an issue when you shift from third to first, but it could be.

- **YOU WILL POTENTIALLY LOSE AUTHORIAL MATERIAL.** I have in mind full omniscience here more than the limited omniscient form, though the latter is not entirely excluded. If you switch your story or novel from the omniscient point of view to two or more first-person narrators, certain authorial statements about the characters might no longer be useful. These might include descriptions of characters' physical appearances, observations about characters' traits, quirks, attitudes, and the like, as well as authorial privileged knowledge of setting. It's a matter of judgment as to how authorially intrusive any of this material might be—even for an omniscient narrator—but the central question for now is: How much of this material will you be able to use? Can all of this material be woven seamlessly into the revised first-person work—for instance, certain larger contexts such as setting and historical background? Choosing the omniscient point of view gives the writer some freedom to comment, as long as authorial commentary doesn't become intrusive—it's a difficult balancing act, of course. Choosing the first person means leaving story materials entirely in the hands of the characters—what is suited to them in all of their particularity: what they can know and be likely to take note of and care about or internalize. If you switch to the first, you may lose some material that worked well in the third but doesn't seem to anymore.

- **THE AUTHOR'S OMNISCIENT KNOWLEDGE OF THE FUTURE WOULD BE LOST.** An omniscient author can look ahead in a character's life and say how this character will view a particular matter years hence. (Of course, one hopes that this is handled with subtlety and not with intrusive commentary.) If you shift from omniscient to multiple I-narrators, this will mean the loss of such omniscience. This means finding ways other than an omniscient author to bring out such future developments. Your other option is to change your story or novel.

If you shift from first to third:

- **YOU WILL LOSE IMMEDIACY AND GAIN DISTANCE.** Will this story work with greater distance? Or is this story meant to be more intimate? Will the narrative distance you achieve somehow keep you from getting close enough to your character's consciousness even if you efface the narrator as much as possible?

- **YOU WILL NOW BE OPEN TO AUTHORIAL MATERIAL.** This may work well for you if you have more than one protagonist and you want to go with an omniscient narrator. You may want to depict a character in ways that are not as available to you in the first person. Perhaps you want to put this character in a certain context, using metaphors or similes that would not have worked in the first person. You may want to bring in setting material or historical background outside of the characters' knowing. Avoid intrusive authorial commentary. Note how successful authors handle this point of view.

If you do change point of view, it's best to apply the new point of view to several pages, as many as fifteen or twenty in a novel, to be sure it will work. You may even decide that changing the point of view from third person limited to omniscient, or vice versa, is the best decision for your short story or novel. Whatever you do, it's best to read good fiction for models of each point of view.

CONSISTENCY OF POINT OF VIEW

Have you gotten out of the voice of your character—or have you inserted yourself into the character's voice? Would your character be likely to know X, Y, or Z, or is this something the author knows instead? With an omniscient POV, the author might step outside the protagonist's consciousness on occasion, as long as most of the drama is left in the hands of the protagonist. With the limited omniscient, it's more of a risk, and yet Dennis Must pulls it off in "Queen Esther," as I've explained. But generally speaking, if you step outside your character's knowing, in the third-person limited especially, your point of view isn't consistent. This can happen even in a first-person narrative if the I-narrator seems to move out of his voice and into an authorial voice, saying and thinking things he clearly would not say or think—or know.

Sometimes, as we've seen, a story or a novel may be written from multiple points of view. In such a story, if the point of view shifts again and again in a particular scene, this may seem cluttered, confusing—or both. Not that you can't shift point of view in a scene. But be sure it's purposeful. Perhaps one perspective provides a context for another. Or perhaps several perspectives are important at this time, place, or set of circumstances. If, for instance, it's a gathering of people—party, wedding, funeral—hopping around from one perspective to another might work quite well. Ask yourself, then, if this is the scene where different perspectives are important to represent.

In some cases, point of view has been consistently in one character's vantage point, or perhaps two, but then the point of view shifts to a third consciousness. A cameo shot. This is certainly doable, but you must make clear why this third consciousness is vital to the story for one short spell. Perhaps it is used to call into question, or to reaffirm, the thinking of the key character or characters, or to provide a contrastive or comparative way of thinking. Be sure you have a good reason to shift the point of view to a minor character.

SUMMING UP

Choose your vantage point carefully. Not every character's take on things is worth exploring. Also choose the narrative mode carefully. First person may not provide the right sound for a particular story. Third person might not be suitable for this novel. Watch especially for authorial intrusion in the omniscient point of view. Nothing makes a story sound more amateurish than an omniscient author telling all—unless this author has a voice we cannot resist. And even then, if the voice gets between the reader and the characters, the reader might tire of the voice.

PROCESS SHEET #6

1. Is your point-of-view character the right choice for this story? Why or why not? Do you plan to change your point-of-view character? If so, what change will you make? How will the new point-of-view character work better than your present one? Will this change yield a more interesting perspective? Or is there a different reason for the change?

2. Do you have a second point-of-view character? Answer questions from #1.

3. If you have two point-of-view characters, whose story is more important? Or, are their stories equally important? If so, how?

4. Which narrative mode (first, second, third) are you using? What is accomplished by this mode? What changes, if any, do you plan to make to narrative mode? Why?

5. Do you see places where you could handle point of view better? For instance, if you're using the omniscient point of view, do you see places where you need to be less intrusive?

EXERCISE 1

Write a passage in either first person or third, using exposition and description. Write from the point of view of Character A. Now write about the same subject from the point of view of Character B, a character with an entirely different personality, with different attitudes and a very different general bearing toward others. Read over what you've written. How are these two passages different? Of the two characters, which do you prefer?

EXERCISE 2

Write a passage using a first-person narrator. Make sure you have some exposition and summary. Change the point of view from first person to third-person limited omniscient. Go over what you've written. What's the difference?

EXERCISE 3

Write a passage in third-person omniscient. Make sure you have some description and exposition. Change the point of view from third person to first person. Go over what you've written. What's the difference?

CHAPTER SEVEN

STRENGTHENING THE CONFLICT

Conflict is the engine that makes the story run. As I emphasized in Chapter Four, conflict is essential to creating a strong character, one that is more than a portrait, one that becomes real by undergoing struggles and coming to some realization about self or world. This is what makes the character interesting—the story interesting. We would find it utterly boring to read a story where no conflict occurred, where everyone got along just fine, where no one lost their job, no one lost out in romance, everyone had absolutely everything they needed, no one ever got ill, never died. Serious fiction, like life, includes many rug pullings. We may not want the grim, but we do want to experience fiction that deals honestly with humans and their condition, and clearly the lot of humans is not sheer pleasure or endless happiness, but pain as well.

Conflict is not, of course, separate from character. You will surely be working with character as you deal with important aspects of conflict.

THE STAKES

Are the stakes high enough? What is the character's investment in his goal? I brought this issue up in Chapter Five, but we will get into this matter more fully here. First, the stakes need to be high enough that the reader cares. Secondly, they have to be believable, given everything we know about this character in these circumstances.

We can think of stakes in relation to one or more human needs and desires:

- **MATERIAL:** In Upton Sinclair's *The Jungle*, the protagonist, Jurgis Rudkus, works in horrible conditions at a meat-packing plant. The stakes are certainly high for this character—basic survival. It may seem too obvious to point out that we have a different expression of material need in D.H. Lawrence's "The Rocking-Horse Winner." But I mention it only for contrast to emphasize that you must consider the make-up of your character, your character's circumstances, and so forth, in deciding on stakes. What's at stake must be firmly grounded in character. What is at stake in Lawrence's story? More and more money is required—an endless supply of it. The stakes may not seem as high as those in Sinclair's novel, but they are indeed very high because of the mother's desperate desire for money and social class. Without this desire we couldn't accept Paul riding to his death on the rocking horse.

- **EMOTIONAL:** Romantic love stories set the stakes high when characters are miserable in love: They must have their beloved or perish. But would a character kill for love—thinking that this is the only way to achieve what she wants? Certainly, the stakes are high enough here to generate reader interest, but now the burden falls on the writer to make sure this action is believable. In *A Wild Surge of Guilty Passion*, Ron Hansen makes us believe that Ruth Snyder is able to convince Judd Gray, driven by his lust for her, to kill her husband, whom she loathes.

- **PSYCHOLOGICAL:** A character may be vulnerable in terms of self-esteem and a sense of personal worth. As I stated in Chapter One, this is the case with Miss Brill of Katherine Mansfield's eponymous short story, which focuses on a personal identity crisis. The identity problem can find a number of expressions, of course. In Alicia Erian's *Towelhead*, her young female protagonist, Jasira, finding no genuine love in either parent, seeks an outlet for her sense of personal emptiness and engages in increasingly dangerous sexual rebellion. Clearly the stakes are high in this story: Will Jasira discover who she really is and steer a path toward self-affirming behavior? For readers, this issue matters, and Erian grounds her character's crisis of self in both character and circumstance.

- **INTELLECTUAL, CULTURAL:** Why is the intellectual and cultural so important to this character? What would happen if he were deprived of intellectual stimulation, art, or culture? Thomas Hardy explores this question with great force in *Jude the Obscure*. For Jude Fawley, Christminster represents the august halls of learning and culture. Much is at stake. To enter the lofty fold he devotes himself to study, to breaking free from his social class limitations as a stonemason, though in Hardy's naturalistic novel, fate has other plans for him.

- **SOCIAL:** For Madame Bovary, the need is both emotional and social. Steeped in sentimental novels and stuck in a marriage with a boring country doctor, Madame Bovary craves excitement and social engagement—grand balls. Her dull, provincial conditions are intolerable to her. She longs to be a gentlewoman. The stakes are truly high for her. It's a life or death proposition for Madame Bovary, and she will have nothing but this life she has sought out. When things go sour, she ultimately kills herself by ingesting arsenic.

When the stakes are high enough, the reader is interested in the character. Of course, readers expect struggle—and this is where a worthy antagonist comes in.

THE ANTAGONIST: A WORTHY OPPONENT

In attempting to achieve what they want, or to avoid what they don't want, protagonists often struggle against antagonists—persons, groups, or whole systems.

What makes a worthy opponent? It's certainly not one who is easily defeated, with little or no struggle. Readers expect an antagonist mighty enough to cause a rug pulling.

Antagonists are often single individuals, with goals of their own that compete with the protagonist's goal. If the resolution is difficult, if antagonists relentlessly stand their ground, they are certainly worthy opponents. Several examples from literature come to mind, and they are all quite different. In *The Scarlet Letter*, there is the arch-villain Roger Chillingworth, who sets out to avenge his lost honor and destroy Arthur Dimmesdale. In *Daisy Miller*, there is Mrs. Walker, who shuns Daisy for her uncultured, unseemly behavior in Roman society. Whereas Chillingworth is a melodramatic figure of evil in Hawthorne's romance, Mrs. Walker is a much more realistic figure, under the illusion that she is doing the right thing to ostracize Daisy from the Europeanized American community in Rome. Put another way, as an antagonist, she is more misguided than evil.

For the most part, we shouldn't think of an antagonist as "the villain" and the protagonist as "the hero" or "heroine." It's best to avoid such simplistic designations. Antagonists can, of course, be very bad people, but be careful not to turn them into clichés. Read your draft carefully for stereotypical treatment. If you find you've rigged things in favor of the protagonist by creating cardboard-character antagonists, look for ways to give them human dimensions. The antagonist doesn't have to be sympathetic, but your reader should be able to appreciate the workings of his mind (if he is a point-of-view character) or be fascinated by his actions (if he is viewed from the outside). If you make antagonists somewhat empathetic, your reader will appreciate the conflict between protagonist and antagonist a lot more. Don't draw the lines too narrowly between the two. Don't create a Roger Chillingworth.

The lines can certainly be blurred in a novel where two protagonists see each other as antagonists. This happens in T.C. Boyle's *When the Killing's Done*. In this novel, an animal rights activist goes head-to-head with an environmentalist. These two point-of-view characters are sufficiently developed, each presented sympathetically as worthy opponents in a battle not easily resolved. If either of the two characters were much less developed than the other, the writing would undoubtedly come off as preachy, as if the author sided with one character over the other. But Boyle avoids this. Through each protagonist's lens, we see the other as antagonist.

Besides individuals, antagonists can be whole systems: social, economic, and political forces pitted against human beings. We find such examples in naturalistic fiction written by such writers as Emile Zola, Theodore Dreiser, and Stephen Crane. In the worlds created by these writers, it's easy to see that these antagonists are worthy opponents. In Zola's *Germinal*, it's the well-entrenched capitalistic system that oppresses the poor, half-starved coal miners; in Dreiser's *Sister Carrie*, Chicago and New York, immense cities, determine the destiny of their inhabitants; in Crane's *The Red Badge of Courage*, the Civil War is a machine itself, much larger than any of the soldiers who fight it.

If your story or novel deals with large societal forces like these, you need to decide what victory or defeat might possibly mean. Are you thinking like the naturalists, who hold that individuals have little or no power over such environmental forces? That they tend to be pawns shaped and molded by forces much larger than themselves? Or are you thinking that individuals can mount a struggle regardless of the odds and achieve some kind of personal dignity? If characters have no power at all, they become merely pathetic. If they mount a valiant struggle and lose, we might see them more as tragic figures. The reader will probably find a tragic figure more sympathetic than a pathetic one—depending, of course, on one's philosophical orientation.

Though fiction involving struggles against such huge external forces isn't exactly "in" today, it's possible that part of your story or novel might include a conflict that goes beyond individual relationship conflicts—probably not the same kind that Dreiser or Zola or Crane concerned themselves with, but perhaps a struggle against an irresponsible corporation (Pork Rite in my novel *Hog to Hog*), against local government (county government in Andre Dubus III's *House of Sand and Fog*), or—turning to a nineteenth-century classic—against a corrupt institution (charity school in Charlotte Brontë's *Jane Eyre*). It's important to decide how you will handle the struggle. The best way is to represent both sides of the struggle as realistically as you can—assuming you're writing realism. Use individual antagonists to represent the larger societal institution that your protagonist is battling against, but give them enough human dimensions so they don't come off as melodramatic villains. If you're writing satire, as I did for my novel, you still need to give your characters human dimensions, though satire is a form based on exaggeration, gross distortion, and the like. Even so, painting characters with a broad brush can put readers off.

BUILDING THE CONFLICT

Conflict enters the story in the form of a complication—a disturbance of an existing equilibrium. This complication can be something good, but only apparently good: It could be followed rather quickly by rug pulling. Consider the bag of money Moss finds in

No Country for Old Men. That discovery is followed by quite the rug pulling. If the complication is something bad, it doesn't have to be monumentally bad. No one has to be maimed or killed. But, as we've already discussed, it does have to matter enough to your character for readers to get caught up in this character's apparent concern over it—whatever the impediment might be. Maybe it's a Dear John letter.

The conflict should be introduced early enough in the story that it has plenty of time to grow, or develop. In stories beginning with exposition (or expository prose), it may be introduced there. Otherwise, it could come out in an opening passage of narrative summary. It doesn't have to happen right out of the gate, but we do look for it fairly early on. It might not appear to be that serious at first, but we suspect it must be in some way and that its seriousness will become apparent later. We should be hooked enough to want to read on to see how serious it will become.

Of course, the conflict needs to build. But how should it build? Incrementally. And as you build it, be sure that if the conflict ratchets up, it remains believable. If it doesn't ratchet up, why doesn't it? Perhaps the conflict itself doesn't increase measurably, but maybe your character's need to deal with this conflict does.

It must be developed in the very fabric of the story. Once we know the conflict, we should feel it threading its way from scene to scene, from story part to story part—or at least we must feel it looming out there, hovering over the world of your characters. But, as I've already suggested, this does not have to be a story with gripping conflict such as Richard Bausch's *In the Night Season,* where killers arrive with an agenda. It can be a brewing marital conflict, as in T.C. Boyle's *The Inner Circle,* where John Milk's relationship with his wife, Iris, is threatened by his involvement with the sex guru Alfred Kinsey. Whether John and Iris are arguing or breaking up, we feel this conflict sustained throughout the novel. It builds, and it undergoes different permutations.

As you revise, working to build and rebuild conflict, think of the different ways that conflict works: through speech and silence, through action and nonaction. Characters sometimes speak of it and share their thoughts with those they think they can trust, or they make mistakes and discuss their troubles with those they later realize they cannot trust.

Characters may remain silent, their troubles brewing in their minds. Internal conflict is essential in character-driven stories. But avoid long passages of exposition, unless these passages are particularly compelling. However you handle this, give a strong sense of interior engagement with perceived troubles.

Dramatic action is essential to heightening conflict. Characters must act and react. What should happen in a scene, each scene, is determined by the nature of the conflict and the specific needs of the character or characters. Some stories, very quiet stories, do not include uproars and do not end with explosive showdowns, but things can still come to a head and have strong emotional impact. Note the conflict apparent in this excerpt from Man Martin's *Days of the Endless Corvette*, which won the 2008 Georgia Author of the Year Award for First Novel:

> Ellen had seen the doctor first thing in the morning, and it was a good job she had, because it gave her plenty of time to compose herself and dry her face before Earl came to get her. Now all she needed to do was to master herself to keep back the tears burning behind her eyes. Thinking he must have done something wrong—it's that frock coat, he told himself—Earl didn't say anything. And Ellen didn't say anything, and so the three of them rode home in silence.

We feel the tension, that third rider, but it's muted, as the two characters say little. The style of the prose itself *feels* quiet.

Look for ways, especially in a novel, to shift the attention now and then away from the central conflict—scenes where characters are not speaking or acting out of concern for the major conflict—their attention apparently directed elsewhere. Such lulls in the storm can be purposeful. People often do not speak of the big conflicts but pick at each other over little things. Characters might even approach the central conflict but draw back. Major conflicts are painful to deal with and often frustrating. This consternation can advance character and, perhaps unbeknownst to readers at this point, actually increase the conflict. Sometimes what is not said is more disturbing to stakeholders than what *is* said. Or perhaps this lull can be an opportunity to develop a subplot in your novel.

Furthermore, scenes dealing with minor conflicts can accomplish two basic things: They can broaden the main conflict of a novel in ways that may not become apparent until later, and, in the absence of this focus on the main conflict, they can create suspense. The reader will want to know what connections exist between these minor conflicts and the main one. And secondly, when will the main conflict surface again? We still feel the key conflict hovering in the air; we know it's not far off.

Another very useful tool for building conflict is foreshadowing. Look for ways to hint at actions that will occur later in the story or novel—later chronologically, or later in the narrative, which could take the form of a flashback. Foreshadowing can come out in a scene or in the mind of a character. Drop hints along the way, teasing the matter out, creating more and more suspense. A character can start to make a statement and then drop it. Another character can make a veiled reference to it. You will need to decide when foreshadowing should end and the event foreshadowed should finally occur. This is a matter of structure, as we'll see in Chapter Eight.

Conflict is also built by *echoes* of different kinds. Characters are reminded of past developments. They remind others of past developments. Repetition creates emphasis. Together, foreshadowing and echoes knit the action together into a strand or plot thread. Watch for both in your fiction reading.

MAKING CONFLICT SUBTLE AND COMPLEX

If you hammer home the conflict too bluntly to make sure that your reader gets it, you will lessen the impact of your fiction. It's best for conflicts to be subtle, and at times even perplexing, just as life is. We can't always say what it is that disturbs us about something. If it's a remark, is it what was said? Is it the way it was said? Is it something *underneath* what was said, some innuendo? In some cases, conflict is quite clear: a robbery at a bank, a physical assault, a messy divorce. But even in these cases, the reasons might vary and be very complex.

Consider Arthur Miller's *Death of a Salesman*, a classic play built around a number of complex conflicts. To oversimply, we could say that Biff's conflict with Willy amounts to Willy's rigid expectations for his son. However, there are several other conflicts bundled into this larger, more obvious conflict: Biff's knowledge of Willy's cheating on Linda, Willy's ill treatment of Linda, Willy's living a lie and expecting Biff to do the same—and more. Conflicts between people are usually complex, and the more you represent this complexity in subtle ways (by suggestion rather than by direct statement), the more you will intrigue your reader. If the conflict can be summed up too easily, it will seem too simple, too ordinary—and not worth the reader's attention or interest.

MAKING ABSTRACT CONFLICTS CONCRETE

An abstract idea is large in scope: war, poverty, salvation. John Bunyan's *Pilgrim's Progress* takes the abstract idea of salvation and makes it an arduous journey on foot. Hawthorne's "The Celestial Railroad" makes it a train ride, representing the streamlined religion of the nineteenth century that Hawthorne wanted to satirize. The abstract conflict—salvation versus damnation—is more important than anything concrete in either story. And yet the concrete does serve the purpose of making the abstract more real to the reader—and provocative in Hawthorne's case.

If your work tends to focus on certain abstract levels—ideas and themes—you must be sure to make these ideas concrete through dramatic event and intensity. The idea informing Shirley Jackson's "The Lottery" would surely not have the impact it does on the reader without the dramatic unfolding of the annual lottery. This makes Jackson's idea very real.

SHORT STORY VERSUS NOVEL

A short story by its very nature is compressed, much like a poem. There isn't room to work out very many conflicts, given the constraints of this form. The short story is a little world, but in spite of its intense focus, it allows for a remarkable depth of character and richness of incident. If you are writing short stories, look over your drafts carefully to make sure you haven't taken on too many conflicts. In the traditional short story, one main conflict and perhaps a few minor conflicts that are tightly connected to the main one—and that are judiciously concise—are all you can handle. In the novel you have much more room to sprawl. Besides your major conflict, you can have several minor conflicts, developed at some length, which contribute either to the main plot or to one of the novel's subplots. The subplots should be related clearly to the main plot.

With both forms, keep in mind that unfocused works tend to make your reader's mind wander. Choose the representative, cut the extraneous, and achieve the best focus you can.

RESOLVING THE CONFLICT BELIEVABLY

A conflict that is resolved too easily is not much of a conflict. The stakes can be high, but somehow regardless of how high they are, and how worthy the antagonist, the conflict is suddenly over, and the character walks happily on. The reader, knowing life doesn't work that way, naturally feels cheated. This is all it came to? This is what I've spent my time for?

If John and Iris's marriage isn't going so well in *The Inner Circle*, T. C. Boyle doesn't cheat it by giving us a happy ending—they still face issues that are probably irresolvable, even after the death of Kinsey. It's tempting to tie things up for your reader, to provide a happy ending. If you do this, make sure it's earned. Make sure you didn't force it. Perhaps on the surface things are better, but not underneath. Some conflicts could still emerge later on, coming up through the floorboards—who knows when? An indefinite kind of ending will probably seem more believable to readers, unless they've lived a very sheltered life. But most people haven't.

Go through your draft and see how you lead up to the ending. Endings are really tough. They must provide closure, but they won't work if they feel as though the author engineered them. To write a good ending may call for some distance from the work, and it may take several attempts. When the ending provides a sense of closure without shutting down all questions, you're getting there. We'll look closely at endings in Chapter Twelve.

PROCESS SHEET #7

1. What are the stakes for your main character? Are they high enough that the reader will care? Do you plan to make any changes regarding your main character's stakes—to make them higher?

2. Does your main character have an antagonist? If so, who? Do you plan to make any changes in your main character's antagonist—to create a more worthy antagonist?

3. Does the main conflict build throughout the story or novel? Spot places where the conflict builds. Do you plan to make any changes so that the conflict builds more?

4. What about lulls in the conflicts? Do you have any? How do these work? Do they provide suspense? Do they provide other benefits, or do they take the story off course? Do you plan to make any changes in terms of lulls in the conflict?

5. Are there places where characters don't talk directly about the conflict, but they still argue—about minor issues? Does it build conflict in some way? If not, do you see ways to make it work better?

6. Are there any places in the story or novel where the conflict is hinted at more than directly stated? Do you plan to make one or more conflicts more subtle—not directly stated but hinted at?

7. Are there any abstract ideas (suggesting conflict) in your story that are not concretely developed? Do you plan to give some abstract ideas dramatic treatment?

8. If you've written a short story, do you have more than one major conflict? Do you plan to decrease the number of major conflicts you have?

9. If you've written a short story, how many minor conflicts do you have? Are they tied tightly to the main conflict? Do they take the story off course? Do you plan to handle minor conflicts differently?

10. If you've written a novel, how many major conflicts do you have? Do you plan to increase or decrease the number of major conflicts you have?

11. If you've written a novel, how many minor conflicts do you have? Do you plan to increase or decrease the number of minor conflicts you have?

12. How is the conflict resolved? Who learns what? Is this resolution earned? How so? Do you plan to redo the resolution of the story? What are you hoping to achieve?

EXERCISE 1

Write a scene of one to two pages in which two people discuss in hushed voices an urgent matter over a hospital bed in the intensive care unit, where a third person lies unconscious or sleeping. Include a clear conflict where the stakes are high.

EXERCISE 2

Rewrite the scene from Exercise 1 making the stakes low, absurdly low, given the location of the discussion.

EXERCISE 3

Rewrite the scene from Exercise 1 making the conversation more oblique. Perhaps the two speakers don't want to face the prospect of the patient's death—or their own. Make the conversation suggestive enough that the reader picks up on this.

CHAPTER EIGHT

RETHINKING PLOT AND STRUCTURE

Plot consists of the logical connections between events in a story. If we ask questions related to plot, we want to know *why* things happen in this way. Why did A cause B cause C?

The structure is the arrangement or order of the story, *how* it's put together. When you revise your manuscript for plot and structure, you need to decide on your main plot—and subplots if you're writing a novel—and choose the structure that gives your story or novel the most impact.

PLOT

Most stories have some sort of plot, unless it's a slice-of-life story, which simply shows how life is for a certain character at a certain time and place. But in this book I want to emphasize fiction with plot—the more traditional kind of story.

Let's focus, then, on connections between story events. Determine what is crucial to the telling of your story. If you're writing a short story, which events do the most to advance the plot? Decide, and eliminate minor ones as much as you can. Remember, tightness! Economy. In a novel, concentrate first on your main plot. Which events are the major ones, the ones that do the most to advance the plot? How do minor events also contribute to the plot? Or subplots? Or do they? What justifies keeping them?

Of course, plot is not separate from the characters whose actions play out the plot, even though in talking about plot, we may seem to treat it as an isolated fictional element. The actions characters perform should do at least one of two things: 1) reveal character or 2) advance the plot, either indirectly or directly. The direct actions are the major ones.

Actions Revealing Character

Not everything a character does will drive the plot. Round characters may reveal themselves in many ways that have nothing to do with the plot of the story but flesh out their avocations, interests, or principles. They may water their flowers, do a watercolor painting, refuse to eat meat. We may see a link between such behaviors and the plot, or we may not. Perhaps some behaviors simply help explain the psychological make-up of the character. In a short story there is much less room for actions meant only to reveal character. In a novel some actions might not advance the plot, even indirectly, but these actions should nonetheless give us a better understanding of the character so that we more fully understand actions that do have a direct effect upon the plot.

When you revise your novel for plot, look for ways to include character actions that will prepare readers for more plot-significant actions to come—actions that will put these key actions in a particular light or context. Be selective. Don't go overboard or lose focus.

Actions Affecting Plot

Actions that affect the plot can be indirect (or contributing in some way) and direct (or major). The indirect ones may be relatively insignificant, but they ultimately contribute in some way to the key ones.

But before we go on any further, I want to emphasize that a believable, credible plot rests on two basic things: believable cause and effect for specific actions and believable cause and effect for the series of actions that make up the short story or novel as a whole. This means rethinking character motivation. Like real people, our characters may not always behave in predictable ways. A train is bearing down on them. They might leap aside; they might stay put; or they might run straight down the track and get run over. But why? When you rethink plot, it's a good idea to check for believable motivation for key behaviors—if not all behaviors.

The kinds of questions you can ask are: What would this character do in this case? Does this series of actions make sense for this particular character? In other words, do we believe the overall character arc?

Actions With Contributing Effects

All actions should reveal character in some way, but some actions do even more—they also indirectly advance the plot. It may be difficult to judge just how much they contribute to the advancement of the plot, but at least you know they're a contributing factor in the character's overall trajectory. For example, excessive drinking on weekends may not cause one to lose one's job, but if it leads to divorce and depression, and one may start missing work, even after one has given up the habit. And so we may say that the drinking indirectly led to loss of job. It was part of a causal chain. An action, considered alone, may not cause something serious to occur, but together with some other action or development it may have a significant impact. Ignoring parents' rules about biking in traffic may not in itself cause a problem. But, if on one particular occasion, a very bad driver is present or bad weather comes, serious consequences could follow.

The key point here is that some actions do more than reveal character. They have an impact on the character's outcome in the story, sometimes a major one.

Actions With Direct Effects

We can think of these actions as the ones central to the basic plot. What is the plot of Dickens' *A Christmas Carol*? It's how Ebenezer Scrooge changes from a miser to a compassionate human being as a result of having met three ghosts: the Ghost of Christmas Past, the Ghost of Christmas Present, and the Ghost of Christmas Yet to Come. The three ghosts' appearances each have a direct effect on Scrooge and advance the plot a notch. Other actions leading up to Scrooge's redemption—Bob Cratchit shivering in the counting house, the urging of the two men seeking money for the poor, his nephew's invitation to come to Christmas dinner—might be viewed as contributing causes, but they are not direct causes in his final redemption. One might see the contributing causes in this narrative working as the bedrock of the work the ghosts perform: What Scrooge has been doing all wrong, he corrects once he sees the light.

As you revise your manuscript, reexamine which actions or events are the key ones shaping your character and advancing the plot. These should stand out in some way so that a reasonably perceptive reader can identify the overall trajectory of your main character.

Identifying Your Main Plot and Subplots

If you're not exactly sure what your plot is, ask yourself what the *emphasis* of your story is. If you had to sum this up in one word, what would it be? The Scrooge story is about *redemption*. What's yours about? Once you've decided on one key word, work from this word into the one-sentence logline I spoke of in Chapter Four. This method can work for both short story and novel. If what you come up with sounds like your plot, then use it to keep your short story tightly focused. For a novel, this summary is the main plot, and any additional story threads, as long as they relate in some way to the main plot, are your subplots. For instance, the two subplots of Tolkien's *The Two Towers*—the Legolas/Gimli and Merry/Pippin strands—allow a broadening of perspective of the main plot: the journey to take the ring back to Mordor and destroy it.

A caution here: As I stated earlier, you cannot separate character from plot. Don't think about a string of actions separate from character as being the plot. Character's motivations determine the actions and reactions that make up your plot.

Consider Tessie Hutchinson's arc in Shirley Jackson's "The Lottery": Tessie Hutchinson begins the story, the same as her fellow townspeople, not questioning the annual lottery, in which one member of the community will be stoned. The tradition of the lottery follows from the belief, "Lottery in June, corn be heavy soon." But when Tessie Hutchinson draws the "winning" ticket, she claims that it's "unfair." Her stake in the lottery changes from unquestioning acceptance to vociferous complaint. If Tessie herself doesn't have a consciousness raising, the reader is meant to. The plot can't be described merely by the two-stage event—conducting of lottery and stoning of victim. We must also trace Tessie's overall awakening, however limited it might be, from gathering stones to being stoned.

What causes Tessie Hutchinson to change? If we say the lottery, this isn't enough. It's the recognition that comes when she herself is about to be stoned—the realization of how unfair this really is. Thus character is integral to plot.

Achieving Focus

Once you've determined your plot, you are ready to begin weeding out extraneous material. Beyond eliminating everything that doesn't pertain to this plot (or in a novel, the subplots as well), you must also consider the kind of fiction you're writing. And, for micromanaging your story or novel, you must consider the question of bloat. First, let's consider the kind of fiction you're writing.

Kinds of Fiction

Fiction is not all of one kind. Knowing the kind of work you're writing gives you a much better handle on what is important and what is not in terms of the plaguing question of what to keep and what to cut. One way to classify fiction is to identify what drives it—whether the driving factor is character, plot, or idea:

- **CHARACTER DRIVEN:** In this kind of story, what counts is the character arc—the trajectory the character makes from beginning to end: the character's needs, wants, and principal goal, the threats to this goal, the final realization the character comes to. What pertains to this goal is what you keep—with less latitude in the short story and more in the novel. Ask yourself this: Is there anything in this story or novel that gets off course in terms of its role in this overall character arc? Are there scenes that seem to go nowhere in terms of this arc? If you spot some, consider cutting them and maybe saving them for another story.
- **PLOT DRIVEN:** This story focuses more on plot than character. Yet this doesn't mean you should ignore character altogether. Readers of plot-driven short stories and novels depend on interesting characters to hook them on the action. But if the focus is largely on plot, then some material on character might become extraneous. The trick is to get the right balance. Does some characterization seem like excess baggage and slow down the momentum of the plot?
- **IDEA DRIVEN:** The main plot is central to developing the central idea of the work. Philosophical novels, utopian works, and satires are idea driven. More emphasis is put on the ideas of the work than on characters or plot. Interesting character and dramatic action are a must, but don't lose sight of the ideas that govern the work.

The Question of Bloat

Once you've determined the kind of story you're writing, you're in a position to consider the second issue: bloat. This question becomes a different question, of course, depending on whether you're writing a short story or writing a novel. But the same general issues apply:

- **TOO MANY SUBPLOTS:** There is no room for subplot in a short story. A novel can include several subplots, but clearly there has to be a limit. When does the work begin to sound cluttered? When do we begin to lose sight of the main plot?

- **TOO MUCH EXPOSITION:** If you are dealing with a character's thoughts about some action—whether it contributes to the plot or not—and you run on too long about it, the story or novel will lose focus. To strengthen the plot, look for places where too much thought slows the momentum of the story.

- **UNNECESSARY SUMMARY:** Could this be handled in shorter fashion? Make sure you keep only what is essential to defining character and/or advancing the plot or subplot. A summary flashback, for instance, that does neither might be interesting, but it will take the work off course, especially in a short story.

- **OVERLONG SCENES:** Is everything in this scene essential to the character or plot? If it's dealing with an action that contributes indirectly to the plot should this much space be given to it? This is particularly important in a short story, with such limited space, but it's an issue for the novel, too. Tightness might not be an imperative, but it's still an important value.

Clichéd Plots

There are a number of clichéd plots on television and the big screen: the serial killer plot, the business tycoon who ignores her family, the hostage crisis. Add to this the abused wife who has to seek a shelter and the alcoholic father who abuses his children. It's hard not to turn out a clichéd plot from these old standbys, but it's possible. It's in the treatment itself, as I suggested in Chapter Four.

First, make your character surprising. Build in contradictions as I mentioned in Chapter Five. To avoid a clichéd plot, you must begin with a complex character. Second, don't focus so much on the familiar plot pattern. Place this pattern in a new, fresh context, one that hasn't been worked to death. Make some other conflict the major conflict and the clichéd one—say the abusive husband or father plot—just one part of this more major conflict. Not that the abuse will be slighted—it will be recontextualized from a different, more interesting perspective.

STRUCTURE

Structure is order and arrangement, and it naturally provides focus. But it would be a mistake to think that if the structure is not absolutely obvious that it's wobbly. It may be much more creative in its order of story parts. As readers, we may have to work harder to understand how its various parts come together to create an overall pattern.

A literary story or novel may make the reader work a little harder, though certainly not every literary story requires this. The structure may be fairly easy to follow. The main thing to remember is this: Each story calls for its own structure. Chris Cleave's *Incendiary* is structured according to the four seasons of the year. Tim O'Brien's *July, July* is organized around a college reunion.

In revising your manuscript, you should consider whether or not your story's present structure helps you achieve the right focus. Consider the following:

- **PROPORTION:** Do some story parts seem to be overlong and others too short? Should some parts be longer than others? This is a matter of emphasis, and this depends, of course, on the purpose of each part in terms of the kind of story you are writing. You might want longer sections of character revelation—whether exposition, scene, or summary—in a character-driven novel. You might want shorter ones in a plot-driven novel.

• **ORDER:** Ask yourself which story section should go first, this one or that one? To decide, try out different orders of story material. If a different order creates more intensity and works better in terms of character arc, you should certainly choose this different order—as long as it won't confuse your reader. Another issue: If you decide to start in the middle of things, will your reader have enough background to appreciate your character and her problems? The best way to decide about matters such as these is to experiment—but save drafts with different file names so you don't lose your original order. Also, read a lot of fiction and see how the pros manage this issue. Finally, should you follow chronological order? Yes, if it provides the most impact for your narrative. But if you need to include flashbacks, you may not be able to do this entirely. I've taken this up briefly in Chapter One, but one thing you can do is trim the flashbacks as much as you can—if they impede the dramatic movement of the story.

• **FORESHADOWING—AT STRATEGIC POINTS:** Do you foreshadow certain key events and developments? If you can hint at things to come at critical points in your manuscript, you will weave together a story which creates suspense. Where are these critical points? They can occur throughout the short story or novel. How much of a mystery do you want to create? How much do you want to keep your reader guessing? Decide, and then look for places to insert hints of things to come or to be revealed (it might be some past action), and then reread your manuscript and see how it works. Perhaps you've done this already. But maybe you will find more effective places to make these insertions, and others you will drop altogether.

- **ECHOES—AT STRATEGIC POINTS:** Note my comment on echoes in Chapter Seven. Try these out in various places and see where they gain the most impact. Look for ways to create the right emphasis so your plot has a kind of beat to it. Listen for when one thing ought to echo another. Is this the right spot? Or is it in the next scene?

These are some of the things you should consider when you are looking carefully at your story or novel's structure. One way to handle structure, especially for a novel, is to do a brief outline, a bird's-eye view. One-sentence chapter summaries will be easier to deal with than searching through the long file that makes up your manuscript. Use your logline as a starting point for your chapter summaries. It should give you an overall direction to follow.

PROCESS SHEET #8

1. Identify your plot, how it works. How does one thing lead to another? Sum up this plot. If your plot is not clear enough, what plans do you have to make it more clear?
2. Does your plot seem in any way clichéd? If you've decided that your plot is too clichéd, what might you do to avoid this problem? List specific plans.

3. Does your plot seem credible or believable? If you've decided that your story could be more credible in places, what specifically can you do to make it so?

4. What are some ways you believe you have achieved focus in this story or novel? If you've decided that you haven't achieved enough focus, what do you plan to do to improve the focus?

5. What is your structure? What plans, if any, do you have to improve the structure? How about flashbacks? Do they lessen the dramatic movement of the short story or novel? Do you see places to work in foreshadowing as well as echoes of earlier actions and developments—without being heavy-handed?

EXERCISE 1

Sum up the plot of a short story or novel you've read. What is the character's overall arc? Explain in a paragraph. Then see if you can do it in one sentence.

EXERCISE 2

Review the summary you've written and examine the character's actions. Are the character's actions credible? Why? If not, what could be done to make them credible? That is, what motivations could possibly explain these behaviors?

EXERCISE 3

Take the same short story or novel from Exercise 1 and identify the overall structure. Is it chronological? Does it use flashbacks? Is the structure of this short story or novel effective? Why (or why not)?

CHAPTER NINE

HONING BASIC PROSE TECHNIQUES

Three techniques essential to good story writing are narration, exposition, and description. Narration, or storytelling, is used for both summary and scene; exposition is used to delve into the character's thoughts, reflections, memories, and feelings; and description is used to make characters and settings visual, sensory. Memorable.

Since you may well have come across different meanings of each of these fictional techniques, I will clarify my use of each term:

- **NARRATION:** Storytelling, stringing events together over time, in summary; covering sequential actions in scene.
- **EXPOSITION:** Expository writing, explaining, not reporting, action; useful in covering the interior of a character. I realize that exposition is used to mean "information" such as story background information. Such information might be conveyed dramatically by scene. Secondary characters voicing their ideas or venting their spleen might serve as valuable expository devices. But in this chapter I'm not referring to this sense of the word. I mean exposition

as a writing technique. For instance, your character's life has taken a 180-degree turn for the worse. Now he tries to assess what went wrong. He thinks it out, analyzes. This calls for expository prose.

• **DESCRIPTION:** Creating a word picture of character, setting, or character's actions.

Let's consider some key elements that you must handle well in order to write narration, exposition, and description. Keep each of these in mind as your revise your manuscript.

RETHINKING YOUR NARRATION

Writing strong summary calls for an ability to telescope events. In other words, choosing the events that matter in some way but are not important enough to warrant a scene. You must collapse time but keep the reader intimately involved in the character or characters. Scene calls for the ability to focus on one event with dramatic intensity. How do you revise your manuscript to improve both scene and summary?

Energetic, Vivid Summary

In your story or novel draft, you may have found it necessary to use narrative summary on various occasions, but maybe the writing tells too much—it lacks dramatic movement. It may sound more like an academic summary instead of fiction. Strong summary engages the reader and is effective when it makes us forget that we're reading summary; we feel "there," involved in the events being narrated. Don't think of summary as story material to "get out of the way" so that you can move on to the more interesting stuff—namely, scenes. It must be vivid and energetic, especially if it runs a page or more. If it's really short, it should still get the reader's attention in some way. But how is this possible? Consider each of the following techniques and use what you can for effective revision.

Voice and Point of View

A strong narrative voice is important. Voice is related to style, but it's also related to point of view. You must be able to handle point of view well to create an interesting voice.

FIRST PERSON: Here you have an advantage—a sense of immediacy. And yet you still face the burden of making your voice interesting. The answer is to give context and color to your summary, which means finding ways to bring out your character's personality. Ask yourself questions like these: 1) Does your character have a unique slant on self, others, or the world? Does your character offer some interesting insights? 2) Is this character struggling with something that we cannot help but find compelling? 3) How do you want this I-narrator to sound? What tone of voice? Bringing out your character's personality, temperament, or slant on things—something deeply and recognizably human about the character—in interesting, striking ways will do much to create an engaging narrative voice in your summary because your character will come alive. Note this passage from Kristen-Paige Madonia's *Fingerprints of You*. The I-narrator has just moved to a new school:

> I spent my first days dodging teachers in the hallways and categorizing students into the distinct groups I'd seen in every school I'd gone to. There were Preps and Hipsters and Weekend-Warrior Partiers with trust funds stitched into their back pockets, the kids who threw ragers at their houses when their parents flew to Vail or Vegas or Key West for vacations. There were the Jocks and the Geeks and the Film Kids, who kept video cameras in their backpacks. The Adrenaline Junkies were the guys who went skydiving or rock climbing on the weekends, and the Low Riders were the country boys who stuck small wheels on big trucks

and cranked rap music from their dashboard speakers. I usually slipped in somewhere between Art Kids and the English Nerds, never committed enough to join the lit magazine staff, knowing we could move again at any time, but too much of a bookworm to be considered an angst-ridden Art Punk or Emo. It always kind of took a while to make friends, but this was the large kind of public school that made it easy to disappear.

This narrative summary, rich with description, tells us what it was like the first days in this new school as the narrator struggles to disappear into the cracks. The summary draws us close, making us experience what the character is narrating. It's the way this narrator pegs her schoolmates—her humorous categories and lively examples—and her air of skepticism about the whole school arrangement that makes this a colorful, interesting passage in a voice we want to listen to.

THIRD PERSON OMNISCIENT: With third person, as you'll recall, there is more emotional distance with the limited form but especially the fully omniscient, which may cause the summary to lack dramatic impact due to a dry and dead narrative voice. How should you handle a revision of such work? Outside of developing a strong prose style, one answer is to capture something distinctive about your character and his circumstances. Consider this passage of backstory in Ron Hansen's *A Wild Surge of Guilty Passion*, written in the third person omniscient:

Judd Gray was sixteen and in the rigorous college preparatory course at William Barringer High School in Newark, intent on attending Cornell medical school. He was president of his high school fraternity, chairman of the Dance Committee, a Newark high schools sports reporter, manager of the basketball team, and in spite of his scrawniness, the quarterback on the football team. Yet he was high-strung and giddy around girls; he thought they could read his dirty mind. And then he met a considerate, pious, slender, solemn, not-pretty brunette named Isabel Kallenbach, of Van Siclen Avenue in New York City. She had a too-prominent nose and a jutting chin and he initially dated her out of chivalry and pity... And Isabel became a devoted but dowdy housewife, finicky in her cooking and cleaning, priggish, overweight, acting ever more disgraced by his job in lingerie sales, and in reaction given to wearing frowzy dresses and farmerish shoes.

Note the fine characterization here, how richly detailed, giving us a strong sense for these two characters. We can't help but be intrigued by how ill-suited Judd and Isabel are for each other. While this passage is written from the omniscient point of view, it doesn't come off as "mere telling." We get caught up in Hansen's vividly rendered characters, who have the fullness of life—and, as a result, help create an interesting authorial voice in spite of the distance of the third-person omniscient form.

Here's another example of compelling summary handled by an omniscient narrator, from Alice McDermott's *At Weddings and Wakes*. The narrator flashes back to a time when a young man's persistent drunkenness plagued his family, especially his mother—a painful time suspended from memory now but brought to the forefront by the omniscient author:

Suspended, too, was the memory of those late nights and early mornings when they had thrown their coats over their nightgowns and gone downstairs to peel him from the sidewalk or from the floor of the vestibule and work his dead weight step by step up four floors and across the moonlit or dawn-lit landing and onto the couch in the living room. Momma would be there in her robe, her long graying braid over her shoulder, and if he was conscious enough she would tell him, her steady voice growing louder and shriller with each word, that she was hardening her heart against him: hardening her heart against the time when she would refuse to spend the night waiting at the window, when she would simply lock the door and turn out the light and go to bed, because she had seen enough tragedy in these rooms, her darling sister cold dead and her husband gone before she'd reached him. She was hardening her heart so that she would never have to see him with that same gray pallor on his lovely face when they brought him home with his neck broken or his liver gone or his flesh frozen stiff in some alleyway.

Clearly, this is powerful, lyrical summary by an omniscient narrator, who provides not only provocative details and striking imagery but also delivers them in a voice that makes us care—and why? Because we get a strong sense for the character of Momma, whose heart speaks its love but also the limits to what it can abide because of this love. This passage escapes dry telling because it captures the deepest feelings of this human being.

SECOND PERSON: Sometimes summary works quite well with the second-person point of view. This is what it is like, the author suggests, to have these things happen to *you*. Or this is what a typical day is like—the events occurring in this order, for you. The author puts you as reader right there—dead center in the narrative. Note this narrative summary from Jay McInerney's *Bright Lights, Big City*:

You have always wanted to be a writer. Getting the job at the magazine was only your first step toward literary celebrity. You used to write what you believed to be urbane sketches infinitely superior to those appearing in the magazine every week. You sent them up to Fiction; they came back with polite notes. "Not quite right for us now, but thanks for letting us see this." You would try to interpret the notes: what about the word now—do they mean that you should submit this again, later? It wasn't the notes so much as the effort of writing that discouraged you. You never stopped thinking of yourself as a writer biding his time in the Department of Factual Verification. But between the job and the life there wasn't much time left over for emotion recollected in tranquility. For a few weeks you got up at six to compose short stories at the kitchen table while Amanda slept in the other room. Then your night life started getting more interesting and complicated, and climbing out of bed harder and harder. You were gathering experiences for a novel. You went to parties with writers, cultivated a writerly persona. You wanted to be Dylan Thomas without the paunch, F. Scott Fitzgerald without the crack-up. You wanted to skip over the dull grind of actual creation.

What makes this summary work so well is the well-handled second-person point of view, but note the compelling human conflict: between the passion to be a fiction writer and the feeling of wasting time doing editorial work. And notice too, a second conflict—quite ironic: the writer "gathering experiences for a novel" yet the desire to avoid the hard work of fiction writing. The "you" works well here because McInerney gives us a character with human traits that most people, at some level, can probably empathize with. Readers of this passage don't have to have the very same aspirations as this character. If they have dreams and have experienced frustrations related to these dreams, if they've been ambivalent at times, they can probably become the "you" McInerney invites them to be. Strong characterization here, as with other points of view, helps create an interesting narrative voice. I don't mean to suggest that it does this alone—much of this depends on style—but it certainly contributes to the voice and tone of the narrative. It breathes the breath of human life into the prose.

Creating Suspense

Suspense is important in all aspects of fiction writing. Suspense keeps the reader with you. To create suspense in narrative summaries, especially if they're fairly long, you need to provoke your reader to wonder about aspects of character, conflict, and plot.

- **CHARACTER:** Do these events suggest something important about this character? Do they point to, or help lay the groundwork for, some future character change or growth? Whether it's backstory, as in the passage from Ron Hansen's novel, or a narrative bridge between scenes set in the dramatic present, your summary should make your reader want to know more about your character. What are Judd and Isabel really like? What made them settle for this marriage, and how will they each deal with it? Suspense in summary is created by planting certain clues but not supplying answers yet—just enough to whet the reader's appetite. Hansen does it.
- **CONFLICT AND PLOT:** As we see with the Judd and Isabel passage, summary also becomes suspenseful when it involves conflict, and we look for its relevance to the plot. In *Rule of the Bone*, Russell Banks provides several

pages of gripping summary, capturing his young protagonist Bone's sense of confinement in a house not his own where he and his companion secretly camp out—the owner being gone. The next few passages come near the end of the summary:

It was no real biggie but we started avoiding each other so to speak. We even took our sleeping bags and put them in separate bedrooms and used different bathrooms and all so we'd some days go the whole day without seeing each other although we no longer even knew if it was day or night except from what was on TV or unless one of us happened to go outside the house.

Of course we'd used up all the weed long ago and didn't have any cigarettes either and that probably contributed to the tension too. When we weren't sleeping we were too wired and too bored for normal conversation. A couple of J's and a carton of Camel Lights and a couple malt 40s would've helped civilize things between us for sure but it still would've lasted for only a day or two. When you've been high for most of your life it's hard to be nice when you're not.

Notice how conflict is revealed: in Bone's boredom, in what he wants and lacks, in his tiring of his friend's company due to their close quarters. As we read this colorful summary, we wonder how the conflicts will be worked out. What's this protagonist's next step? What about his drug use? What part does this camping out in another person's house play in the overall plot? In other words, readers are left with questions.

Conflict might be pretty subtle, just hinted at. But don't lose the opportunity to work in conflict in your story or novel wherever you can—including in narrative summary passages.

Overlong Summary

Russell Banks's summary is long, but not overlong—it sufficiently captures one period of his protagonist's runaway existence. But how long can a summary run? In the case of backstory summary, ask yourself how much the story or novel depends on the impact of the past on the main character or characters. If not very much, then trim or exclude these summaries altogether. Even if backstory summaries are crucial to the storytelling, keep them to a length that doesn't impede the forward momentum of the story. In the case of present-time-frame summaries, ask yourself if the summary is essential in making clear something in the present—in terms of character, plot, or perhaps idea. Even if the summary is essential, can it be trimmed and still make the same point? Does the summary length make the reader impatient for a scene? Banks's summary provides plenty of provocative detail to keep us reading.

Specific, Concrete Writing

To avoid the appearance of mere telling, be sure to put your reader in the world of the five senses. Summaries can be quite visual, as we've seen. Consider the following summary from Richard Bausch's *Rebel Powers*:

> He sits in his small cell, with its one bunk bed and its toilet and sink, its thick walls the color of gray water, and because he believes he is without love anymore, his strength has begun to abandon him. Each long day is filled with the increasingly frantic effort to avoid being noticed and to get along. He moves among the other inmates with a nervous quickness, and the other inmates, having noticed this, are finding ways of getting to him and at him—they trip him up whenever they can, doubtless hoping to provoke him into some response. They tamper with his food, they jostle and elbow him in crowds, they soil his sheets, they pilfer

his laundry. There have been several sexual advances, which he has managed to fight off. He's been buffeted and knocked around by guards. His bones ache; he has bruises under his clothes.

Because of the many specific details here, we can picture this prisoner and his depressing surroundings. We can sense the various threats he is dealing with. When you revise your narrative summaries, go for this kind of visual imagery. Surely it would be much less effective if Bausch had said this prisoner was being harassed by his fellow inmates—and left it at that. The impact is much greater if the reader can picture the specific ways he's being harassed.

Vivid, Compelling Narrative Scenes

Narration is also used in creating scene. If specific and concrete imagery is important in summary, it is surely important in scenes. Make your reader feel *present*. We might think of scenes as being driven largely by dialogue, and certainly many are. But scenes can also include action only, with perhaps a line or two of dialogue—or none. In this chapter, we're dealing with narrative prose, so we'll consider scenes without dialogue. We'll take up scenes with dialogue in the next chapter. When you revise for narrative scenes, what should you consider?

Conflict

If conflict is the heart of fiction, scenes, more than any other fictional device, thrive on conflict. As you revise your narrative scenes, ask questions like these:

- What is the nature of the conflict? Is it physically intense and heated? Or, on the other hand, is the surface of the scene relatively quiet, with conflict and tension apparent mostly in the character's thoughts?

- What more could be done to heighten the tension? Or even lessen it in places if it seems overdone?

Notice the impact in the following narrative scene from Daniel Woodrell's *Winter's Bone*:

> Ree reached for the steaming cup, smiling, and said, "I'm not really—" And the world flushed upside down in her eyes while her ears rang and she staggered, then the world flushed again and again and she stumbled across the gravel. One of Mrs. Thump's rollers had jerked loose and dangled springy around her head as she pulled her big hand back to whack Ree another in the face, and Ree swung a fist at those blunt teeth in a red mouth but missed. The other women closed in with boots to the shins while more heavy whacks landed and Ree felt her joints unglue, become loose, and she was draining somewhere, draining to the dirt, while black wings flying angles crossed her mind, and there were the mutters of beasts uncaged from women and she was sunk to a moaning place, kicked into silence.

The conflict here is mostly physical but internalized in Ree as she sinks into unconsciousness. This is an action scene, packed with great energy.

But scenes vary in purpose. In some scenes, the conflicts are more internal. Notice how the following excerpt from Ellen Sussman's *On a Night Like This* involves emotional conflict in her protagonist, Blair:

> She waited, turned away from him, until she heard him leave. When the door clicked closed behind him, she lay in bed for a moment, contemplating sleep. But she thought about the cancer in her body and felt heavy,

weighed down by so many black cancer cells, pressing
her into the mattress. She pushed herself upright and
began to tremble.

On the surface this scene is quiet, but internally it's filled with
tension. Sussman vividly captures the sense of hopelessness and
dread this woman feels. Note how, in the next passage, Blair's
cancer threatens her romantic relationship:

"On a night like this, I could fall in love."

"Don't bother," Blair said. "I'm dying."

She immediately regretted it, cursed herself for
ruining a good time. When was the last time she
had a good time with a handsome, straight man?
She looked down at the table, thought of saying,
"I'm only kidding. I like you; let's start over." And she
thought, for a terrifying moment, of dying. She imagined the black sea pulling her down—not a night-
mare, but something very real. She heard the words
as Luke Bellingham might hear them and felt her
pulse pound in her head.

The waiter arrived. Blair looked up, though she
knew her face was flushed, her hands on the table
now trembling.

In this excerpt, the scene has dissolved from dialogue into
prose narrative, giving force to Blair's own internal thinking,
hearing, and feeling—then her physical, observable reaction.
What we have, then, is a forceful handling of internal conflict
in the midst of scenic action. The heat and the tension here are
mostly internal.

As you revise your scenes, be open to different kinds of conflicts. Where there is pain, suffering, discomfort, dissatisfaction,
and disharmony, there is conflict.

It's true that not every scene must have conflict. A few scenes, especially in a novel, might simply develop character, theme, or idea, but when you see the opportunity to introduce conflict, do so. It might be something very small: an antagonist's irritating habit, a sense of unease, a feeling that things could be a little better. Firecrackers don't have to go off. People are plagued by many little things, and so might your characters be. Heighten the tension only when the conflict calls for it. Lessen it when it doesn't. To decide, look closely at character motivation. Is my character stirred up enough? Is he too stirred up?

Reporting Conflict With Point of View

Of course, it's certainly as important in scene, as it is in summary, to create an interesting character, which will help create an interesting voice. But beyond that, let's consider how point of view might work in a scene.

A narrative scene usually works through one character's point of view, whether in first person or third. This point of view determines which actions are narrated. But we could have two characters with alternating or even competing points of view, each noticing something a little different. You might choose to use an omniscient narrator or multiple points of view.

- **FIRST PERSON OR THIRD-PERSON LIMITED OMNISCIENT:** If your point of view is limited to one character's consciousness, this means you are limited to this one character's experience of the narrative action. Problems are more likely to occur with third person than with first. It may be tempting with the third to shift to the authorial mode and narrate an action or two outside of the character's consciousness. Perhaps you feel cramped by the limited consciousness: You want to be able to report more actions. But if you shift to the authorial mode, exerting omniscience, and report action outside of the character's consciousness, you risk confusing your reader: How can this character know this? This character isn't *there*; he's *here*. This constitutes a point-of-view shift—and seen negatively it's authorial intrusion. But no hard, fast rules. If it becomes purposeful to the story, then you may want to expand the authorial omniscience beyond the protagonist's consciousness. But take heed: It must be done skillfully. It's a risk.

• **OMNISCIENT POINT OF VIEW:** With this point of view, you could have two or more characters' actions to report, written from these characters' different vantage points. If so, it needs to be clear where one character's viewpoint ends and the next begins. Be careful to avoid a scattered effect. Also, with this point of view, the author can introduce information into the scene that the characters cannot possibly know—an impending disaster, say, or a piece of good fortune soon to be revealed. But use good judgment here. It may well come off as authorial intrusion. It takes a strong authorial presence—usually one with stylistic brilliance—to make this kind of omniscience work well. If you want to do this, study the masters to see how they handle it. One fine example is Ron Hansen's *A Wild Surge of Guilty Passion*.

Focus

Whichever point of view you use, keep the focus sharp. Eliminate extraneous material. Ask yourself: What is the purpose of this scene? Is it to convey something about the character? Is it to advance the plot? How will it advance the plot? Will it deal with a contributing cause of some kind or a main one? If you have two points of view, what does each character contribute to the scene? Should one character play a dominant role, or should the two characters share the scene, their viewpoints being of equal weight? Would the scene be better written from one point of view or vantage point?

EXPOSITION

First, a few words of caution: As a general rule, make sure that expository sections aren't substituted for dramatic action. Fiction is scene, movement, drama. Second, if you do need expository sections, make sure that your exposition doesn't run too long. If it does, it's likely to threaten the dramatic intensity of your work. Outside of these two cautions, I do want to emphasize that exposition can serve two important functions: exploring character consciousness and developing story themes or ideas. It doesn't have to be mere "telling." It can be arresting and provocative.

Characterization

Exposition—again, I mean *expository prose*—can be used to delve into a character's feelings, thoughts, and reflections. Through exposition you can bring out your character's attitudes, expectations, assumptions, and beliefs. This can happen in first person, second, or third. And yet, can't thoughts and feelings be saved for scenes? Sometimes, but in certain cases exposition seems the right tool. The reader wants to experience the mind of the character sorting things out, working things over. Imagine the following expository passage. Do we feel this sorting out, this working over?

> Bill was the lonely type. He had no parents. He was an only child, and he didn't have one friend he could really count on. Holiday seasons were the hardest for Bill.

The answer is no. There's simply too much distance here. This is the standard expository passage as "telling" only, which gives exposition a bad name. But consider this passage from Robert Garner McBrearty's "The Edge He Carries":

> Josh Daniels was short and he was pissed. He didn't know if he was pissed because he was short, but he

knew that he was short, and he knew that he was pissed. He did not like this about himself. He thought of himself, all in all, as a gentle and kindly sort, but he was aware that this was a self-reflection, something he might be totally wrong about. He might be, in fact, just short and pissed, and at the age of thirty-four, he did not look forward to decades of being angry.

This expository opening is comic and lively! It isn't "mere telling." We feel like we're inside the character—not outside of him, reading authorial explanation, as with my prior example. It might be possible to bring this inner conflict out in a scene, but this opening passage, because of its frankness and intimacy, certainly pulls us into this character. It's exposition that works.

Here's an example of first-person exposition from *Catcher in the Rye*. It's quite different in tone. Note how engaging Holden Caulfield's voice is:

I don't like any shows very much, if you want to know the truth. They're not as bad as movies, but they're certainly nothing to rave about. In the first place, I hate actors. They never act like people. They just think they do. Some of the good ones do, in a very slight way, but not in a way that's fun to watch. And if any actor's really good, you can always tell he *knows* he's good, and that spoils it.

What draws us in? Clearly, Holden's frankness and strong opinions, the way he speaks as though his personal opinions are totally authoritative. And he's speaking of something that catches most people's attention. Who doesn't have an attitude about actors? This is expository prose, and it's interesting because it captures the thought life of Holden Caulfield with force.

Developing Theme and Idea

Narrative commentary by an omniscient author is one way to bring out a story idea, but it will probably come across as too authorial. It's better to turn the reins over to a character. One thing is clear: If your idea is developed through exposition, the exposition must command the reader's attention. This passage from Don DeLillo's *White Noise* certainly does:

> Department heads wear academic robes at the College-on-the-Hill. Not grand sweeping full-length affairs but sleeveless tunics puckered at the shoulders. I like the idea. I like clearing my arm from the folds of the garment to look at my watch. The simple act of checking the time is transformed by this flourish. Decorative gestures add romance to a life. Idling students may see time itself as a complex embellishment, a romance of human consciousness, as they witness the chairman walking across campus, crook'd arm emerging from his medieval robe, the digital watch blinking in late summer dusk. The robe is black, of course, and goes with almost anything.

While this passage contains description and narration, the primary prose mode here is exposition. The I-narrator's purpose is to get across an idea: the nature of time "as a complex embellishment, a romance of human consciousness." It might be rather difficult to take up such a philosophical idea in a scene without overplaying it. It belongs to the mind of the narrator, to his internal ponderings.

DESCRIPTION

Describe only those things, places, or characters that are important in some way to the telling of your story. Is this object important enough to describe? If you provide many visual details, you will signal to your reader that whatever you are describing will figure into the plot—or that it's symbolic in some way.

Don't spend an entire paragraph on a minor character unless there is a good reason to do so. Is the character going to be a foil for the main character? Or an antagonist? Just keep in mind that description must be relevant to your overall character, plot, and key ideas. When you revise your manuscript, you will probably see places where description seems pointless, but in other places it answers to your purpose. Assuming it is purposeful, how do you handle description well? Let's focus on description of setting. Here are three techniques to consider.

Make It Vivid

Make use of one or more of the five senses. This means choosing details that make your reader see, hear, touch, taste, or smell something. Do this, and your reader will be able to enter the world you're creating or get up close to your characters. Here's an example from Mark Wisniewski's *Show Up, Look Good*, where his harried protagonist meets Etta, an aging woman with a room to rent in her Manhattan apartment:

> Etta's building wasn't a high-rise though I wasn't there to quibble, and she had no apparent health problems and didn't seem shocked by my appearance despite my lack of a shower in thirty-eight hours. Her apartment smelled of eucalyptus and had ceilings that were some two feet higher than I'd imagined, her living room more hip than geriatric. In her kitchen, on an antique farm table, she'd laid out blue and white china, ornate but unpolished silverware, pumpernickel bagels cut in thirds, and nickel-thin slices of liverwurst...

The diction here is precise and the details varied. Note how rich the description is. Wisniewski situates his readers in this place, using two of the senses, visual and olfactory.

How many senses you should represent varies according to purpose. Here's a description of a school restroom in Alice McDermott's *At Weddings and Wakes*:

> She knew in an instant that the place was empty. It was gray and green and smelled of disinfectant and old paint and the floor seemed to vibrate dimly with the droning recitation of the fourth-grade class downstairs. She went to one of the small sinks and scooped some cold water onto her face and then grabbed a harsh brown paper towel.

Sight, smell, touch, sound—four senses. In some cases, it would overload a descriptive passage to include this many senses. But here it works beautifully. The passage evokes a picture of the restroom and even connects it to the classroom below. There's no overload.

Notice the technique in the opening to Dennis Must's "Typewriter":

> The room had one window, a metal cot, a lime-green chest of drawers, and a mirror that hung on the backside of its shellacked door. The distance between the bureau and the bed was the width of a heavyset man. Twelve pairs of shoes placed toe to heel its length.

Must provides specific details, location, and a concrete sense for the distance between bureau and bed. It's one thing to say how many feet; it's another to imagine a "heavyset" man or a dozen pairs of shoes filling that space.

Metaphors and similes make for vivid writing. Note this description of an "A-frame cottage" from Geoffrey Clark's "A Place for Your Guests," from his collection, *Rabbit Fever*:

> Built carefully amid a sturdy lilac grove by craftsmen who had grumbled at Jay Blount's refusal to let them clear any more shrubbery than was absolutely necessary, the single high severely-angled gable of the A-frame rose skyward from the lilac thicket, presently in bloom, like the blade of an ax.

The specific and concrete details alone are vivid and compelling, but it's the closing image of the ax blade that really empowers this descriptive passage. An apt simile or metaphor like this can energize your prose. Just make sure it's not a cliché.

Be Selective—Create a Dominant Impression

Generally, you should pick and choose a few details that create a dominant impression of your character or setting. A strong dominant impression will grab your reader's attention. Look at this one, from Leonard Gardner's *Fat City*, describing professional boxer Ernie Munger's place:

> It was a low, white frame house with a sagging porch roof supported by two chains that through years of stress had cracked the overhang of the main roof where they were attached, pulling it downward at so noticeable an angle that everything—overhang, chains, porch roof—appeared checked from collapsing by nothing more than the tar paper over the cracked boards.

Dominant impression? *Collapsing.* And consider the words and phrases that advance this idea: "sagging," "pulling it downward," and, finally, "collapsing"—explicitly naming the idea.

Choose the Appropriate Place in the Story to Describe

Description of setting in advance of scenic treatment can provide important character context. In *The Marriage of Anna Maye Potts*, winner of the Peter Taylor Prize for the Novel, DeWitt Henry describes Anna Maye's candy factory work space. Notice how thorough it is and how Henry contextualizes his character within this particular setting:

> Just inside the icebox door, her office was to the right. Because of metal walls and glass windows around three sides, the girls called it her toll booth, but it was really called the sample room. That was another task: she must prepare the sample cases for the sales department, varnishing all the items of candy and arranging them in special boxes. Overhead, the long fluorescent light came on—showing the desk bank and shelves inside, and the adding machine and porcelain dishes (full of hairpins and combs), the scales, the punches, the matching planter with bright red geraniums in it, a spare umbrella, two old sweaters, another white cap hanging beside the mirror on the back wall, and there, the large green cushion on her swivel chair. These things and others had been together so long that what was hers seemed to be the company's and what was the company's, hers.

This description of the office contributes to a fairly lengthy narrative summary that establishes Anna Maye's typical day at the factory, her duties, her co-workers, and so forth. It's possible to parcel out such details in scenes, but in a character-driven, psychological novel like Henry's, this, as well as other introductory setting description, helps to establish early on both an external and internal landscape for his character—as we note especially in Anna's sense of relatedness to the company captured in the nicely balanced closing line.

In Leonard Gardner's *Fat City*, setting details provide context for an upcoming scene:

> The Lido Gym was in the basement of a three-story brick hotel with a façade of Moorish arches, columns, and brightly colored tile. Behind the hotel several cars, one tireless and up on blocks, rested among dry nettles and wild oats. In a long, narrow, open-end shed of weathered boards and corrugated steel, a group of elderly men were playing bocce ball with their hats on and arguing in Italian. A large paper bag in his hand, Ernie Munger went down the littered concrete stairs. In a ring under a ceiling of exposed joists, wiring, water and sewage pipes, a Negro was shadowboxing in the light of fluorescent tubes.

This is where Ernie Munger will fight. The setting details—outside, then inside—locate us concretely. But Gardner also works in setting details as the scene unfolds:

> They walked on their heels through the shower room, the floor wet from a clogged drain. In a narrow, brick-walled, windowless room smelling of bodies, gym clothes and mildew, several partially dressed Negroes and Mexicans glanced up and went on conversing.

Two strategies to keep in mind, then. If you're describing setting, you may want to provide details first to give context for an upcoming scene. Or you may want to weave the details in as the scene develops. If too many initial setting details—in advance of scenes—slow down the pace of the story or novel, you may want to choose the second method.

SUMMING UP

Good fiction depends largely on dramatic scene with dialogue, but it also depends on the ability to create strong prose, whether it's exposition, narration, or description. In the next chapter we'll see how these modes come into play in scenes containing dialogue. If scene makes you think of dialogue only, take a closer look. It's often interwoven with prose, and that prose needs to be well handled.

PROCESS SHEET #9

1. How would you describe your narrative voice when it comes to your handling of summary? Read several passages of summary before answering this question. What is your main character's apparent slant on things? Do you see ways to bring out your character's personality more—to enliven the narrative voice?

2. Which elements of suspense do you create in your narrative summary passages? If they're backstory summaries, what do readers now want to know or expect to happen? What makes readers want to keep reading? (Even with short summaries, do they seem to bog down a little?) Do you see places where you could embed or heighten conflict to increase the suspense a little more?

3. How long are your summaries? Why did you give them this amount of space? Do you see any summaries that might be trimmed a little—or a lot?

4. Are your summaries specific and concrete? What pictures do you create? Do you see where you might be more specific and concrete?

5. Are your scenes written from one character's point of view or from more than one? How do you achieve focus in the scene so that the narrated action doesn't seem scattered? If you find some of the action scattered, pinpoint where the confusion occurs. A scattered effect is not a good thing unless you want to create a sense of mayhem and disorientation. Otherwise, look for ways to strengthen the focus in your narrative scenes—gauging the quality of the prose as the focus is strengthened.

6. How would you describe the conflict in your scenes? Are they scenes with explosive action or scenes which hint at explosive action to follow? Or are they quiet scenes, which nonetheless involve conflict? Do you find any scenes where the narration seems dull because conflict is missing?

7. Do you find your expository prose interesting or uninteresting? Why? Are there places where you could bring in more character revelation and conflict to make exposition more interesting?

8. Do you find your expository prose sections about right in length or overlong? In which parts of your story or novel do these sections seem overlong? Do you see places to cut and achieve more impact?

9. If you've described setting at any length in your story or novel, what is the purpose? Do you see places to cut?

10. Are your setting details specific and concrete? Could you be more specific and concrete?

11. In your descriptions of setting, what dominant impression will the reader most likely take away? Do you see places where you could create more of a dominant impression?

12. Do you see places to set up scenes with initial description? Do you see places to feed in description in scenes as they unfold? Decide on the most effective method as you examine each scene.

EXERCISE 1

Using first person write a narrative summary of about 300 words. Go over it for the following: voice, elements of conflict and suspense, and concrete and specific details. Rewrite your narrative summary in second person. How does the voice change?

EXERCISE 2

Write a narrative scene of about 300 words in which a character encounters trouble of some kind—at home, at work, in the mall, or wherever you wish. Make the scene as concrete as you can. Then try this out: Either heighten or lessen the tension in the scene.

EXERCISE 3

Write a passage of exposition of about 200 words representing a character's thoughts about self, others, or some aspect of the world. Then, experiment some: If the piece is serious, make it quirky. If it's quirky, make it serious.

EXERCISE 4

In 100 to 200 words, using specific and concrete description, give your reader a word picture of a particular setting. Go over what you've written. What dominant impression have you created of this place? Add details to make this impression sharper. Delete any details that detract from this impression.

CHAPTER TEN

SHAPING GREAT SCENES

Scenes externalize the internal, as in real life. They create strong dramatic movement. Scenes advance present conflicts and can be used to bring in backstory. It would be quite rare for a short story or novel to be written without a single scene. We might imagine, I suppose, an extremely interior, meditative kind of work, employing mostly summary, exposition, and description to delve deeply into the inwardness of the character. For such a story to be successful, the style would really have to pull us in. A focus on inwardness, though, doesn't mean a lack of scenes. A character given to memory, thought, reflection, and imagination will surely have some sort of life involving other people and, in his mind, could flash back to remembered scenes.

Fiction often works from summary to scene. If summary must engage the reader, scene must directly *involve* the reader. Scenes draw readers in because they are highly dramatic: Characters act, are placed in motion, and, of course, talk.

One of your most important revision aims should be to create great scenes. If you will think back to Chapter Four, conflict is crucial in developing strong characters, ones with range and depth. Scenes, more than any other element in fiction, make this conflict possible.

What follows is a two-part approach to revision: First, the function of scenes in a literary work; second, the nature of great scenes.

SHAPING SCENES WITH THE WHOLE WORK IN MIND

Scene must contribute meaningfully to the whole fictional work: That is, they must help develop round, dynamic characters; help flesh out the plot; and contribute in some way to the themes and ideas of the work.

A caution here: We know that scenes, in general, should have conflict, but certainly not every story part that involves conflict can be made into a scene. Some conflict might be better internalized in the mind of the narrator through exposition or summary—or a mix of the two. Perhaps this could be true of a tortuous period of a character's life; even though some of the events of this period might produce great scenes, others will be better explained via summary. But not every great scene should be written because dramatic intensity alone should not determine what you select for scenic treatment. You must also consider the needs of plot. A scene can be good, even powerful, but if it takes the plot off course, you need to drop it. This gets back to one of our revision principles—tightness or focus.

If you're writing the short story, think tightness. If you're writing the novel, think looser but not too loose.

Short Story

Due to its compression, scenes in a short story tend to do double duty: They help develop character as well as plot, directly or indirectly. Character-wise, through scenes, we see firsthand what a character is like. Plot-wise, a few scenes may have less impact than others, but all scenes should contribute in some way to the tensions in the work. Theme-wise, does this scene hint at key ideas in the work? As you revise your story, you should ask yourself: How important is this scene? What if I dropped it? What would I lose as far as characterization goes? How central to the plot is it? If it indirectly advances the plot, what would I lose if I dropped it? Would I tighten the story by finding another way to handle this matter—perhaps by character thought or reflection?

Novel

In a novel the same questions come up, but there is more room to play with. Most scenes should develop character in some way. If not all of your scenes advance the plot, certainly most scenes should, either directly or indirectly. It's impossible to put a number on this. But one thing is certain: Even with the large canvas of a novel, you have to be judicious about creating scenes. If your novel is mostly character driven with a minimal plot, you might find more room for some scenes that develop character only. A novel short on plot and heavy on idea would surely call for a sufficient number of engaging scenes to develop both character and ideas. Certainly this would be the case with a philosophical novel.

MAKING GREAT SCENES

Strengthening Your Dialogue

If you want to write strong scenes, you need—more than anything—to be able to write strong dialogue. Many scenes call for dialogue. As I noted in Chapter One, dialogue needs to sound real, not fake—not like prepared speech (unless you mean for it to be ironic or comic or for it to relate to a particular kind of character). But how do you know what to include? How do you give your scenes palpable energy? Movement? The breath of life? Consider the following.

Handling Dialogue With Subtlety

Conflict energizes scenes. Dialogue reveals the conflict and moves it forward. When there's serious friction between characters, something is about to boil over or is boiling over. Readers need to feel the heated emotion welling up in the words of each character. This doesn't mean characters must say *everything* on their minds. Like in real life, they may hold back, engage in innuendo, or make veiled threats. Dialogue often packs more of a punch when it's a bit elliptical. When there's an air of mystery about it all. Characters are leaving ideas hanging out there, and more will come of it. This creates suspense.

Dialogue can be effective if it presents conflicts as only provisionally settled. Problems in life aren't usually wrapped up in neat packages with all the answers or options clear. Living in this world, surviving in it, is more complex than that, as most of us know. Consider the end of Richard Bausch's *In the Night Season*, where, after a dangerous encounter with dark forces of criminality, the characters demonstrate an urgent need to believe in a better future:

> "It isn't ever going to go away, is it?"
>
> "No," she said. She would not lie. "I can't believe it will. Not completely."
>
> "We can't ever be like we were before."
>
> "No."
>
> He was quiet, looking out. The silence of the house took on an expectant quality, as though they were both listening for something.
>
> She put her hand on his shoulder.
>
> "What will we do?" he said.
>
> "Love each other as best we can, and go on."
>
> "Then they lose."
>
> "Yes," she said, feeling the tears come.

Presently, he said, "I did it. I came up here and looked out."

"What did you see?" she asked him.

"Nothing. The field."

She knelt and put her arms around him. "Look again, sweetie," she said. "See?" She indicated the faintly rose-colored horizon. "See it, darling?"

"Yes."

"What do you see?"

"Dawn," he said.

This dialogue captures the characters' sense of loss and hopelessness as far as ever redeeming the past. But it also captures their need to have hope for the future, and of course the coming of the dawn symbolizes such hope. Bausch avoids explicit commentary. Dialogue isn't an occasion to let characters vent everything they think, believe, feel, and know. Less is often more.

Personality of Character

If the personality of your character is important in narrative summary and scene, it is clearly important in dialogue. Personality invigorates dialogue. You can establish your character's personality through intonation or tone of voice. I'll talk more about this in Chapter Thirteen, on style. Granted, once readers know the personality of your character, they will likely fill in a little on their own, hearing the character's voice in terms of what they know about this character. But don't depend on this. Do as much as you can to make your character's personality come through in her speech.

If a personality is coming through, one that's engaging in some way, then readers will be more likely to stay with the dialogue. The more the dialogue sounds like abstract thoughts of a disembodied character, the worse.

Note how the personality of Adam Newman, the protagonist of Man Martin's farce, *Paradise Dogs*, comes through in the following excerpt, where Adam is entrusted with a bag of diamonds:

> "Two and a half to four carats. I mixed them up—there's a couple of emerald cuts and a princess cut in there." Ernie bent behind the counter and retrieved a sheaf of twenty-four papers, two for each diamond in Adam's hand. "I'll need you to sign these papers before you can take them out of the store."
>
> "That's right," Adam said. "I guess it wouldn't do for me to go losing these, would it? Ha-ha."
>
> "Ha-ha." Foreboding swelled in Ernie again, and a serious look fell over his face like a damp rag. "I want you to be careful out there, boss."
>
> "I'll be careful."
>
> "I mean, you're one of the nicest people I know, boss, but sometimes you trust people too much. There's some bad people out there." Mr. Newman was a good man; Ernie hated thinking of his friend getting taken in. "The fact is," Ernie added, "I'm kind of in a tight spot myself right now. I owe some money. If anything happened to these—"
>
> "I'd make it good," Adam finished.
>
> "What I'm saying is I'm really out on a limb here."
>
> "Nothing's going to happen to them." Adam applied the Newman autograph on the indicated spaces.
>
> "This is going to thrill her," Adam said.

Note the difference between Ernie's mood here and Adam's. Ernie's laugh isn't the same as Adam's. Adam is an unstable kind of man, not trustworthy but quite endearing, and Ernie likes him. Ernie's private thoughts as well as what he says to Adam also bring out Adam's character. And if Adam comes off as rather flighty about such valuables as diamonds, we can't help but appreciate his romantic sentiment: "This is going to thrill her." This scene functions to create character as well as advance the plot, providing suspense. How will this woman react?

Context

Every remark your character makes has some context, internal or external. It comes out of the character's personality, need, desire, goal, hope, or aspiration. Or circumstance. Even if a character is chattering on inanely, doesn't this say something? He is feeling good, inspired—or has just taken an upper. If you think about your dialogue as expressive of your character's way of thinking, take on the world, or present circumstances, you will have a good chance of making this dialogue work well for your reader. It points to something. It comes out of character. It's not just there for the reading. If it's a face-off with an antagonist, it relates to a personal, philosophical, social, religious, or cultural context—what is it? Why would your character say this? Why would the antagonist respond in the way she does? What is her take on the world? And again, be subtle: Capturing this context in dialogue without explicitly naming it makes for invigorating reading.

Provocative Ideas

Characters that introduce ideas about people, society, nature, or God often stimulate reader interest. If a character talks about the psychology of the aberrant and the pathological, this can certainly generate reader interest. Or black holes or parallel universes or alien abductions. In real life, our interests are often stirred by such subjects, and they certainly are in fiction. But don't insert provocative ideas simply for shock effect. Your character's interest in them must be believable, and the ideas need to make sense in terms of where the short story or novel is going as a whole, in terms of its themes and premises. Perhaps further exploration of your character will uncover some provocative ideas this character might believably inject into dialogue.

Consider the young black man in the dentist office who comes in conflict with the black preacher in Ernest Gaines's "The Sky Is Gray." Note what this young man says about his questioning of everything:

> "I'm not mad at the world. I'm questioning the world. I'm questioning it with cold logic, sir. What do words like Freedom, Liberty, God, White, Colored mean? I want to know. That's why you are sending us to school, to read and to ask questions. And because we ask these questions, you call us mad. No sir, it is not us who are mad."

Soon the young man challenges the preacher's faith. The preacher is outraged by what he views as sheer impudence, and he strikes the young man. This scene is one of the most memorable scenes in the story.

Dialogue that introduces conflicts over fundamental values and beliefs is naturally going to interest many readers—those who are perceptive, thoughtful readers at least. Such conflicts energize dialogue. But again, a strong caution: These ideas must come out of the fabric of your work—through character, plot, and theme. Don't engineer them from without. But what better way to introduce provocative ideas that do belong to the essential substance of your work than by dialogue—*if* the dialogue is compelling and not merely academic. The rich dialogue in Gaines' story is compelling indeed: It makes us visualize the strong-willed young man unequivocally speaking his mind.

Dramatic or Objective Point of View Scenes

With the objective or dramatic point of view, action and dialogue dominate the scene, making conflict entirely external—readers are privy only to what characters say and do. A few details of setting might be included. Dialogue has to be particularly strong to carry the scene. Consider this excerpt from Flannery O'Connor's "A Good Man Is Hard to Find":

> "Let's go through Georgia fast so we won't have to look at it much," John Wesley said.
>
> "If I were a little boy," said the grandmother, "I wouldn't talk about my native state that way. Tennessee has the mountains and Georgia has the hills."
>
> "Tennessee is just a hillbilly dumping ground," John Wesley said, "and Georgia is a lousy state too."
>
> "You said it," June Star said.
>
> "In my time," said the grandmother, folding her thin veined fingers, "children were more respectful of their native states and their parents and everything else..."

Notice how there isn't anything internal here. The dialogue, which is rich with conflict between the children and the grandmother, drives this excerpt.

Here's a particularly stripped-down scene from Cormac McCarthy's *The Road*:

> There are other good guys. You said so.
> Yes.
> So where are they?
> They're hiding.
> Who are they hiding from?
> From each other.
> Are there lots of them?
> We dont know.
> But some.
> Some. Yes.

Is that true?

Yes. That's true.

But it might not be true.

I think it's true.

Okay.

You dont believe me.

I believe you.

Okay.

I always believe you.

I don't think so.

Yes I do. I have to.

Dialogue only. A number of the scenes in this novel contain sections like this of bare dialogue, with no action. A second issue is the lack of quotation marks, which is a matter of style. Note, though, how when we read this we get a sense for the characters by what they say and how they say it. We have nothing internal here—no private thoughts or feelings. We're left with the bare bones dialogue and the sound of the characters' voices. The boy sounds concerned, the father reserved, patient.

The O'Connor excerpt is fairly traditional, the McCarthy passage more extreme. Why would an author strip a scene down this much? Because as readers we are right there hearing people talk; absolutely nothing slows the dialogue down. There's an intensity about this back and forth exchange.

Scenes With Point-of-View Characters

When you're not working with the dramatic point of view, you need to attend to both external and internal spaces. External: action, speech, and details of setting. Internal: character thought and reflection. But how much of each should you use to create a strong scene? To decide, read your scenes with and without action, description, and thought interspersed. What is needed? What is the right proportion? Which version has more impact?

Action

In your story or novel draft, narrative spurts of action may interrupt the dialogue. A character gets up, leaves the room, returns. This may be necessary material. Beyond this, it can serve a dramatic function: The reported action can work either to relieve the tension—creating a kind of interlude—or enhance the tension, building suspense. What's going to happen when this character returns? Will things truly fall apart? Just be sure that you don't interrupt the dialogue too long. The question is, when does the reported action lessen instead of enhance the dramatic intensity of the scene?

Narrative action can certainly make the scene more vivid. The character taps the table with a pencil. Stands up, sits down. Takes off gloves. Such actions remind us we're not in the presence of disembodied spirits but real people. Decide on what is essential, and don't go overboard. How much action does it take to make the scene concrete? How much is needed to help with characterization? Which actions advance the plot? Dump the extraneous.

Physical Details: Character and Place

Concrete imagery can draw your reader in. For character, consider body language: *how* a character adjusts himself in a chair, *how* he places his hands on the table, *how* he picks up a pen. *How* he rubs his nose, lips, forehead. As readers, we can sense the character's thoughts, feelings, or attitudes when we see these things.

How much body language do you need? It depends on your purpose. If you want to emphasize some aspect of character, you may bring in quite a bit of body language—but you must make sure you don't slow down the dialogue, unless it is your intention to slow the dialogue for some reason. Space or proportion is usually connected to purpose. If a lot of space is given to something, we're naturally going to think it is important. A few descriptive brushstrokes may be enough to suggest the attitude of your character and also give the reader something visual.

Setting details may or may not be important. If they're not all that important, you might supply only a few visual details to situate your reader. If setting is really important, you must clue your reader into certain prominent visual details. Perhaps these details suggest something about the character's likes and dislikes, or something important theme-wise. They might even provide foreshadowing. But again, don't use so many details that they lessen the dramatic force of your dialogue.

Character Thought and Reflection

You may have written a number of scenes where the protagonist's thoughts and reflections are revealed—either through a first-person narrator or a third. In this case, you must work back and forth between the external and the internal, the spoken word and the unspoken. Unless your character's thoughts provide strong characterization or help fuel scenic action, go light on this.

If a character recalls, in the midst of a conversation, some inspiring place, with visual imagery that makes us take notice, then this may actually contribute to the scene and not detract from the dialogue, as long as you don't go on too long. If you do, you will sidetrack your scene.

A thought that evokes a remembered event can sometimes strengthen a scene. Here's an example from Ellen Sussman's *French Lessons*:

> "What do you write about?" Chantal asks. Her face lights up—this is the Chantal he fell for weeks ago, the woman who listened to him tell a long story about his first girlfriend in Normandy and who asked him, with so much kindness, "Will you always love her best?"

No," he had told her, "I hope not." He did not say:
Maybe I will love you best.

"It's a series of poems that are all about the same
story. . ."

This remembered event becomes a half-scene *within* this scene,
and it helps flesh out the present scene. The momentum of the
scene continues and even picks up with this intriguing memory.

Thought can evoke memory, which you would write as summary. A flashback within a scene can grab the reader's interest,
but it's best not to let it go on too long. As with other dialogue interruptions, there must be sufficient reason to evoke this memory. Is your character avoiding conflict for some reason? If so, this
could work well dramatically because instead of *saying* that your
character is avoiding the matter, you show it by having the character daydream in the middle of a conversation.

A character also could be distracted by some pressing need
in the present. Note how distraction works effectively in the following excerpt from Man Martin's *Paradise Dogs*. Adam, the protagonist, is on the phone with his fiancée. She's trying to set up
premarital counseling, while he's busy looking for his misplaced
bag of diamonds worth over $200,000:

"I have called Father Peel to arrange an eleven o'clock
appointment."

"Father Peel?"

"The priest, Adam. St. George's has a strict pro-
vision against performing marriages without a counseling session with the priest. It's very mandatory."

"Wonderful." Where were they? The zebra-
striped ceramic alligator that served as a doorstop of-
fered no clues in its yellow-pupiled eyes. The framed
black-and-white photos of Adam shaking the hands
of governors and celebrities were similarly unhelpful.

> "We have to meet today if we are going to have
> the ceremony as soon as you say."
>
> Adam made a nonverbal grunt of inquiry, reach-
> ing down the front of his pants. Could the diamond
> be in his boxers?

Adam's preoccupation with his missing diamonds adds vitality to the scene. Aren't we often occupied by other matters in the midst of conversation? Character thought revealing conflict of one kind or another can help fuel a scene.

It's possible that character memory, thought, or reflection could run fairly long, interrupting a scene in one long passage or interspersed in segments throughout the scene. If you find this happening, be sure to read the whole scene with an eye toward passages you might trim or eliminate.

Half-Scenes

Half-scenes are very short, clipped scenes. Why include these? Short scenes are sometimes more useful than long ones. If you want a quick take on something—whether it's a quarrel, a matter of fellow feeling, a moment of angst, or a moment of triumph, a quick scene can focus it. Raymond Carver's "Why Don't You Dance?" (from which the Will Ferrell movie *Everything Must Go* was based) includes several half-scenes. Here's one—utterly offbeat:

> Arms about each other, their bodies pressed to-
> gether, the boy and the girl moved up and down the
> driveway. They were dancing. And when the record
> was over, they did it again, and when that one ended,
> the boy said, "I'm drunk."
>
> The girl said, "You're not drunk."
>
> "Well, I'm drunk," the boy said.

The man turned the record over and the boy said, "I am."

"Dance with me," the girl said to the boy and then to the man, and when the man stood up, she came to him with her arms wide open.

The man, who's moved all of his stuff out of his house and into his yard, has in the scene just previous to this one invited the boy and the girl to dance. They do. It's a quirky story, and this short, highly compressed scene ratchets up the quirkiness even more. With brevity and economy, it offers a quick take—like a miniplay.

PROCESS SHEET #10

1. Look over your scenes. Are they all needed? Do you think any of them should be dropped?
2. If you've written a short story, do your scenes help develop character as well as plot? What might you do to make sure they do both?
3. If you've written a novel, which of your scenes directly affect the plot or subplots? How do they stand out from other scenes? Is there more you could do to make them more prominent?
4. If you've written a novel, do some of your scenes develop character and/or indirectly develop plot or subplots? If not, do you see ways to make sure they do these things?

5. Is your dialogue subtle enough? Are there things you could do to make it more subtle? Could you be more suggestive in places instead of having your characters vocalize too much?

6. Does your protagonist's personality come through in the dialogue? How about other characters? Can you find ways to make personality come through better?

7. Do your characters seem motivated to say what they say? Are there places where the dialogue seems good but where you realize your character probably wouldn't say this? Can you think of ways to make the character's speech more credibly motivated?

8. Do you find any provocative ideas in your dialogue, the kinds of ideas that suggest conflict as well as larger themes for your story or novel? Do you see places where ideas might be introduced—but not forced?

9. Do some of your scenes use the objective or dramatic point of view? Is the dialogue strong enough to carry the scene? Do you see ways to improve it?

10. How much do you intersperse character action, setting description, and character reflection in your dialogue? How necessary are these details? Should you trim any of this?

11. Do you have any half-scenes? Can you see places where you might fit in some half-scenes for effect? Do you see any longer scenes that might work better as half-scenes?

EXERCISE 1

Write a scene of about 300 words of dialogue only. Make your characters come alive by introducing a direct conflict between them—perhaps over money, a belief, politics, or a job. Go over this piece and improve the dialogue by making the interchange more subtle. Which version do you like better?

EXERCISE 2

Take the scene in Exercise 1 and add character action, some description of character and setting, plus character thought or reflection. Go over this and strike out anything that seems excessive. Is this edited version better than the unedited version? Why or why not?

EXERCISE 3

Take the scene in Exercise 2 and imagine a complete story where this scene is a key scene. Outline a story around it, and place this scene anywhere in the story. What have you learned about the function of scenes in terms of developing character and plot?

CHAPTER ELEVEN

WHAT ABOUT SETTING?

How important is setting in your short story or novel? Don't describe place just to describe. In some stories place isn't all that important—meaning that just about any city or town would do to tell the character's story. In other stories setting is quite important—in terms of plot, character, mood, and theme or idea.

SETTING AND STORY

Certain story types call for a strong setting. A journey plot, which is often episodic, may call for a strong setting. Other stories with plots centered on setting include institution stories, war, and regional fiction.

Journey Stories

Journey stories tend to call for a developed setting. This is true in *Huckleberry Finn*, where Huck and Jim are rafting down the Mississippi, away from slavery for Jim, away from Pap as well as stifling societal convention for Huck. Their journey is an escape. At Cairo, Illinois, they intend to take a steamboat up the Ohio River to freedom; but when they miss Cairo, ironically they are forced to head further south, to Louisiana, the heart of the South and slavery. Consider the rich setting details in this passage, which occurs just before they miss the Ohio River:

> Well, the second night a fog begun to come on, and we made for a tow-head to tie to, for it wouldn't do to try to run in fog; but when I paddled ahead in the canoe, with the line, to make fast, there warn't anything but little saplings to tie to. I passed the line around one of them right on the edge of the cut bank, but there was a stiff current, and the raft come booming down so lively she tore it out by the roots and away she went. I see the fog closing down, and it made me so sick and scared I couldn't budge for most a half a minute it seemed to me—and then there warn't no raft in sight; you couldn't see twenty yards.

Through carefully selected details, this narrative passage gives us a strong sense of the river environment: the fog, the towhead (or sandbar), the swift current, the saplings to tie up to. These visual details make us feel like we're right there with Huck.

If Twain's *Huckleberry Finn* is a classic nineteenth-century journey/escape novel, James Dickey's *Deliverance* is surely a classic twentieth-century one. Set in the Georgia wilderness, four men take an adventure away from their normally civilized lives and canoe down a treacherous river. At first the river itself seems harmless enough:

> The river opened and was there. It was gray-green, very clear and yet with a certain milkiness, too; it looked as though it would turn white and foam at rocks more easily than other water. It was about forty yards wide, and shallow, about two and half or three feet deep. The bed was full of clean brown pebbles.

Harmless, but notice the suggestive statement about how the water would more easily turn color and foam—foreshadowing of white-water rapid trouble. Now notice how the wilderness around them is soon depicted as creepily ominous:

> I could hear the river running at my feet, and behind my head the woods were unimaginably dense and dark; there was nothing in them that knew me. There were creatures with one forepaw lifted, not wanting yet to put the other down on a dry leaf, for fear of the sound. There were the eyes made for seeing in this blackness; I opened my eyes and saw the dark in all its original color.

Through this "Nature, red in tooth and claw" imagery, Dickey foreshadows the danger that lies ahead for these adventurers. The real danger is not the white-water rapids, which will certainly pose a serious threat, but the clannish, menacing locals who will soon make their wilderness event a hellish experience. Dickey's strong sense of place is integral to this journey/escape novel.

This is surely the case as well in Tim O'Brien's *Northern Lights*, which includes a wilderness survival story as a key element of the plot. O'Brien describes two brothers in the deep Minnesota wilderness in the dead of winter. Notice how the setting details create interest and build tension:

> They strapped on their skis. The bluffs fell to a natural valley that burrowed southwest and then opened on to a meadow surrounded by more trees. The trees were very old, mostly pine but some birch. The birch were slim and tall, and the white bark stretched in large sheets around the trunks, crinkling at the black seams. There was nothing moving. Perry looked once

at the closing sky then decided to ignore it and followed Harvey's orange rucksack. A palpable, bitter
air kept him going.

For a time it was easy skiing again, but then again
the forest thickened and they were forced to walk.
Harvey followed a chain of moraines that gradually
flattened and gave way on the rim of an ancient gully.
It was getting dark.

This carefully nuanced detail gives us a picture of the two brothers, on skis, in the midst of a cold, beautiful, but stark, unforgiv-
ing terrain. The journey they make wouldn't be complete without
the vivid setting O'Brien portrays here and elsewhere:

For a time Harvey kept a fairly straight course and
the trees filtered out the falling snow and the day
was dismal gray. Weaving and picking the way, Harvey
led him through a stand of old pine, then through a
natural clearing and into dense birch, then into more
pine. The country was flat. It was all the same, and
Perry followed the orange rucksack.

Action mixed with landscape: trees, clearing, more trees. Flat-
ness, sameness. O'Brien anchors us in the particularities of place.
If we are to enter fully into this journey, strong sensory details
of place are essential.

If you've written a journey story of some kind, be sure your
story's setting is vividly rendered. Sometimes this takes only a
few sharp details. The reader will fill in the rest. I do want to emphasize that not every journey or trip requires a vivid setting. It
may be enough to say your character took the red-eye from New
York to L.A. and leave it at that. But if something important occurs on this flight, then you will probably need to evoke a visual
sense of the setting.

The Institution Story

A story centering on an institution of some kind also calls for a strong sense of setting. I'm not speaking of societal institutions in the abstract sense (such as slavery) but a particular institution with physical environs. Whether it's the TB sanatorium in Thomas Mann's *The Magic Mountain*, the health sanitarium in T.C. Boyle's *The Road to Wellville*, or the Siberian forced labor camp in Alexander Solzhenitsyn's *One Day in the Life of Ivan Denisovich*, a strong sense of setting is essential to telling such stories.

Consider Mann's stunning description of the mountainous surrounds of the TB sanatorium. Hans Castorp views this sublime natural setting from the moving train as he makes his arrival:

> Magnificent vistas opened onto regions toward which they were slowly climbing, a world of ineffable, phantasmagoric Alpine peaks, soon lost again to awestruck eyes as the tracks took another curve. Hans Castorp thought about how he had left hardwood forests far below him, and songbirds, too, he presumed; and the idea that such things could cease, the sense of a world made poorer without them, brought on a slight attack of dizziness and nausea, and he covered his eyes with his hand for a second or two. This passed. He realized that their climb was coming to an end, that they had taken the crest. The train was now rolling more comfortably along the level floor of a valley.
>
> It was almost eight o'clock, but still daylight. A lake appeared in the distant landscape; its surface was gray and from its shores black pine forests climbed the surrounding slopes, grew thinner toward the top, and gave way at last to bare, fog-enshrouded rock.

This rich setting imagery, early in the novel, functions like an establishing shot in a film: the remote mountainous region where Hans Castorp is about to take residence as a patient.

Here's a sweeping description from *The Road to Wellville* of the Kellogg Battle Creek Sanitarium:

> Twenty-eight hundred patients annually passed through its portals, and one thousand employees, including twenty full-time physicians and three hundred nurses and bath attendants, saw to their needs. Six stories high, with a gleaming lobby half the size of a football field, with four hundred rooms and treatment facilities for a thousand, with elevators, central heating and cooling, indoor swimming pools and a whole range of therapeutic diversions and wholesome entertainments, the San was the sine qua non of the cure business—luxury hotel, hospital and spa all rolled into one.

Here, setting includes, as setting sometimes does, the patients as well as the various medical professionals. If we entered this institution, it would be hard to separate the place from the people that inhabit it—they make it what it is. This is the world that Kellogg rules over with an iron hand and the world that his patients struggle to endure. If we couldn't visualize this place, it would be much less real to us.

Alexander Solzhenitsyn's *One Day in the Life of Ivan Denisovich* is set in a Stalinist Siberian labor camp. As the novel unfolds, we piece together the various details the author supplies: the barracks, the searchlights from the watchtowers, the dispensary, the mess hall, the many prisoners and guards that make the setting what it is. The author describes a moment of relaxation:

> He ran at a dog trot to his barracks. The whole parade ground was deserted, the camp looked empty.

> It was that brief moment of relaxation when, al-
> though everything has been decided, everyone is
> pretending to himself that there will be no march
> to work. The sentries sit in warm quarters, their
> sleepy heads propped against their rifles—it's not
> all milk and honey for them either, lounging on the
> watchtowers in such cold. The guards at the main
> gate tossed coal into the stove. The campguards in
> their room smoked a last cigarette before searching
> the barracks. And the prisoners, now clad in all their
> rags, a rope around their waists, their faces bound
> from chin to eyes with bits of cloth against the cold,
> lay on their bunks with their boots on and waited,
> eyes shut, hearts aquake, for their squad leader to
> yell: "Out you go."

This passage of summary, with its carefully chosen detail, gives us a brief shot of camp routine—both of the prisoners and the guards—and in doing so, a sense of place. A vivid picture of this forced labor camp is central to the novel's purpose.

If you've written a story or novel centering on an institution of some kind—perhaps a hospital, a nursing home, a psychiatric facility, a military base, a university—find ways to make this institution as real as you can for your reader. You can provide specific, concrete description, using the direct method. Or you can make use of the more indirect method, supplying selected specific details as the story proceeds, depending mostly on your reader to create a picture in his own mind.

War Story

If war is an *action*, it is nonetheless a setting as well—a setting that includes all the forces of war, material and human, as well as the physical place where the war is conducted. The question is, how do you create such a setting? How do you make it real to your reader? Look at this opening passage of summary mixed with vivid description from Stephen Crane's *The Red Badge of Courage*:

> The cold passed reluctantly from the earth, and the retiring fogs revealed an army stretched out on the hills, resting. As the landscape changed from brown to green, the army awakened, and began to tremble with eagerness at the noise of rumors. It cast its eyes upon the roads, which were growing from long troughs of liquid mud to proper thoroughfares. A river, amber-tinted in the shadow of its banks, purled at the army's feet; and at night, when the stream had become of a sorrowful blackness, one could see across it the red, eyelike gleam of hostile camp fires set in the low brows of distant hills.

This concrete, energetic prose does much to establish the setting for this novel—the landscape, the river, the enemy camp-fires. Crane, who was born after the Civil War, made this novel so real to readers that some Civil War veterans thought he had surely fought in it.

Setting is also richly evoked in Erich Maria Remarque's *All Quiet on the Western Front*, a classic work set in World War I. Note this vivid passage:

> These are wonderfully care-free hours. Over us is the blue sky. On the horizon float the bright yellow, sunlit observation-balloons, and the many little white clouds of the anti-aircraft shells. Often they rise in a sheaf as they follow after an airman. We hear the muffled rumble of the front only as very distant thunder, bumble-bees droning by quite drown it. Around us stretches the flowery meadow. The

> grasses sway their tall spears; the white butterflies
> flutter around and float on the soft warm wind of
> the late summer.

The beautiful and ugly are blended here with stunning concreteness. The "muffled rumble of the front" foreshadows the scarred battleground, the trenches, the brutal machinery of war. A strong evocation of setting is crucial to the telling of this story.

If you've chosen this subject, you're taking on a lot, perhaps too much, if you haven't been in a war in some capacity (perhaps as a journalist, if not a soldier) or haven't done considerable research. How can you create a believable setting working in a vacuum? And research, while necessary, surely isn't enough. You must transform research materials into lived reality, contextualizing (if not directly stating or dramatizing) the conflict in terms of all the military, political, economic, and social forces at work. This takes thorough research but also a fertile and active imagination. Still, historical novels about war are, of course, plentiful. If you're drawn to writing about war, any war, dig in—don't flinch from the task, but do expect considerable work.

The Regional Story

Fiction sometimes focuses on a specific region of the country, evoking in the reader a strong sense of the physical environs as well as the local culture. There are Southern writers, New England writers, Midwestern writers, and others, but do keep this in mind: In terms of thematic scope, regional writing doesn't have to be limited to a specific region. Great literary works that focus on region embody universal themes. Such is the case with Geoffrey Clark's story collection *Schooling the Spirit*, which portrays the provocative mix of beauty and brutality in rural Michigan in the 1950s.

In this work we get a strong visual sense for the countryside, the roads, the tavern, the small Michigan town, the tourist spot on the lake. Clark interweaves story line with specific details of character and place. In the following passage from "Ice Fishing," the narrator lists the many supplies for the fishing adventure:

> Details began to fill paucities: they had gotten their stuff together ... minnow bucket, tackle box, short ice fishing rods, half a fifty pound sack of crushed oyster shells, a spud, a sieve for an ice skimmer, the stainless steel thermos ... full of coffee, a couple of Spam and cheese and mustard sandwiches apiece ... and had stood there on the shore, looking out toward their shanty, a dot barely distinguishable from other dots in what seemed a vast whiteness.

This passage, depicting all the gear packed for the occasion, together with that "vast whiteness," paints a pastoral vision of the Michigan rural winter landscape—and life. But elsewhere, Clark's vision is not so pastoral. It's in fact anything but idyllic. By story's end, the protagonist's brother is dead in a senseless killing by an old schoolmate, a bully turned trooper. Clark's vision of this region is complex. The region that inspires the earthiness and beauty of ice fishing is the same region that breeds senseless violence. The rich imagery of the setting at the beginning of this story prepares us for an ironic rug pulling at the end. But if Clark's physical setting is Michigan, his moral arena is humankind itself, an inseparable mix of good and evil. Like all great writers with a regional emphasis, Clark moves us beyond the specific region to universal themes. This is something to think carefully about if your story or novel emphasizes region—seek the universal in the particular.

If you've written a regional story or novel—perhaps about Appalachia, the Midwest, or the South—make sure you capture the ethos of this region by dramatizing it in the characters' lives, speech, and mind-set. Clark's work zeroes in on 1950s Michigan locals with such specificity and concreteness that we can't help but feel the locals' presence as individual living creatures and at the same time reflective of their cultural milieu.

SETTING AND CHARACTER

Character may be mirrored in the setting itself: the house, paintings on the wall, rugs covering the floor. Naturally, if we emphasize how affluent the house or gated mansion, the reader will undoubtedly see these details as revelation of the owner's values. Jay Gatsby's mansion and possessions clearly gauge his sense of self-worth.

Possibilities abound for connections between setting and character. Consider Hemingway's "A Clean, Well-Lighted Place." The older waiter, a philosophical nihilist, closes up the café late at night. This clean, well-lighted café provides, for him, a haven from the darkness of *nada*. When he shuts down the place late at night, he thinks:

> It is the light of course but it is necessary that the place be clean and pleasant. You do not want music. Certainly you do not want music. Nor can you stand before a bar with dignity although that is all that is provided for these hours.

When this waiter is about to leave for the night, the narrator provides his internal thoughts:

> He disliked bars and bodegas. A clean, well-lighted café was a very different thing. Now, without thinking further, he would go home to his room. He would lie in the bed and finally, with daylight, he would go to sleep.

For this older waiter, a clean, well-lighted place answers to his need for a refuge; a dark bar is the opposite of what he needs. Setting is an expression of character—of need. Hemingway, in his characteristically spare style, selects a few details at the beginning of the story—a tree, an electric light, the dusty street—to situate the café setting in our mind, but the rest is expressed through drama and interior monologue.

Setting may be an important part of a character's cultural and emotional make-up, as we see in Thomas S. Whitecloud's "Blue Winds Dancing." Feeling isolated and alienated from his Native American roots, Whitecloud's protagonist makes his way home at Christmastime from southern California, where he attends a university, to his native Wisconsin. The author provides rich setting imagery to link his character's spirit to this important place:

> Laughing, I go into the woods. As I cross a frozen lake I begin to hear the drums. Soft in the night the drums beat. It is like the pulse beat of the world. The white line of the lake ends at a black forest, and above the trees the blue winds are dancing.
>
> I come to the outlying houses of the village. Simple box houses, etched black in the night. From one or two windows soft lamp light falls on the snow.

Home is connected to this character's sense of self, his very being tied to this place. Away from his Native American heritage he suffers a deep sense of alienation. His whole identity as a person is rooted here.

As you revise your manuscript, look for ways that setting might be related to your character. Does this setting reflect your character's values? Does it answer to certain psychological or existential needs? Does it tie in with your character's basic roots and sense of self?

Setting might also be used metaphorically. If all the clocks in a character's house are wrong, this might suggest something larger than the timepieces being off. It might be used, if developed sufficiently, to suggest the character's basic disorientation.

The question for your present manuscript is how important setting is. Don't come on too strong or heavy-handed, but do look for any possible connections between your character and setting. Deep emotional connections, if they apply, can give your character more depth and breadth. Metaphorical uses of setting, if subtle, not only strengthen characterization but can also give your work more levels and dimensions.

SETTING AND THEME

If setting can be important to plot or character, it may also play an important role in developing theme and idea. Let's consider setting as it relates to three American classics dealing with the American Dream.

In Rebecca Harding Davis's *Life in the Iron-Mills*, we see first-hand the desolation of the urban environment in which the characters live. The novella calls into question the attainability of the American Dream, in that some people are utterly disempowered and excluded. Notice these provocative setting details:

> The idiosyncrasy of this town is smoke. It rolls sullenly in slow folds from the great chimneys of the iron-foundries, and settles down in black, slimy pools on the muddy streets. Smoke on the wharves, some on the dingy boats, on the yellow river,—clinging in a coating of greasy soot to the house-front, the two faded poplars, the faces of the passers-by... Smoke everywhere!

Having presented this detailed description of a horrific setting, the author invites us to read the story of her protagonist,

Hugh Wolfe, whose gripping poverty makes for an utterly futile existence. This authorial approach is nineteenth century in style but nonetheless illustrates how concrete details of setting can situate a character like Hugh Wolfe within a context of grim socio-economic circumstances and in this way point to the story's theme.

Consider how important setting is to a naturalistic work of fiction like Dreiser's *Sister Carrie*. In Dreiser's novel, Chicago is portrayed as an immense urban environment, having the power to crush or make the individual. When Carrie is on foot seeking employment, note how Dreiser gives us a sense of the immensity and sheer power of this city setting:

> The entire metropolitan centre possessed a high and mighty air calculated to overawe and abash the common applicant, and to make the gulf between poverty and success seem both wide and deep.
>
> Into this important commercial region the timid Carrie went. She walked east along Van Buren Street through a region of lessening importance, until it deteriorated into a mass of shanties and coal-yards, and finally verged upon the river. She walked bravely forward, led by an honest desire to find employment and delayed at every step by the interest of the unfolding scene, and a sense of helplessness amid so much evidence of power and force which she did not understand. These vast buildings, what were they? These strange energies and huge interests, for what purposes were they there?

These setting details do much to advance Dreiser's claim that the environment—in this case, Chicago—has the power to mold and shape the destiny of the individual. In Dreiser's naturalistic, or deterministic, vision, there is little personal freedom to chart one's own future, to enjoy the fruits of the American Dream. One is a pawn—for good or ill—in the hands of larger social forces. Setting is tied to theme.

In *The Great Gatsby*, what is the meaning of the green light across the bay from West Egg to East Egg, the light Gatsby so passionately observes? What do Dr. T.J. Eckleburg's eyes looking out over an ash pit stand for? Together, green light and ash pit point to the dual nature of the American Dream: the green light suggesting the pure Dream itself; the sign with Eckleburg's eyes the American Dream spoiled—a veritable ash pit of desolation, materialism, sterility. This novel relies greatly on these two setting details to make a critical statement about the American Dream.

When linking setting to theme, you do need to be very careful not to symbol hunt. Not every green light means something, but in *The Great Gatsby* it certainly does because when Gatsby looks across the bay at night from West Egg to East Egg, he is looking in the direction of Daisy Buchanan. Gatsby's goal is to win her over—and in the America of the 1920s, this means money. "Her voice is full of money," says Gatsby at one point. In Fitzgerald's novel, setting contributes significantly to the theme of money and privilege. These are what the American Dream has been reduced to.

Setting can serve many thematic uses. An urban setting with a subdivision of cracker-box houses can suggest uniformity and sterility. A rural setting can suggest either beauty or bleakness— or a mix of these two, as in the work of Geoffrey Clark. An idyllic, imagined setting can suggest the longing of the human spirit for beauty and goodness. If you think about your setting carefully as you revise your story or novel, you may see some definite possibilities. Which embryonic ideas do you see embedded at this point in your work? See what might come of these with further treatment. But if you find that setting isn't all that important, don't work it. Maybe it's important in some way to theme, but maybe character and conflict are much more important. If so, give it the proportion of space that it's due—and no more.

SETTING AND MOOD

A grim setting certainly creates a grim mood, as we see in the passage from Rebecca Harding Davis's novella. One might say that the mood of melancholy and gloom in Poe's "The Fall of the House of Usher" is pretty grim, but certainly it's a different kind of grim—and coming from a different source. Take note:

> During the whole of a dull, dark, and soundless day in the autumn of the year, when the clouds hung oppressively low in the heavens, I had been passing alone, on horseback, through a singularly dreary tract of country, and at length found myself, as the shades of the evening drew on, within view of the melancholy House of Usher.

Even though this style is a far cry from contemporary prose style, there is still much to learn from it. It embeds several mood-creating words and phrases. It's autumn, symbolic of age and mutability. Note how the clouds "hung oppressively low"—the opposite of buoyancy and uplift. The tract of country is "singularly dreary." The house is "melancholy." The mood this setting creates is oppressive and melancholy, and prepares us for the doom that follows.

In a different vein, notice the mood created by details of setting from "The Yellow Wall-Paper." The protagonist studies the wallpaper, its design and color:

> One of those sprawling flamboyant patterns committing every artistic sin.
>
> It is dull enough to confuse the eye in following, pronounced enough to constantly irritate and pro-

voke study, and when you follow the lame uncertain curves for a little distance they suddenly commit suicide—plunge off at outrageous angles, destroy themselves in unheard of contradictions.

The color is repellant, almost revolting; a smouldering unclean yellow, strangely faded by the slow-turning sunlight.

It is a dull yet lurid orange in some places, a sickly sulphur tint in others.

Published in 1892, this story was written in a surprisingly modern style. The mood evoked by these setting details, filtered through the protagonist's mind, is one of amazement, confusion, and disgust—quite fitting to the mood of the protagonist in her progressive deterioration of mind.

Now consider this passage from *Deliverance*. The four adventurers are about to spend their first night in the woods. The I-narrator describes the situation:

They tried to be useful, but Drew and Bobby did not seem to be getting much done, and I saw the folly of just standing around and letting Lewis do everything, though it would have been all right with him if I had. I was sleepy, and I went to the equipment that had to do with that. I blew up the air mattresses with a hand pump, all four of them; it took a good half an hour, and I was pumping steadily all the time, while the river lightened in front of me and the woods at my back got thicker and thicker with blackness.

We can't help but sense the narrator's anxiety and sense of danger. But Dickey avoids telling. He lets the setting details—the woods becoming increasingly dark—suggest this.

The mood of a story or novel is extremely important. Mood may change from one section of a story to another, and it must be appropriate to character and plot. Search out places where you want to achieve a given mood—perhaps a feeling of lightness. This may be expressed via setting by noting a glider in the sky, a hot air balloon, a kite flying high—your characters can see these things or imagine them. If you work them a little, giving them some dramatic attention, they might become symbolic. If such devices don't seem to fit in your story or novel, don't add them. But when you do find possible figurative uses of setting details to contribute to mood, be attentive to them.

PROCESS SHEET #11

1. Does your story or novel have a journey plot? Is your setting sufficiently developed? How concrete? Can you see places to add more details?

2. Does your story or novel center on a specific institution of some kind? Is your setting sufficiently developed? Do you see places to add more details?

3. Is your story or novel set in wartime? Have you made the war setting sufficiently real? Can you see places to develop it further?

4. Does your story or novel focus on a certain region of the country or on a certain culture? Is the setting sufficiently developed? Can you see places to add more details? Can you see ways to give your regional story or novel universal themes?

5. Does your story deal with a plot different from the types mentioned in questions 1-4? Is your setting sufficiently developed? Can you think of more details to add?

6. Do you use setting in your story or novel to reflect character or to help develop character? Can you see additional places to connect setting to character?
7. Does setting in your story or novel contribute to theme? Do you see places to make various connections you haven't yet made?
8. Does setting in your story or novel contribute to mood? Can you see ways to connect setting to mood?

EXERCISE 1

Write a short narrative of about 300 words. Write a journey story or a story centering on an institution or on a particular region of the country. Begin with setting details that physically place your reader there. Rewrite this piece, furnishing setting details as the narrative proceeds. Which version do you prefer?

EXERCISE 2

Write a narrative of about 300 words, creating a particular character. Bring in specific setting details to help develop this character. Go over this piece. How would changing the setting details alter a reader's perception of this character? Try it.

EXERCISE 3

Take the narrative passage in Exercise 2 and try to embed a thematic idea or two—by suggestion, not direct statement. In a second version, state the theme explicitly. Which version do you prefer?

EXERCISE 4

Write a narrative passage of about 300 words. Use setting details to create mood. Go over this piece. What mood have you created and which details did you use to create this mood? Rework the piece with different setting details to create a different mood.

CHAPTER TWELVE

RETHINKING OPENINGS AND ENDINGS

As you revise your short story or novel, go back and reread the first several pages of your manuscript. Does your present opening work as well as it should? Does your opening draw the reader in quickly enough, or would it be better to lop off the first paragraph or even the first few pages? Does it set the right tone for the work?

Examine your final pages and paragraphs. Did you end the story in the right place? Is your present ending too obvious? How can you achieve the maximum impact and still "say" what you want to say? How can you provide closure without too much closure?

The emphasis in this chapter is on what makes a good opening or closing, not on what makes good expository or descriptive writing or what makes good summary or scene—we've dealt with this already in Chapters Nine and Ten. And yet the quality of the writing itself is important, and I will comment on that as well.

RETHINKING OPENINGS

Different readers expect different things. Some readers enjoy a story that begins with a gradual buildup. Others want a fast start, and this often means scene. Agents and publishers tend to go for scenic openings, which pull us right into the story. Beginning with summary may be an option, as long as it's lively and energetic. Whatever you do, your writing needs to hook your reader. If the opening doesn't do this, your story or novel may not get read at all.

Expository Openings

As I pointed out in Chapter Nine, if handled well, expository prose can be as energetic and lively as any other prose technique. And when it is energetic, it gets a story or novel off to a good start.

Character Background

Sometimes an expository opening provides a character's background, or, in the case of an omniscient narrator, a whole town's historical background. Russell Banks begins his novel *Rule of the Bone* with teenage Bone's intriguing comments about his past life:

> You'll probably think I'm making a lot of this up just to make me sound better than I really am or smarter or even luckier but I'm not. Besides, a lot of the things that've happened to me in my life so far which I'll get to pretty soon'll make me sound evil or just plain dumb or the tragic victim of circumstances. Which I know doesn't exactly prove I'm telling the truth but if I wanted to make myself look better than I am or smarter or the master of my own fate so to speak I could. The fact is the truth is more interesting than anything I could make up and that's why I'm telling it in the first place.

This is expository prose, but note its strong dramatic quality—note the way Bone intimately addresses the reader. We want to read on. What bad things have happened to Bone? What has he done? Why is the truth more interesting than something he could make up? This opening makes us seek answers to questions about this character's mysterious background. Questions create suspense.

Key Character Qualities

A work can begin with provocative character traits. Here's an example from Megan Mayhew Bergman's "Housewifely Arts," appearing in *The Best American Short Stories 2011*:

> I am my own housewife, my own breadwinner. I make lunches and change light bulbs. I kiss bruises and kill copperheads from the backyard creek with a steel hoe. I change sheets and the oil in my car. I can make a pie crust and exterminate humpback crickets in the crawlspace with a homemade glue board, though not at the same time. I like to compliment myself on these things, because there's no one else around to do it.

Notice the repetitive structure here: "I make"; "I kiss"; "I change." This enumeration creates an interesting cadence. We are surely drawn in by the specific details, plus the sheer range of this woman's many tasks—her resourcefulness and varied capabilities. What's next? What challenges can she not handle?

Present Predicament

Nick Hornby begins *High Fidelity* with his I-narrator's "five most memorable split-ups, in chronological order." Rob, his protagonist, provides a numbered list of five women's names. He continues:

> These were the ones that really hurt. Can you see your name in that lot, Laura? I reckon you'd sneak into the top ten, but there's no place for you in the

top five; those places are reserved for the kind of humiliations and heartbreaks that you're just not capable of delivering. That probably sounds crueler than it is meant to, but the fact is that we're too old to make each other miserable, and that's a good thing, not a bad thing, so don't take your failure to make the list personally.

This quirky expository opening establishes Rob's present disgruntlement over his past romances. Note how he speaks (in his mind) directly to Laura—this adds to the dramatic quality. It's like dialogue, but it's *not* dialogue—it's internal monologue. Like other strong openings, it provides suspense: What part has Laura played in his romantic loves gone sour? Why would she qualify for the top ten but not the top five?

Expository prose doesn't have to be dry. It can be provocative. It can be witty. It can invite questions that provoke readers to read on. The authors I've quoted provide information, but it's handled in a lively, intriguing manner.

Descriptive Openings

If it's vivid and energetic, description of character or place can grab the reader's attention. If you haven't tried a descriptive opening, consider it. If you have, look at the following examples, plus find more on your own, and try to improve your descriptive opening.

Character

A story or novel can open with description of character. Here's a famous one—*Lolita*:

> Lolita, light of my life, fire of my loins. My sin, my soul. Lo-lee-ta: the tip of the tongue taking a trip of three steps down the palate to tap, at three, on the tenth. Lo. Lee. Ta.

This is fairly abstract except for the aural as well as tactile imagery gained by the description of the tongue uttering these syllables. But it certainly creates interest in Vladimir Nabokov's famous fictional character and his passion for this young woman.

Place

If you begin with place, will the plot of your story or novel center on this place? Will it be important to theme?

Rick Moody's *The Ice Storm* begins with amusing expository commentary mixed with description of setting:

> So let me dish you this comedy about a family I knew when I was growing up. There's a part for me in this story, like there always is for a gossip, but more on that later.
>
> First: the guest room, with the orderly neglect of all guest rooms. Benjamin Paul Hood—the dad in what follows—in the guest room. In the house belonging to Janey and Jim Williams, just up the street from Hood's own comfortable spread. In the most congenial and superficially calm of suburbs. In the wealthiest state in the Northeast. In the most affluent country on earth. Thanksgiving just past and quickly forgotten. Three years shy of that commercial madness, the bicentennial.

This opening passage—with its repetitive phrases hammering an interesting beat—reflects a strong attitude and provides an initial time-place frame, a sociohistorical context, for this novel. It draws us into the messed-up lives of the characters that people this work. As description this is more specific than concrete, but because of the engaging narrative voice, it certainly has impact.

Description can also draw us in with concrete, visual imagery. In Chapter Eleven, we saw how Crane's opening to *The Red Badge of Courage* establishes, in short order, the reality of war. Hemingway's opening to "In Another Country" establishes what it's like to be away from the war:

> In the fall the war was always there, but we did not go to it any more. It was cold in the fall in Milan and the dark came very early. Then the electric lights came on, and it was pleasant along the streets looking in the windows. There was much game hanging outside the shops, and the snow powdered in the fur of the foxes and the wind blew their tails. The deer hung stiff and heavy and empty, and small birds blew in the wind and the wind turned their feathers.

This is as much description as summary. Note how concrete: the snow powdering the foxes' fur, the wind blowing their tails. How deer hang outside the shops. How the wind turns the small birds' feathers. We can't help but see these things, and we are drawn in to find out more. What will happen to the "we" who have a present refuge from the war?

Rethink your own opening. A descriptive passage can locate your reader concretely in your fictional world. It can also provide suspense.

Summary Openings

As we saw in Chapter Nine, summary must be written in a strong voice, it must be vivid, and it must create suspense. Janet Burroway distinguishes between two kinds of summary: "sequential" and "circumstantial." Sequential means a time line, or one event following another. Circumstantial is the way things tended to happen over a given time period. Here's an example of the sequential type, from David Cates's *X out of Wonderland,* a satire on free-market capitalism:

> Not long ago, in the belly of a big-bellied land called Wonderland, there lived a young man who, in order to protect from unwanted commercial solicitations, we'll simply call X.
>
> X grew up with loving parents in a prosperous time of peace. He attended public schools from kindergarten through the university, and after ten years in the building trades, he earned a graduate degree from the prestigious School of Ecology and Economics.
>
> After graduate school, X remained at the university and became well known for his public radio show, *Home Renovation and Repair Issues.* He built himself a beautiful house in the country down a long driveway through the grove of Lombardi poplars. In those days the sky was mostly blue and the grass very green. There were brook trout in the creek and pretty horses in the neighboring pasture. X read of injustice and evil in the newspaper, and he saw it on the evening news, but, sitting on his water-sealed redwood deck in the evening after a day discussing with curious and energetic callers concrete slabs, vent spaces, blown-in cellulose, wall mold, and capillary flow through foundations, injustice and evil seemed far away indeed.

This opening has a fairy-tale quality to it, and certainly Cates's novel, based on Voltaire's *Candide,* isn't a realistic work of fiction. What we have here is X's history rendered vividly in capsule form and his present, naïve sense of personal security from evil and injustice—which we assume is about to change. And thus suspense: What will be the nature of this rug pulling, and when will it occur?

Hemingway's *A Farewell to Arms* begins with the circumstantial kind:

> In the late summer of that year we lived in a house in a village that looked across the river and the plain to the mountains. In the bed of the river there were pebbles and boulders, dry and white in the sun, and the water was clear and swiftly moving and blue in the channels. Troops went by the house and down the road and the dust they raised powered the leaves of the trees. The trunks of the trees too were dusty and the leaves fell early that year and we saw the troops marching along the road and the dust rising and leaves, stirred by the breeze, falling and the soldiers marching and afterward the road bare and white except for the leaves.

Here's how it was that summer. This by-now famous opening passage demonstrates how energetic summary can be. We can credit Hemingway's concrete description and the lyrical movement of his prose. Circumstantial summary can serve different functions throughout a story, but as a device for openings, it most likely tells us what it was like before something important happened—something that changed the present equilibrium. This could be something bad or good.

If your present manuscript begins with summary—or if you are thinking about using a summary opening in your revised manuscript—make sure you accomplish four things: Make your writing vivid, get your reader interested in your character or characters, make your reader wonder what will happen to them, and create a compelling voice and tone. I'll talk more on that in the next chapter.

Scenic Openings

A reminder from Chapter Eight: If you begin with a scene and you have backstory to deal with to any extent, you will either have to use flashbacks or find some way to include this backstory through dramatic means. Having said that, scenes make for strong openings as long as they include conflict and suspense.

Note this startling opening from Kafka's *The Metamorphosis*:

> As Gregor Samsa awoke one morning from uneasy dreams he found himself transformed in his bed into a gigantic insect. He was lying on his hard, as it were armor-plated, back and when he lifted his head a little he could see his dome-like brown belly divided into stiff arched segments on top of which the bed quilt could hardly keep in position and was about to slide off completely. His numerous legs, which were pitifully thin compared to the rest of his bulk, waved helplessly before his eyes.

Surely this scenic opening commands the reader's attention. Samsa has awakened to find himself a giant bug. How did this happen? What else will happen to this character?

You may not be planning anything this odd or bizarre, but the scenic method may still be the best choice for your opening—and perhaps you have already chosen it.

This is a popular method today to involve the reader immediately in the action of the story. Notice what happens in Eric Miles Williamson's novel *Two-Up*:

> Yesterday Broadstreet saw a laborer from the union hall lose a finger in the gunite pump.
>
> The laborer reached into the hopper after a rock that made its way into the batch, and the churning paddle blades chopped his finger off and slapped it down into the concrete.

"Ah," the laborer screamed.

This horrifying opening scene establishes what it's like to be a gunite (or concrete) worker, the hard, dangerous work this novel focuses on. If page 1 opens with this occurrence, what's next?

Of course, an opening doesn't have to be as shocking as this. Consider this opening from Nathaniel West's satire *The Day of the Locust*:

> Around quitting time, Tod Hackett heard a great din on the road outside his office. The groan of leather mingled with the jangle of iron and over all beat the tattoo of a thousand hooves. He hurried to the window.

This narrative scene is concrete, it moves, and it also places us in Tod Hackett's new environment, 1930s Hollywood. The last sentence creates suspense: What will he see?

Here's a short opening scene, from Ian McEwan's *Amsterdam*, a British satire:

> Two former lovers of Molly Lane stood waiting outside the crematorium chapel with their backs to the February chill. It had all been said before, but they said it again.
> 'She never knew what hit her.'
> "When she did it was too late.'
> 'Rapid onset.'
> 'Poor Molly.'
> 'Mmm.'

Who's Molly? What happened to her? What is each speaker's stake in her demise? The writing is stripped down, tight, which makes the scene move.

If you begin with a scene, make sure it has conflict. Make sure it gets the reader's attention in some way, but don't overwrite it. Leave the reader with some questions.

RETHINKING ENDINGS

Except for summary, the same methods—exposition, description, and scene—apply here. Let's look first at endings for the sense of closure and impact and then look more closely at the closure question itself.

Exposition

An expository closing is a bit risky, but in the hands of a good writer, it can have real force. Consider this expository ending from "The Sleep" by Caitlin Horrocks that appears in *The Best American Short Stories 2011*:

> Now we are the people of Bounty, the farmers of dust and cold, the harvesters of dreams. After the lumber, after the mines, after the railroad, after the interstate, after the crops, after the cows, after the jobs. We're better neighbors in warm beds than we ever were awake. The suckers of the last century, but not of this one.

This *feels* like a wrap-up. And notice the forceful parallel structure with the sequence of "after" phrases—which hammer home the narrator's point. The succinctness of the final line creates impact.

Here's the end of Alexander Solzhenitsyn's *One Day in the Life of Ivan Denisovich*:

> Shukhov went to sleep fully content. He'd had many strokes of luck that day: they hadn't put him in the cells; they hadn't sent his squad to the settlement; he'd swiped a bowl of kasha at dinner; the squad leader had fixed the rates well; he'd built a wall and enjoyed doing it; he'd smuggled that bit of hacksaw blade through; he'd earned a favor from Tsezar that

> evening; he'd bought that tobacco. And he hadn't
> fallen ill. He'd got over it.
>
> A day without a dark cloud. Almost a happy day.
>
> There were three thousand six hundred and fifty-
> three days like that in his stretch. From the first clang
> of the rail to the last clang of the rail.
>
> Three thousand six hundred and fifty-three days.
>
> The three extra days were for leap years.

In spite of the third-person narrative point of view, we're placed squarely inside the consciousness of Shukhov as he rehearses the events of his day with satisfaction and then contemplates the seemingly interminable length of time still to be served in this labor camp. An expository ending in which a character analyzes, with some notable satisfaction, what's been accomplished so far, yet what still remains in the long road ahead, can surely make for a fine ending—depending, of course, on what's being contemplated and if it's contemplated with such fine detail and style as we see here. Make sure the matter isn't trivial. Certainly it isn't in Shukhov's case.

Description

A descriptive ending can be equally gripping if it leaves us with something concrete to take away. Consider this ending to Lauren Groff's "Eyewall," from *The PEN/O. Henry Prize Stories 2012*:

> Houses contain us; who can say what we contain? Out
> where the steps had been, balanced beside the drop-
> off: one egg, whole and mute, holding all the light of
> dawn in its skin.

Here, a sentence of expository prose is followed by a passage of concrete description in language with a brilliant flourish of finality to it. This closing image makes us want to rethink everything that's happened in this story.

Note this closing to E.L. Doctorow's *The March*:

> Later, back on the road, the shadows began to length-
> en as the afternoon wore on. The green of the land
> grew softer, and the road, in a slow descent, passed
> into a valley. And then there was a dark, thick grove
> of pine where some of the war had passed through.
> A boot lay in the pine needles, and the shreds of a
> discolored uniform. Behind a fallen log, a small pile
> of cartridge shells. There was still a scent of gunfire
> in the trees, and they were glad to come out into the
> sun again.

This is scenic, but the characters are relatively absent, with the dominant mode being a descriptive passage of the landscape, providing striking evidence of the ravages of war: the boot, the shreds of the uniform, the cartridge shells. This one tight passage delivers a powerful sense of closure.

Scene

A story or novel can end with a short scene. Consider the ending to James Thurber's classic tale "The Secret Life of Walter Mitty":

> He took one last drag on his cigarette and snapped
> it away. Then, with that faint, fleeting smile playing
> about his lips, he faced the firing squad; erect and
> motionless, proud and disdainful, Walter Mitty the
> Undefeated, inscrutable to the last.

This comic story ends with actions we can't exactly ignore. The double adjectives, paired off—"erect and motionless, proud and disdainful"—give an intensity to the prose, and on the heels of that, with Thurber's snappy authorial one-liner, the story feels closed. We've come to a distinct end.

Consider the ending of John Updike's *Rabbit, Run*:

Rabbit comes to the curb but instead of going to his right and around the block he steps down, with as big a feeling as if this little sidestreet is a wide river, and crosses. He wants to travel to the next patch of snow. Although this block of brick three-stories is just like the one he left, something in it makes him happy; the steps and windowsills seem to twitch and shift in the corner of his eye, alive. This illusion trips him. His hands lift of their own and he feels the wind on his ears even before, his heels hitting heavily on the pavement at first but with an effortless gathering out of a kind of sweet panic growing lighter and quicker and quieter, he runs. Ah: runs. Runs.

Rabbit's a man who has always run from commitment, and Updike shows him running to the last. The passage is a play-by-play close-up of his aims, desires, and physical movements. The novel ends with impact, especially with those last few words giving such fine emphasis to the central idea.

Eric Miles Williamson's *Two-Up* also ends with impact:

In the distance he sees the Geary Street tunnel. It looks like a tiled white throat.

He slows to a jog. He slows to a walk. He breathes heavily. His throat burns and feels shredded. His nose runs. His ears are hot.

He stops at the edge of the tunnel.

"Two-up," Broadstreet says.

He counts paces.

Cars stream past. Their engines boom against the tiled white walls.

Broadstreet stops. He lifts the pickaxe from his shoulder and holds the head in his right hand, the base of the handle in his left. He stares at the tiled white wall.

Broadstreet hoists the pickaxe.

Broadstreet swings.

Two tiles shatter and fall to the pavement.

Broadstreet hoists the pickaxe.

He swings.

A chip of concrete falls to the pavement.

He hoists.

He swings.

"Yes," Broadstreet says.

Hoist.

Swing.

The hole widens. The hole deepens.

Broadstreet hoists.

Swing.

The concrete breaks in chunks.

The hole widens and deepens.

Broadstreet hoists the pickaxe and swings.

"Two-up," Broadstreet says.

Hoist.

Swing.

The pickaxe breaks through the concrete.

A puff of dust.

"Bones," Broadstreet says.

For Broadstreet, gunite work has meant horrific death and maimed bodies of laborers. The term "two-up" (a signal to blast away with the gunite hose) is Broadstreet's signal to remedy the exploited labor of oppressed workers by destroying the product of this exacted labor. This vivid scene in which Broadstreet settles the score in his own way ends this novel with great force, and it feels just right.

A scenic ending can provide dramatic impact. It needs to give the reader a sense of closure without being anticlimactic.

This doesn't mean it should answer all the questions the reader might have.

The Closure Question

Short story endings are often quite elliptical or opaque, or enigmatic—causing the reader to puzzle it out. What does this ending really mean in terms of what's happened so far in this story? Groff's "Eyewall," as I pointed out earlier, requires interpretation and is a good example of a suggestive ending. Novels tend to be less suggestive than short stories, though one certainly can't overgeneralize about this.

Endings should give a sense of closure and create impact, as we've seen in the above examples, but the question still remains: How do you close *without* closing—that is, without shutting off all further reader involvement? And without tying everything up in a neat little bundle? What are some techniques you might employ to create an "open" ending?

Suggestive or "Open" Endings

One clever technique Richard Ford employs in "Rock Springs" is explicit questions:

> And I wondered, because it seemed funny, what would you think a man was doing if you saw him in the middle of the night looking in the windows of cars in the parking lot of the Ramada Inn? Would you think he was trying to get his head cleared? Would you think he was trying to get ready for a day when trouble would come down on him? Would you think his girlfriend was leaving him? Would you think he had a daughter? Would you think he was anybody like you?

Like many fine endings, this one has a real snap to it. This is the expository mode, but it's all in the form of questions: "Would you..." The reader is left to puzzle out answers on his own, especially the answer to the last question.

A second method is symbolism. Here's the ending of Cormac McCarthy's *The Road*:

> Once there were brook trout in the streams in the mountains. You could see them standing in the amber current where the white edges of their fins wimpled softly in the flow. They smelled of moss in your hand. Polished and muscular and torsional. On their backs were vermiculate patterns that were maps of the world in its becoming. Maps and mazes. Of a thing which could not be put back. Not be made right again. In the deep glens where they lived all things were older than man and they hummed of mystery.

The brook trout become symbolic for what's now missing—and can't be replaced—in this postapocalyptic world. With their smell of moss and their shape and muscle and their ancient biological history, preceding man, they represent an essential life force. The demise of the brook trout suggests the demise of many biological forms that will likely occur once a major catastrophe takes place. Symbolism gives the reader something tangible to focus on and yet that tangible something has numerous possible meanings beyond the obvious one.

A third method is metaphor. Notice how Fitzgerald closes *The Great Gatsby* with direct as well as indirect statement:

> Gatsby believed in the green light, the orgastic future that year by year recedes before us. It eluded us then, but that's no matter—to-morrow we will run faster, stretch out our arms farther. ... And one fine morning—
> So we beat on, boats against the current, borne back ceaselessly into the past.

This is direct statement up to a point, stating what Gatsby believed, according to Nick Carraway, but then the boat metaphor: We have to decide what this ending really means. What about "ceaselessly into the past"? Be careful with direct statement. A direct statement can destroy the vitality that comes from compelling characters, events, and a plot that has moved us to its conclusion. Indirect statement, as with this metaphor, gives the reader something to work on after he puts the story or book down.

Hemingway employs a fourth method in the closing scene of *A Farewell to Arms*. It operates on understatement. Frederic Henry shows up at Catherine Barkley's hospital room:

> "You can't come in now," one of the nurses said.
>
> "Yes I can," I said.
>
> "You can't come in yet."
>
> "You get out," I said. "The other one too."
>
> But after I had got them out and shut the door and turned off the light it wasn't any good. It was like saying good-by to a statue. After a while I went out and left the hospital and walked back to the hotel in the rain.

Understated here is the emotion, but then this fits with the Hemingway code of hero's stoicism: One doesn't show emotion in the face of tragedy. Even if you don't share Hemingway's code, you can certainly tone down a closing scene so that the emotion must come from the reader, not the author—and not even from the character, at least not openly. You create a gap between the dramatized world of the character and the emotion elicited from this felt experience, which the reader himself can fill in.

Ironic Endings

An ironic ending is certainly suggestive. Irony requires that we "see double": the disparity between expectation and result. Irony also has an edge to it. Twain, the great satirist, ends "The War Prayer" with this statement from the "aged stranger" regarding what it means to pray for war:

> "Ye have prayed it; if ye still desire it, speak! The messenger of the Most High waits."
>
> It was believed afterward that the man was a lunatic, because there was no sense in what he said.

There *wasn't?* What the aged stranger has said to the church congregation is that each war prayer delivered to God has two meanings: the spoken meaning (asking God for victory) and the unspoken meaning (asking for unmerciful mayhem and suffering for the defeated). The aged stranger attempts to disabuse the congregation of the belief that they are praying only the spoken one. It's quite ironic, suggests Twain, that they are so easily able to ditch what the aged stranger has told them, writing him off as a "lunatic."

Irony can be lighthearted or savage. It reflects a certain skepticism about what others might accept without careful judgment. If you end on an ironic note, don't explain it for your reader; lay it down and leave it there.

A Final Word on Endings

An ending should open us up, in some way, to a world greater than the sum of the parts of the story. A good story gets us beyond a simple bromide. It provides both depth and range: Perhaps we saw only one planetary system before beginning this story; now we see a host of them.

As you revise your story or novel's ending, look for ways to make this ending more suggestive. If you can inspire your reader to think further about your story, to return to it, to wonder what it all means, that's an accomplishment! I don't mean to write it in a half-baked way. I mean to write it in a complete and coherent way but without everything nailed down. Leave room for interpretation, for thinking about ideas, for making connections between one thing and another.

PROCESS SHEET #12

1. Look at the opening to your story. If it's expository, does it provide one of the following: character background, key character qualities, or the character's present predicament? Or does it provide some other information? Should this information be brought out elsewhere instead of here? If so, where would you put it? If not, is the writing lively enough to grab your reader? Is it overlong? Should it be trimmed? Can you think of ways to more effectively pull your reader in?

2. Do you use a descriptive opening? Is it character or place? Would it be better to bring this material out later, or does it seem important to bring it out here? If it's a place, how will it function in the story? Does the story center on this place? Does it have symbolic importance? How does the opening pull the reader in? What dominant impression are you trying to create? Would it help to add more concrete details? Should some details be deleted?

3. Do you begin with summary? Could you bring this material out in another place in the story? If the summary seems fitting here, is it compelling enough to pull your reader in? Is the character interesting? Does the summary create suspense? Is it concrete? Can you see places where you might add and/or trim to make it work better?

4. Do you begin with scene? Is it narrative only, or does it include dialogue? Does this scene work well here, or would it be better to place it elsewhere in the story? Is it lively enough to draw the reader in? Does it present a conflict, suspense? If there is dialogue, how subtle is it? Do any provocative ideas come up? Does the personality of the character come through the dialogue? Is the pacing of this scene right for this story? Does it set the right tone? Can you think of anything to add to this scenic opening or any way to reshape it?

5. Is your ending expository? Is it lively enough? Provocative enough? Can you think of ways to make it more lively and retain the overall tone of your story?

6. Is your ending descriptive? Is it concrete enough? Can you see ways to make the imagery more compelling?

7. Is your ending scenic? Is the dialogue energetic? Does it provoke thought? Can you see a way to make the scene stronger?

8. Does your ending provide a sense of finality? Is it a suggestive ending? Or does it sum up the story so that the reader is left with nothing to interpret? Can you see ways to make it more indirect and suggestive? Do you use any of the techniques I suggested to create an open ending or one that is ironic?

EXERCISE 1

In approximately 200 words, write one of the four kinds of story openings: expository, descriptive, narrative, or scenic with dialogue. Try to draw your reader in, using this mode as well as you can, keeping in mind the various techniques to consider and attend to. Go over what you've written. Choose a different kind of story opening and compare this version to your first one. Which do you prefer? Which has more impact?

EXERCISE 2

Choose one of the three modes for closing a story: exposition, description, or scene. Write 100 to 200 words and make it direct, lively, and provocative. Choose a different mode for closing your story and compare this version to your first. Which do you prefer? Which has more impact?

EXERCISE 3

Redo Exercise 2, first version or second, but this time write it in a much more suggestive way, leaving more room for interpretation. Compare the two endings. Which do you prefer?

CHAPTER THIRTEEN

IMPROVING STYLE, MOOD, AND TONE

Style is the manner of expression in a literary work, and it is integral to the story's inner workings—it permeates the story or novel through and throughout. It is not something to be added like frosting on the cake. Sometimes style is hardly noticeable; it's a clear glass though which we see a world. Sometimes the glass itself is interesting. In both cases style is as important as any other fictional element.

Your story or novel probably calls for different moods, or emotional states, to match different occasions. It also calls for a particular tone. Tone is affected by everything that occurs in a story, but it is also shaped by the narrative "voice," which is largely a result of the style. Tone can change from story part to story part, but even so, there should be an overall tone that these different parts contribute to.

STYLE

As you revise your story or novel, consider whether the style seems appropriate. Many of the changes you make will probably come from experimentation, based on your intuitive sense of what sounds right—in other words, your ear for it. Even so, if you understand how style works in fiction, you can work more consciously to revise areas that might need attending to in your draft. Let's begin with prose style. We can speak of prose style as having several distinct features.

Prose Style Features

As you study each prose style feature, remember that this aspect of style needs to work in harmony with the world you're creating. It must help create the appropriate tone for your story or novel.

Spare Versus Fully Textured

One of the most noticeable prose style features is the amount of detail the author furnishes. In fact, stylists are sometimes classified according to how spare or how dense their style is. A classic contrast is Ernest Hemingway and William Faulkner, contemporaries and both Nobel Prize winners. Here is the opening to Hemingway's *The Sun Also Rises*, written from Jake Barnes's point of view:

> Robert Cohn was once middleweight boxing champion of Princeton. Do not think that I am very much impressed by that as a boxing title, but it meant a lot to Cohn. He cared nothing for boxing, in fact he disliked it, but he learned it painfully and thoroughly to counteract the feeling of inferiority and shyness he had felt on being treated as a Jew at Princeton.

The writing is typical Hemingway, direct and spare, with a few well-chosen details. Now contrast this with Faulkner's opening to *Absalom, Absalom!*:

> From a little after two o'clock until almost sundown of the long still hot weary dead September after-

noon they sat in what Miss Coldfield still called the office because her father had called it that—a dim hot airless room with the blinds all closed and fastened for forty-three summers because when she was a girl someone had believed that light and moving air carried heat and that dark was always cooler, and which (as the sun shone fuller and fuller on that side of the house) became latticed with yellow slashes full of dust motes which Quentin thought of as being flecks of the dead old dried paint itself blown inward from the scaling blinds as wind might have blown them.

Clearly, there is a significant difference between the styles of these two passages: sparse versus full-blown. Is one style better than the other? No, but each style meets the author's purpose. According to Hemingway's iceberg analogy, in which much less is visible to the eye than what is actually there, in fiction writing less is more. Much is unstated in Hemingway's work—much left to the reader to fill in on his own. Faulkner's prose style, on the other hand, works oppositely: Almost every nuance of perception, thought, and feeling is captured in Faulkner's intricately textured style. Through this dense, heavy prose style Faulkner creates a haunting sense of the Southern past.

In general, with dense prose—depending on the author, of course—character, action, and setting can be fully explored in language. Character might include details of physical appearance, traits, personality, thoughts, and feelings. Action might include detailed descriptions of dramatically experienced—or remembered and distilled, even imagined—events. Setting might include past, present, and imagined places. The dense style is full-bodied, orchestral.

With the spare or lean style, on the other hand, we lack such linguistically constructed fullness. What fullness of harmony there is—to extend the metaphor—must be supplied by the reader to "hear" this on his own, based on carefully selected "notes," or details. The works of Raymond Carver and Cormac McCarthy exemplify the spare style at its extreme—a stripped-down or minimalist style that in spite of the scarceness of detail nonetheless calls up a whole visual world for readers to enter.

Many or even most authors today write somewhere in the middle, their prose more detailed than the stripped-down style but not as detailed as the dense or fully textured one.

Which style is fitting for your short story or novel? How much detail should you include? How long should the sentences be, how complex? To answer such questions, you have to consider this question: Which style goes best with your character, your setting, and your themes or ideas? Which style creates the right tone? There isn't a magic formula for this. You have to get a sense for style as it relates to all the story elements. Does it sound right? A heavily textured style tends to add an air of sophistication that might not be fitting to your story. A stripped-down one might seem at odds with your particular character. Maybe a style in between these two will work better for your story.

But keep in mind that prose can change throughout a story or novel as the need arises. Note the opening to Karl Taro Greenfeld's "Mickey Mouse," from *The PEN/O. Henry Prize Stories 2012*:

> After our triumphant winter, the pink-white cherry blossoms already budding on mossy branches, the first cicadas buzzing in the late afternoons, our Empire's prospects boundless, our fleets triumphant, our soldiers valiant, our Divine Emperor infallible, I received in my third-floor office on our deserted campus a visitor, my former classmate Kunugi.

This is rather detailed. But notice how the style moves to the spare near the end of the story:

> She said my name.
>
> I nodded.
>
> She said she was Kunugi's widow and that she was pleased that I was showing my work.
>
> My husband often spoke about you as classmates.
>
> I bowed slightly.

Style meets the needs of the story as a whole as well as particular story parts. In the beginning, the narrator is summing up the various triumphs of Japan at this point in the war. The more detailed, more formal style works well. But he chooses a more clipped, informal style to narrate his encounter with his former friend's wife after some bad baggage of war. Style goes hand in hand with purpose. What kind of tone do you want to create?

Formal Versus Informal

As with the amount of detail, most writers today choose a neutral path in terms of both diction and syntax. But the formal style is sometimes used. Part One of Ian McEwan's *Atonement* is quite formal, reflecting the aristocratic bearing of the characters. Consider the opening to the novel:

> The play—for which Briony had designed the posters, programs and tickets, constructed the sales booth out of a folding screen tipped on its side, and lined the collection box in red crepe paper—was written by her in a two-day tempest of composition, causing her to miss a breakfast and a lunch. When the preparations were complete, she had nothing to do but contemplate her finished draft and wait for the appearance of her cousins from the distant north.

This has an air of sophistication about it due largely to the syntax as well as the diction. Note the "for which" and the detailed passage set off in dashes. Note words like "tempest," "composition," "preparations," "contemplate," and "appearance." This isn't conversational English. In Part Two, where the setting switches to World War II, the opening passage is also somewhat formal in syntax and diction:

> There were horrors enough, but it was the unexpected detail that threw him and afterward would not let him go. When they reached the level crossing, after a three-mile walk along a narrow road, he saw the path he was looking for meandering off to the right, then dipping and rising toward a copse that covered a low hill to the northwest.

Not exactly the vernacular: "There were horrors enough"; "dipping and rising toward a copse." But notice how, a few pages into Part Two, the language becomes much more informal, not only in diction but also in sentence construction:

> He didn't owe them explanations. He intended to survive, he had one good reason to survive, and he didn't care whether they tagged along or not.

Stripped-down and utterly conversational, this is the language of the soldier, of the man facing the threat of death. The sophistication of aristocratic life doesn't fit here. McEwan can write in the dense formal style or the stripped-down informal one. He chooses style according to the purpose he wants to achieve. Here, setting helps determine the question of formality.

Note the informal style in Amy Hempel's "Tonight Is a Favor to Holly":

> A blind date is coming to pick me up, and unless my hair grows an inch by seven o'clock, I am not going to

> answer the door. The problem is the front. I cut the
> bangs myself; now I look like Mamie Eisenhower.

No complicated syntax. No formal word choices. It's spare, stark. In the hands of minimalists, the spare style tends to go with the informal.

Be sensitive to this issue of formality. If the diction is relatively formal, is this fitting to your character? Are your characters relatively formal? Would it be out of "voice" to use such formal language? But perhaps you want a third-person, relatively formal narrative voice to serve an intermediary role between reader and character. This is what we have in *Winter's Bone*:

> Ree's grand hope was that these boys would not be
> dead to wonder by age twelve, dulled to life, empty of
> kindness, boiling with mean. So many Dolly kids were
> that way, ruined before they had chin hair, groomed to
> live outside square law and abide by the remorseless
> blood-soaked commandments that governed lives led
> outside square law.

This voice is almost exclusively authorial, somewhat formal in places ("dulled to life"; "blood-soaked commandments") with but one phrase—"boiling with mean"—serving as an embedded voice suggesting the language of the locals.

Here's the spoken language of the locals—Ree Dolly, in this case—which is quite different from the author's:

> "Get," she said. "Get your book satchels'n get. Get
> down the road'n catch that bus. And put your stocking
> hats on."

Woodrell's omniscient narrative voice gives him more control over the material. He's not limited to the language of the locals, but neither does he crowd out their voices. Such a balancing act is not easily managed.

Concreteness: Direct Versus Indirect Methods

In Chapter Five I took up the direct versus indirect method of characterization. We're back to these two methods, but now my emphasis is on style itself—on how these two methods relate to the issue of concreteness of style.

DIRECT METHOD: Perhaps your style tends to be rich with detail. You make your reader "see" by use of specific and concrete detail and figurative devices such as metaphor, analogy, and simile. Notice E. Annie Proulx's opening passage to "On the Antler":

> Hawkheel's face was as finely wrinkled as grass-dried linen, his thin back bent like a branch weighted with snow. He still spent most of his time in the field and on the streams, sweeter days than when he was that half-wild boy who ran panting up the muddy logging road, smashing branches to mute the receding roar of the school bus. Then he had hated books, had despised everything except the woods.

This writing is specific, concrete, and laden with figurative language. The opening line gives us similes, fresh ones—these aren't overworked comparisons or clichés. The language makes us see pictures: the muddy roads, the branches, the school bus.

Here's another example of a passage replete with specific and concrete detail, drawn from T.C. Boyle's story "Big Game":

> Bernard Puff pushed himself up from the big mahogany table and flung the dregs of his coffee down the drain. He wasn't exactly overwrought, but he was edgy, his stomach sour and clenched round the impermeable lump of his breakfast cruller, his hands afflicted with the little starts and tremors of the coffee shakes. He lit a cigarette to calm himself and gazed out the kitchen window on the dromedary pen, where

one of the moth-eaten Arabians was methodically peeling the bark from an elm tree.

Look what we have here: a coffee drinker, a smoker, a man with a sour stomach and bad nerves. And note such rich imagery as "little starts and tremors of the coffee shakes." We see the camel "methodically" eating the bark off the elm tree.

In these two excerpts, the specific and concrete details are furnished for us, and how can we help but visualize the characters? But what if the author doesn't use the direct method? What if the language of the story is not concrete—specific, yes, but it doesn't include concrete imagery such as we see above? Is this style lacking in some way?

INDIRECT METHOD: Authors who have mastered dramatic methods can still make us "see" and "hear" even if the prose style itself is not, on the whole, all that concrete. But you have to be a master of the language to pull this off.

An excellent example is Alicia Erian's novel *Towelhead*, a New York Times Notable Book, which gives sparse, specific details about characters and place, nothing particularly concrete about visual appearance, and yet, because of Erian's incredible ability to dramatize, we come to know quite well the various characters that people this book.

As an example, when Jasira, the young teenage protagonist, meets her father at the airport, she notes:

> Daddy met me at the airport in Houston. He was tall and clean-shaven and combed his wavy, thinning hair to one side. Ever since my mother had ground up his glasses, he'd started wearing contacts. He shook my hand, which he'd never done before. I said, "Aren't you going to hug me?" and he said, "This is how we do it my country." Then he started walking really fast through the airport, so I could barely keep up.

We have a few sketchy specifics: tall, clean-shaven, thinning hair, and how he combs it. But the rest is managed by dialogue and action: a few words, and then his hurrying off on his own, leaving his daughter to catch up. Sparse as the description is, we can picture this father quite well.

Here's another example—a scene where a neighbor and his son stop by Jasira's father's house so that the son can apologize for calling Jasira a "towelhead." Notice how the characters come fully alive before us:

> While we were planting, Mr. Vuoso and Zack came over. We were kneeling on the ground with our backs to their house, so we didn't see them until they were right in front of us. "Good morning," Mr. Vuoso said.
>
> Daddy looked up. He was wearing dirty green garden gloves and holding a trowel. "Yes?" he said.
>
> Mr. Vuoso cleared his throat. "Zack and I were wondering if we could talk to you and Jasira."
>
> Daddy looked over at me, then back at Mr. Vuoso. "Aren't you talking to us now?" he said, and he laughed a little.
>
> I could see Mr. Vuoso was getting irritated. "There's no need for that," he said. "We're just here as friends. That's all."
>
> "What friends?" Daddy asked then, looking around. "Where are the friends?"

Notice how when the neighbor and his son arrive, Jasira's father looks up and remarks, "Yes?" He doesn't rise. His tone of voice sounds abrupt and challenging. Mr. Vuoso appears nervous. Then because Jasira's father laughs—mockingly—Mr. Vuoso grows irritated, the protagonist tells us. When Mr. Vuoso tries to smooth things over, saying they're here as friends, Jasira's father pointedly demands to know where such friends are—he doesn't see any. His voice is again mocking and brusque.

We get to know the characters in this novel mostly by their gestures and voice intonation. But this is enough. We can vividly picture them in our minds via these two senses. But why not depend a little more on the direct method? In this novel it makes perfect sense. Jasira notes specifics, but as an adolescent she isn't one to flesh out concrete details of physical appearance. It's fully in character for Jasira to note a few specific details about a character and move on.

Milan Kundera, whose most famous novel is *The Incredible Lightness of Being*, is an inveterate user of this indirect or dramatic method. On the whole, his style is more abstract than concrete. Consider this example from *Ignorance*, where Kundera's two main characters, Irena and Josef, meet:

> One day at the Paris airport, she moved through the police checkpoint and sat down to wait for the Prague flight. On the facing bench she saw a man and, after a few moments of uncertainty and surprise, she recognized him. In excitement she waited till their glances met, and then she smiled. He smiled back and nodded slightly. She rose and crossed to him as he rose in turn.
>
> "Didn't we know each other in Prague?" she said in Czech. "Do you still remember me?"
>
> "Of course."

All general—actions noted only. Few specifics, no concrete details, no use of figurative language. And yet once we get caught up in Kundera's novel, or I should say novels, and read on, we feel we know his characters in the flesh—though at some remove. Perhaps since his work is largely philosophical, this relatively abstract style helps his readers focus a little less on the particular and more on the general.

It's something of a risk to depend on this more indirect method. Your scenes must be rich and full or your reader won't "see" or "hear" anything. Read plenty of examples from professional authors. Notice how minimalists like Hempel, Carver, and McCarthy make us picture characters based on what they say and do. This means studying scenes closely for characterization. In prose sections you need to get *inside* characters. Read your own work over—do your characters come alive? When you get feedback, be sure to ask writer friends if they can picture your characters. If they can't, you know you have a problem.

Pacing or Tempo

A story's pacing or tempo can vary widely. Certain tempos fit certain moods:

FAST: When there is heightened emotion in a story, the author can capture this by quickening the pace or tempo. Here's a rich excerpt from Robert Garner McBrearty's "The Comeback," from his collection *Episode*, which won the prestigious Sherwood Anderson Foundation Fiction Award:

> The call came unexpectedly. I recognized the voice. Phlegmy. Breathy. Too many years of chewing tobacco. Too many years of spitting hard. Coach's question was simple: "Can you still hit the fast one?"

McBrearty's narrator decides he'll try:

> The kids promised they wouldn't do anything outlandish. I jogged through our suburban neighborhood. I sweated. I started to wheeze. When I got home, the belly was still there. It glistened with sweat.

Notice the fast pace, how the writing captures the protagonist's excitement in bursts of short sentences and one-word fragments. In these bizarre, comic passages, we get a strong sense for the narrator's ambition and demonstrated drive, in spite of the odds against him. We sense his worry—will he make it? In a different story, with a more meditative, quiet narrator, the comeback events might be handled quite differently—the pacing perhaps slow, leisurely, in a matter-of-fact voice. But the comic tone is established early in this story, and the fast, furious pace fits this character perfectly.

Unless you have a fast-paced story like McBrearty's, which isn't a very long story, you don't want the pace to be continuously fast. Even in a highly suspenseful novel, you need to let up a little now and then, let the pace slow, and give your reader a chance to catch his breath.

MEASURED, STEADY: A measured, steady pace can reflect calm, resolve, acceptance—or even a studied sense of imminent doom, as in the opening to Mark Wisniewski's *Show Up, Look Good*:

> I know of a secret murder, and I've loved a speechless man, and sometimes I'd like to tell someone about how death and love have changed my life, but any of three thoughts give me pause. For one, if I talk about the murder, I myself could be killed. I can't know how true this is, but the speechless man said it was, and even though he's disappointed me, I trust him. Two, if someone's murdered, she's murdered, and talking about her will never change that. Then there's the reality very few people care to face: unless you have majestic beauty or power, your secrets rarely matter to anyone but yourself.

Notice the steady, rhythmic beat of the sentences as the narrator thinks about this murder, assessing her situation. Her studied analysis belies the sense of urgency she feels. It's a way of trying to place it under the microscope to examine it objectively, to break it down into its component parts—to get a firm grip on it.

Here's a steadied, measured pace in a passage from James Dickey's *Deliverance*, where the narrator recalls his panic when threatened by one of the deranged hill people who shoved a shotgun in his chest:

> My heart quailed away from the blast tamped into both barrels, and I wondered what the barrel openings would look like at the exact instant they went off: if fire would come out of them, or if they would just be a gray blur or if they would change at all between the time you lived and died, blown in half.

One might think that this kind of tension would be represented by a string of short sentences, reflecting an adrenaline rush. Instead, we have a long, intricately woven sentence, measured steadily out, beat by beat. But we must read the pacing of this passage with the point of view of the novel in mind: The narrator is looking back on this event, years hence, and so he has had time to distill it in his memory and reflect on it. Yet notice how he feels threatened. It's reflected in language with emotional impact ("at the exact instant they went off"); the series of "if" clauses which drive home the sense of alarm; and finally, the flourish— "blown in half"—which delivers quite a punch. These rhetorical devices, though measured out in this fairly lengthy sentence, create thrusts like pistons firing—a tempo appropriate to fear.

JARRING: Sometimes the prose style seems quite jarring, and if considered alone, out of context, this might seem like bad writing. But that's not so *if* it's taken in context. A jarring syntax can create a character's sense of disorientation, frazzled nerves, or anxiety. Consider this passage from DeWitt Henry's *The Marriage of Anna Maye Potts*:

> At the back door, he opened the screen, which squawked on its spring, and stopped, and peered in-

side, shading the window with his hand. Then pulled out keys, right one, slid it slowly in the lock and turned, and slowly swung the door; inside, then, pocketed his keys, and just as slowly, silently, closed the door, locked it, listening. Wiped his feet. Kitchen was empty, surfaces dully gleaming in half-light. His footsteps squeaked on the linoleum; the floor creaked. He felt a gathering, crawly apprehension, steeled himself, as he moved into the hall...

The jarring rhythm we see here helps to establish the character's anxiety over his all-nighter and now, back home, having to face his sick wife. Henry doesn't need to say his character is anxious. He demonstrates it in the jarring tempo of the passage itself.

The staccato rhythm in this passage from Stewart O'Nan's *Songs for the Missing* establishes the sense of urgency the family feels when their daughter suddenly goes missing:

> The first person her mother called was Nina.
> The second was J.P.
> The third was Connie at the hospital.
> The fourth was the police.

These short, abrupt sentences awaken us to the seriousness of the event. They are jarring in a different sense than the passage from Henry's novel, where the effect is created more by the sometimes-broken syntax. Here the one-liners pound away—one, two, three, four—like a fist beating a tabletop. You won't be likely to employ a staccato rhythm like this very often, but store this technique away for when you want to create strong emphasis. Perhaps you'll see an occasion for use in your present manuscript.

LYRICAL: The opposite of jarring is lyrical, smooth flowing, rhapsodic. Note how Stewart O'Nan's *Songs for the Missing* begins:

> July, 2005. It was the summer of her Chevette, of
> J.P. and letting her hair grow. The last summer, the
> best summer, the summer they'd dreamed of since
> eighth grade, the high and pride of being seniors
> lingering, an extension of their best year. She and
> Nina and Elise, the Three Amigos. In the fall they
> were gone, off to college, where she hoped, by a
> long and steady effort, she might become someone
> else, a private, independent person, someone not
> from Kingsville at all.

Note the smooth, rhythmic swing of the sentences, the way repetition of "summer" expresses the character's excitement. In lesser hands, this might end up as purple prose. We soon discover that it sets up a rug pulling: The girl who has such rhapsodic feelings goes missing.

SLOW, SLUGGISH: If the prose style slows down, even becomes sluggish, we may sense that the character is feeling inertia or ennui, is depressed, or is incapable of action. Long, labored sentences—I don't mean bad ones—slow the pace. Note this passage about Mary Kingsley from Richard Bausch's *Hello to the Cannibals*:

> 100 Addison Road, in the cold and damp of a day in
> January. Winds sweep down coal ash and the dust of
> chimneys, swirling. The sky is the color of iron, and the
> swollen folds of a dark cloud at its edge move with a
> sluggish, chilly sullenness, letting so little of the sun's
> light through that one can't tell if it is almost day or
> almost night.

The depressing winter scene comes through here. The long sentence with phrases parceled out, the word *sluggish* itself, and the way the phrase "sluggish, chilly sullenness" impedes the easy flow of speech all help create a sense of lethargy. Sound matches sense.

Grammatical Features

We have looked at several noticeable features of style and prose style types. You will need to get the right feel for your story or novel to see what works the best. This means not only reading your own work carefully but reading good professional models as well. It means being sensitive to language for its many possibilities. Does your style fit your purpose? Would a different style work better?

Besides the various stylistic features I've covered, there are certain grammatical features that also contribute to style. These grammatical features don't belong to a particular style; they are simply useful in various ways.

Ellipsis

Ellipsis creates a pause. Note how it's used in a passage from Robert Garner McBrearty's "The Helmeted Man":

> Alex wrote down: "Left house at six-thirty in the morning ... Beth and Dan still sleeping ... jogged down street ... cool fall morning ... It seemed like any other Saturday, I always went jogging early Saturday morning ... Ran about two miles ... nobody out..."

This creates a disjointed syntax that is quite appropriate to what's going on here. The character is freewriting in a writing class. Through ellipsis, McBrearty makes us experience the fragmentary thoughts yielded by his free-association process.

Ellipsis is sometimes used to suggest hesitation, as we see in DeWitt Henry's *The Marriage of Anna Maye Potts*:

> "Look ... I..." He cleared his throat.

Or, quite differently, it might suggest an intent to coax:

> "Hey ... hey ... come on, now. Enough." She pushed herself free and glanced around.

Note how the pauses convey the sense of coaxing and soften the blow, just slightly, of the action that follows. Henry shows this instead of saying it.

Italics and Capitalized Words

It's nothing new to say that italics and capitalized words are used for emphasis, but how they're used is another matter. In Mark Wisniewski's "3 X 5 Steve," note how emphasis is created:

> She had a familiar look on her face: *Men owe me love regardless of my weight.*

The use of italics registers what is apparent in this character's facial expression. Putting this in italics is close to the character herself speaking it, but she doesn't. The observer speaks for her. It functions as the observer's internal monologue.

In this same story Wisniewski uses capitalization—and italics as well—in one line of dialogue:

> Something about him was frightening. "I'M A WHOLE FLOOR BELOW SLEEPING," he yelled. "AND I WAKE UP AT THREE-THIRTY IN THE MORNING TO THE SOUND OF ALL YOUS *LAUGHING*?"

The all caps makes the yelling seem all the louder, with the final italicized word a double whammy. You can't do this all the time—and Wisniewski doesn't. But certainly both capitalization and italics are tools that create emphasis which will naturally affect the tone. Remove these two grammatical features and reread the passage. Different?

Alliteration

Alliteration (the consonant type) is an effective tool in creating certain beats in a sentence as the reader lands from one consonant to another. Consider this opening passage to Geoffrey Clark's *Two, Two, Lily-White Boys*:

I stood watching as my mother, Gracious Carstairs, backed our pearl gray '47 Chevy two-door cautiously out of Camp Greavey's parking area, paused, then slowly drove out the wide gravel road by which she'd brought me here. Sunlight flashed on the windshield, then on her silver-blue hair.

Notice the repetition of *c* sounds (*Carstairs, Camp, cautiously*); the repetition of *p* sounds (*parking, paused*), the repetition of *s* sounds (*slowly, sunlight, silver*). Alliteration creates a distinct beat from one consonant to another. The language gains force that way.

Repetitive Words and Structure

Repetition in words can work as a structuring device, creating echoes. Note this dialogue from T.C. Boyle's *The Inner Circle*:

"Do you know any roadhouses? Have you ever been to one?"

"Sure," I lied. "Sure, dozens of times."

"And then what?" she asked, fixing me with a teasing look.

"We eat, drink and make merry."

"And then?"

"And then?" I said, leaning into her, the wind tearing at my collar, a flurry of students hurrying by with pale numb faces, "then afterwards we can drive off into some quiet, dark lane and, well, and have some real privacy."

Notice the words and phrases repeated: "sure," "and then," "and." This kind of repetition creates an interesting cadence. It keeps us reading. Like alliteration, it creates a beat as we land on familiar sounds—in this case words, not letters.

Some Stylistic Techniques

Also related to style are certain rhetorical techniques that authors sometimes employ. Two that work quite well for irony and humor are juxtaposition and listing. Both are the satirist's stock in trade.

Juxtaposition

Juxtaposition is the placing of two things together, usually of an opposite nature, creating irony. Here's an example from Don DeLillo's *White Noise*:

> Heinrich's hairline is beginning to recede. I wonder about this. Did his mother consume some kind of gene-piercing substance when she was pregnant? Am I at fault somehow? Have I raised him, unwittingly, in the vicinity of a chemical dump site, in the path of air currents that carry industrial wastes capable of producing scalp degeneration, glorious sunsets? (People say the sunsets around here were not nearly so stunning thirty or forty years ago.)

Note the juxtaposition of "scalp degeneration" and "glorious sunsets." The author doesn't provide logical transition such as *but* between these two phrases because this would ruin it. By juxtaposing these two, he creates humor and irony. The reason for beautiful sunsets may well be toxic waste, anything but beautiful.

Listing

One effective stylistic technique is creating a list, sometimes quite long, to give the reader a sense of how varied or profuse something is. I will draw upon DeLillo's *White Noise* here, too. Note how the author writes about the appearance of the students at the beginning of a semester:

> The roofs of the station wagons were loaded down
> with the carefully secured suitcases full of light and
> heavy clothing; with boxes of blankets, boots and
> shoes, stationery and books, sheets, pillows, quilts;
> with rolled-up rugs and sleeping bags; with bicycles,
> skis, rucksacks, English and Western saddles, inflated
> rafts. As cars slowed to a crawl and stopped, students
> sprang out and raced to the rear doors to begin re-
> moving the objects inside; the stereo sets, radios, per-
> sonal computers; small refrigerators and table ranges;
> the cartons of phonograph records and cassettes; the
> hairdryers and styling irons; the tennis rackets, soccer
> balls, hockey and lacrosse sticks, bows and arrows;
> the controlled substances, the birth control pills and
> devices; the junk food still in shopping bags—onion-
> and-garlic chips, nacho thins, peanut creme patties,
> Waffelos and Kabooms, fruit chews and toffee pop-
> corn; the Dum-Dum pops, the Mystic mints.

The protagonist regards all of this as a "spectacle," and what better way to show such a spectacle than a plethora of things—of
innumerable kinds? A list this long gives an overwhelming sense
of a particular reality and creates a comic effect.

Style and Dialogue

Dialogue comes in two forms: direct and indirect. A writer's style
can be apparent in either of these. With direct dialogue, writers
sometimes depart from the standard punctuation. With indirect
dialogue, the writer's prose style can vary significantly as with
any prose passage.

Direct Dialogue

Standard dialogue is handled by double quotation marks, with
reported conversation in single quotes. But alternative methods
can achieve interesting results.

DASH INSTEAD OF QUOTATION MARKS: We see this in Rick Moody's *The Ice Storm*:

> —Where have you been? she called across the gloomy landscaped expanses of Silver Meadow.
> —Something with my mom, Mike said, hauling his bike alongside him.

We also see it in Chris Cleave's *Incendiary*:

> —Football fan are you? said Jasper Black.
> —What do you think?
> —I think you're beautiful, said Jasper Black. So do my friends. They bet me 20 quid I couldn't get your name. So tell me your name and I'll split the cash with you and never bother you again.

This dash creates a more distanced effect, perhaps because it's different from what we're used to (the double quotes). If you want to create a kind of haze over your fictional world, this might be a good choice.

ABSENCE OF QUOTATION MARKS: An even more distanced effect is created by the absence of quotation marks, which is often the case in Cormac McCarthy's novels. Note its use in Banks's *Rule of the Bone*:

> Listen, Mom, just give me the money. I need the money.
> What are you saying?
> Give me the money.
> What?
> The money.

Note too how Banks mixes exposition with dialogue, with no punctuation marks:

> Thanks, I said, and I gave her a kiss on the cheek. I'll be back later, after I get my stuff from Russ's.

It's important to emphasize here that style isn't bound by the rules of grammar handbooks. It's what works that counts. It's what works best with character, voice, and overall tone. Experiment with punctuation in dialogue in order to find the right sound or tone for your characters.

Indirect Dialogue

Sometimes indirect dialogue works better than direct dialogue. The spoken word might be less effective than a narrative reporting of what's being said. Note this example from Alice McDermott's *At Weddings and Wakes*—it begins with indirect dialogue and moves to direct:

> At dinner the mailman's face was flushed again and he praised every morsel of the meal, remarking again and again how many years had passed since he'd had creamed onions such as these, sage dressing, mashed potatoes so light and giblet gravy as rich as this; since he'd had buttermilk biscuits—"Not since the last batch my own mother made, God rest her soul" . . .

Note how nicely the indirect method works here. In a way we can hear the mailman exclaiming the wonders of the meal, but the added advantage is that we have McDermott's rich prose style to relish. And the movement from indirect to direct is also a pleasure. The distance gained by the indirect method is then suddenly closed: We hear the mailman speaking himself.

Indirect dialogue may serve you well, at least in portions of your manuscript. If your prose style is strong, it will help carry the scene. But be careful: It does have to be strong prose. If not, your reader will feel like you are simply telling what happened in a scene and not allowing the reader to *experience* the scene.

Speeding Up Dialogue

Sometimes dialogue drags. If you see places in your manuscript where this is happening, try these techniques:

- Write shorter sentences—in a series of back-and-forth interchanges.
- Use fragments. People speak in fragments, don't they? Have characters give a one-word or phrase answer.
- Have characters interrupt and jump in.
- Intersperse very little character thought or action.
- Intersperse very little description of setting or character.

Dialect

This is certainly an issue for dialogue, but it's also a more general stylistic issue because a narrative voice can also be in a particular dialect. Convincing dialect isn't easy to write. If you do use dialect, you have to be careful to make sure you know what you're doing. Mark Wisniewski creates a believable Polish dialect in *Confessions of a Polish Used Car Salesman*. Note how this character speaks:

> "...and she's got the ten kids," Anna said. "You knew that, inna?"
>
> "The Indian lady has ten?" my grandmother said.
>
> "Why sure."
>
> "Ten I didn't know. I knew kids, but not ten."
>
> "She's got that son. You've heard about the son, inna?"
>
> "With the measles?"
>
> "*Oh* no. Thirty-seven years old, this one is. Malcolm, I think she named him. You haven't heard?"

You might try to fake this, but it wouldn't come off. Either you have to be in the culture, or you have to study the rhythms, the special features of the language to get it just right. And you had better hear it spoken.

In *The March*, E.L. Doctorow creates a believable character in Pearl, in part because of the authentic-sounding black slave dialect. Here's Pearl recognizing she is now free:

> I free, I free like no one else in de whole worl but me. Das how free.

MOOD

To create mood you need to find the appropriate diction, syntax, and pacing. Note the mood of suspense in this passage from Mark Wisniewski's *Show Up, Look Good*:

> Then I heard footsteps in the corridor outside my door, which stirred memories of the evening the woman had been dragged. Headed toward me, the footsteps stopped just outside my door, and I wanted to turn on the light to make sure my locks were secured, but whoever was out there knocked.
>
> I groped for my cell phone, hoping it was on the floor near the couch. But it wasn't. On the TV? I thought, and I crawled as quietly as I could over the bleached floorboards, then heard another knock. Someone, I thought, who knows the woman who was dragged. I found the light switch and turned on the light but couldn't see my cell phone anywhere.
>
> Then I heard scratching on the other side of the door—someone trying to pick a lock?

Clearly there is a suspenseful mood here, though this novel isn't the typical thriller. It has a distinct element of the comic running through it, which comes out even here as the narrator speculates who is outside the door. The sentences are rather fluid, reflecting the narrator's processing of details in the midst of what might be serious danger; certainly these sentences are more fluid than we might expect in a heightened moment of danger in a serious thriller. But despite the element of comedy, this is suspense. Notice the overall structure, the patterned pacing: each paragraph initiating a new action—threat or response—driving the scene forward.

What mood is apparent in this passage from Marilynne Robinson's *Gilead*?

> No sleep this night. My heart is greatly disquieted. It is a strange thing to feel illness and grief in the same organ. There is no telling one from the other. My custom has always been to ponder grief; that is, to follow it through ventricle and aorta to find out its lurking places. That old weight in the chest, telling me there is something I must dwell on...

The mood of the speaker is a harried one, a feeling of great unease. The syntax works, in part, to create this: Notice the fragment that starts it off, followed by the short sentence. This creates emphasis. His "disquieted" condition is likened to an illness, and notice the diction: "grief" and "weight." Readers can't help but sense his distraught condition.

For a third example, consider the mood in this passage from Vladimir Nabokov's *Pnin*:

> "Doesn't she want to come back?" asked Joan softly.
>
> Pnin, his head on his arm, started to beat the table with his loosely clenched fist.
>
> "I haf nofing," wailed Pnin between loud, damp sniffs, "I haf nofing left, nofing, nofing!"

The despair is unmistakable. But let's analyze: It comes through in the way Joan speaks to the broken-hearted Pnin. It comes through in Pnin's body movements. It comes through most force-fully in the language itself, in the repetition of *nofing*.

As you look closely at your manuscript, be attentive to mood. Which emotions should the characters be feeling? Is it a sad mood you want to create? A sense of urgency? A joyous mood? Certainly thought, speech, and action contribute to mood. But beyond these, you will need to decide on which stylistic features and techniques will best enable you to create the desired mood. In a work of fiction, you don't have the added benefit of a sound track as you do in a film production. You must create moods with words only. And the same goes for tone.

TONE

Tone, as I stated in Chapter One, is the apparent attitude of the narrator toward the characters and the world created in the work as a whole. But as I also stated, every aspect of a fictional work contributes in some way to the overall tone.

From a creative perspective, the exact tone you want may not be easy to achieve. What tone do you desire? Impassioned, urgent, quiet, nostalgic, ironic, offbeat? Sometimes, in a burst of creativity, everything seems to be working: You find your voice—the right one for this character, this place, this story. But ... sad to say, when you read it over, when you step back and take a critical eye to it, it's not what you thought it was. It's amateurish, horsey, bouncing all over the place. Or it's somehow devoid of emotion. Or it's overwritten, laying on the emotion way too thick.

Several things might be responsible for this—lack of character and plot development or thin scenes. Perhaps the work's lack of substance creates a weak tone. The work seems limp, shaky. But style can certainly be a factor. The language doesn't seem to fit the characters, and the pacing seems wrong in places. To create the right tone, you may have to experiment with style. Take a page or two and play with the language. Once you do this, though, be ready to make other changes. As I suggested earlier, you may even begin to see your character differently.

HARD-AND-FAST GENERALIZATIONS ABOUT PROSE STYLE

Hard-and-fast generalizations about style are hard to make. For instance, it may be tempting to say that a stripped-down style means a succession of simple sentences. Yet this is too broad of a generalization. Note the variety of sentence types in this passage from Raymond Carver's "They're Not Your Husband":

> The two men sitting beside Earl exchanged looks. One of them raised his eyebrows. The other man grinned and kept looking at Doreen over his cup as she spooned chocolate syrup over the ice cream. When she began shaking the can of whipped cream, Earl got up, leaving his food, and headed for the door. He heard her call his name, but he kept going.

This is the spare style, but it isn't a succession of simple sentences. It contains three of the four sentence types: simple (first two sentences), complex (second two), and compound (last). The spare style doesn't have to be a string of simple sentences, though it can be.

Instead of relying on a hard-and-fast generalization, study the work of writers with spare styles and those with dense styles. Analyze their use of sentence types, and note examples of sentence variety.

But can't we generalize about the uses of style? Any hard-and-fast generalization we make about this matter won't really hold. There's always an exception. For instance, it might seem reasonable to say that the fully textured style would not work very well in a high-intensity event, for instance, a murder; you would surely need fast-moving, spare prose. But if the psychology of the character is forefront—that is, the intricate workings of the murderer's mind in the midst of killing another human being—then the fully textured style might work quite well.

Another example: It might seem that if a character is caught up in a quandary and is trying to make a rational decision, the fully textured style would be best. But perhaps you want to represent the character's fragmentary attempts to solve the problem, and a spare style, a succession of machine-gun-like thoughts, might be perfect. My point is, study each style and decide what seems to work best for your character in this particular place in the story. Everything in fiction is a matter of function. You can write in either the spare or the fully textured style as a general practice as long as you can make it work in terms of character and everything else in the short story or novel. If the tone seems off, that's a good reason to rethink your style.

With the issue of formality versus informality we again run into the same problems of making hard-and-fast generalizations. One might think that a grand ball would surely call for a formal style, but what if your protagonist, though aristocratic in class, is decidedly informal? A rodeo would probably call for a rather informal style, but what if the story is filtered through a narrator with a formal voice? If the story deals with certain ponderous issues, maybe a formal style would work quite well. But again, the nature of the protagonist will make all the difference.

The same issues arise with pacing. A fast pace might be right for a funeral setting if you're dealing with a character's intense shock. A slow pace might be appropriate in the midst of a riotous, carefree party if your character is engrossed in his private thoughts.

The only hard-and-fast generalizations I will make about prose style, in general, are:

- Style depends on purpose or function.
- Stylistic choices vary widely.
- Study the masters to see how they handle style.
- Learn to trust your own ear.

PROCESS SHEET #13

1. How would you describe your style? Is it detailed or spare? Is it formal or informal? Does it achieve the tone you want to achieve in this story or novel? What changes, if any, would you make?

2. How specific and concrete is your style? Do you see changes you'd like to make? If you depend more on indirect or dramatic methods, do you think your reader will be able to visualize your characters by what they do and say? Where are some places you could make a character's tone of voice more apparent?

3. How would you describe the pacing or tempo in your story or novel? Do you see places where you might make the pacing or tempo fit the story mood better?

4. Do you see places where you can make use of grammatical features like ellipsis, italics, capitalization, repetition, and alliteration to good effect? Do you see places where you might be able to use stylistic techniques like juxtaposition and listing to good effect?

5. Can you spot different moods in your story or novel? Do you see places where you might create mood more effectively without overdoing it?

6. How would you describe the overall tone of your manuscript? Is this the tone you wanted to achieve? How does character contribute to the tone? How does the plot itself contribute to the tone? How does style? Without forcing things, what changes, if any, do you plan to make to develop the overall tone you want in this work?

EXERCISE 1

Write a piece of about 300 words with a character dealing with an internal or external conflict. Write this in a spare style with informal diction. Decide on the appropriate pacing. What tone is achieved? Rewrite this piece in a more fully textured or detailed style, with more formal diction. How does the tone change? Which of the two versions do you prefer?

EXERCISE 2

Write a scene of about 300 words, with dialogue, and include specific and concrete details to describe a character or two—perhaps secondary characters. Then rewrite the scene where the characters come alive more by voice intonation and gesture than by concrete description. Which of the two versions do you prefer?

EXERCISE 3

Write a scene of 300 words, with or without dialogue, developing a mood of frustration in your character. Then rewrite the scene and increase or decrease the frustration level of your character. Try to account for what contributed to the change in mood (something you added or something you took out?).

CHAPTER FOURTEEN

WORKING THEME AND IDEA

When you write a first draft, you may not have themes or ideas in mind. It's quite possible that your focus is more on character or plot. But read your draft carefully now. Is this story suggesting something universal about the human lot? About constrained choices human beings have? Compromises they end up making?

Whatever the case, theme must emerge naturally from the materials of the short story or novel, and the fiction itself must be an experience for your reader, not just an abstract idea you hammer home in didactic fashion. If the theme of your work is presented like the thesis of a nonfiction work, then the work will be second-rate fiction. Keep in mind what a character says in Solzhenitsyn's *One Day in the Life of Ivan Denisovich*: "Art isn't a matter of what but of how." This is something every writer should heed well.

Assuming your work has some sort of theme, which fictional elements contribute to it? In a short story, because of its compression, every vein can be loaded with ore, especially when the style is heavily figurative, dense with metaphor and simile. In a short story or novel, character, plot, and style all contribute in some way to theme.

CHARACTER AND THEME

Since character is essential to fiction, it only makes sense that themes and ideas embodied in the work will be deeply rooted in character. What a character is, what a character says or does—all of these things can suggest central ideas of the work itself, especially if the character is the protagonist, but even if the character is a secondary character.

Character Make-Up and Theme

A character's general make-up—who this character essentially is—can become thematic in different ways: Holden Caulfield may stand for all the disaffected youth who want something real or genuine—not phony. Randle P. McMurphy of *One Flew Over the Cuckoo's Nest* represents the rebel figure against societal authority and tyranny. Madame Bovary stands in for women who have succumbed to the pernicious influence of sentimental, romantic trash. Or one might say more generally, she stands for those who have been duped and are subject to the destructive nature of their romantic dreams. Flaubert was, after all, a realist. Each of these characters is carefully individualized, though they have become types and symbols. Danger lies in making your characters types only—seeking the thematic representation first at the expense of individualized character. Heed what is, by now, a famous Fitzgerald dictum from "The Rich Boy":

> Begin with an individual, and before you know it you find that you have created a type; begin with a type, and you find that you have created—nothing.

Whether or not your character becomes symbolic of larger ideas, it's absolutely essential to begin with "an individual," as Fitzgerald states. He also says, "There are no types, no plurals," and that's because each character, if the character is real, is unique. And yet out of the wellsprings of this uniqueness may certainly flow a type if your character also partakes of the universal.

Study your character closely. What universal qualities does this character have? What might you add to the character to make her more universal? Another way of putting the question: In the particular, where is the universal? In the universal, we find the basis for key thematic ideas.

Character Statements and Theme

It's possible for characters to make statements that suggest a main theme or principal idea of the work. Statements can be direct or literal, or they can be indirect or metaphorical. Either of these statements, direct or indirect, can—if we see them in context—contribute to our seeing the story or novel in larger terms than the actual, than this character having this problem in this particular place at *this* particular time.

Direct Statements

Direct statements can be quite compelling if they don't belabor the obvious. If you will recall the scene I quoted from *The Road* in Chapter Ten, the dialogue establishes the nature of McCarthy's postapocalyptic world. There are some "good guys," but they're "hiding"—from "each other." It's not known how many so-called good guys are left in this world. But one thing is certain: You can't trust anyone. You're on your own. This may be direct statement, but it doesn't answer all questions. How many are there? And where are they?

In a scene from James Dickey's *Deliverance*, the narrator is speaking to Lewis Medlock about the present state of affairs: A killer is hunting them down. Lewis advises the narrator to find and kill the man, and the narrator assures him that if he can find him, he will kill him. Note how this excerpt from the scene makes a thematic statement. Lewis speaks:

> "Well," he said, lying back, "here we are, at the heart of the Lewis Medlock country."
> "Pure survival," I said.

"This is what it comes to," he said. "I told you."

"Yes. You told me."

This scene crystallizes the key idea informing this work, that of pure survival when all the structures we count on in so-called civilized society are removed—a theme taken up in Conrad's *Heart of Darkness*. Dickey doesn't overwork it. Saying it once is enough.

Figurative Statements

In Tom Bissell's "A Bridge Under Water," a metaphor suggests a thematic idea. When the newlywed wife asks her husband what if they can't get through what's standing between them and their happiness together, the husband responds: "Then I guess it's a bridge under water." This occurs fairly early in the story, inviting the reader to imagine whether or not their marital relationship will be this water-covered bridge. Metaphorical statements are intriguing—as long as they're not clichéd—because they give us an image to reflect on. They concretize an idea.

Literary Allusions

Characters, or authors, can make literary allusions. In probably the most memorable passage from *The Catcher in the Rye*, Holden tells his sister, Phoebe:

> "Anyway, I keep picturing all these little kids playing some game in this big field of rye and all. Thousands of little kids, and nobody's around—nobody big. I mean—except me. And I'm standing on the edge of some crazy cliff. What I have to do, I have to catch everybody if they start to go over the cliff—I mean if they're running and they don't look where they're going I have to come out from somewhere and catch them. That's all I'd do all day, I'd just be the catcher in the rye and all. I know it's crazy, but that's the only thing I'd really like to be. I know it's crazy."

To Holden Caulfield, this rescuing of little kids seems the most genuine, nonphony kind of thing he could do. If it's deeply romantic for such a skeptic as Holden, the other side of skepticism might just be romanticism—affirming the ideal when the real is so unappealing. Holden has ironically gotten the Robert Burns poem itself wrong, thinking it's, "If a body *catch* a body... " (italics mine) instead of, "If a body meet a body coming through the rye." This is significant. Holden wants more than meeting, or acquaintance; he wants to *do* something profoundly important, to be useful to those who need someone—innocent children, that is, who aren't yet corrupted by all the phoniness he detests. The literary allusion becomes a springboard for Salinger's key idea.

Character Actions and Theme

In some cases, characters' actions can become symbolic, suggesting key ideas and themes. When Daisy Miller, because of her innocence and brashness, goes to the Roman Colosseum and catches malaria and dies, we cannot help but see this tragic end as some sort of symbolic retribution for Daisy's breaking the restrictive social codes of the Europeanized American community in Rome. Thematically, her action represents American innocence, a freshness and naïveté that Henry James himself valued.

Consider other symbolic character actions from famous American novels:

- Huck rips up the letter to Miss Watson that reveals Jim's whereabouts. Huck's action represents Twain's concept of the sound heart versus the deformed societal conscience. Huck recognizes Jim's humanity and rejects slavery.
- Jay Gatsby flamboyantly displays his fine shirts, symbolizing the shallowness of the American Dream, which has come to be equated with wealth and extravagance only.
- Holden Caulfield leaves school, symbolically rejecting society and all its phoniness.

An interesting combination of action and thing, both symbolic, is found in Robert Garner McBrearty's satire "First Day." In this comic work, the young protagonist, on his first day on the job at a loading dock, dutifully follows the absurd orders of the overbearing boss, who scornfully addresses him as Einstein, Edison, Balzac—and more. The poor young guy is charged with pushing a "big thing"—which McBrearty knows better than to describe—a considerable distance on the street to another warehouse loading dock. It would be gross understatement to say the journey is a rigorous one, but our hero does what he can and feels hopeful:

> It was getting easier. The big thing was starting to roll. The big thing bounced to the left, and the big thing dragged to the right, and I tried to move it from side to side. We rolled out the gate and on to the street. Cars started honking. People were yelling. A guy shouted out his window, "Get that big thing out of the street, you moron!"

He rolls it and rolls it and at one point lands in a ditch:

> It was starting to sink. I was starting to sink too. I'd gotten my foot caught underneath the big thing and now we were sinking together.

When he finally gets to his appointed destination, his big thing is rejected because he lacks a warehouse form. He must push the big thing back to its point of origin, where his boss gives him a tongue-lashing.

On the plot level, this story is a comic riot, and the boss's scorn for college-boy types is harmless and amusing, but clearly this story is meant to be read more on the figurative than on the literal level. The big thing itself becomes symbolic: the heavy, ponderous load of first-day-on-the-job responsibilities, the burden of being a newbie, and so forth. But more universally, this is life—the burden of human existence, that boulder that Sisyphus must forever roll up the hill. The act of rolling is also symbolic. It's the endless wrestling with the burden. Sometimes one ends up in the Slough of Despond; sometimes one overcomes the problem, but there's always more trouble on the horizon, and the protagonist of this bizarre story takes it all in stride, with Chaplinesque resilience.

"First Day" is idea driven, but it depends on a compelling character. It's doubtful that theme could carry this story on its own. We get interested in the theme because of the interplay between insolent boss, with his quirky name calling, and sympathetic protagonist, who gives it his all without complaining. The lesson here is that if you have a theme-driven story, whatever it might be—satire, farce, philosophical work—you must have interesting characters.

Something else: Watch out for symbol hunting. If in a short story, because of the compression of this form, a character wrestles with a boulder, we'll probably find something thematic about this action, even if it occurs only one time. If it's the central action of the story, we can't help but read the story on a symbolic or metaphorical level. In a novel, if it occurs once, we probably won't make much of it. If it occurs three times, that's a different matter.

As you revise your manuscript, look closely for characters' actions that suggest a universal idea or theme—actions that may be seen as more than what they literally are. What are they suggesting?

NATURAL AND MAN-MADE OCCURRENCES

In Stephen King's *Dolores Claiborne*, on the evening the solar eclipse is to occur, Dolores is planning to make her husband, Joe St. George, stumble into an abandoned well and die. Though the solar eclipse is a plot device, it also becomes a metaphor for Joe's own eclipse. Thematically, the natural eclipse becomes a symbol of righting the moral order—bringing Joe St. George to account for his abominable sexual behavior toward his daughter.

Is an earthquake, a tornado, or a tsunami symbolic? Can it point to theme? Only if you make it do so—if you associate it with catastrophes of a more general kind: disruptions in the social order, in relations between humans, and the like. But don't be heavy-handed about this. Find subtle, metaphorical ways to connect it to a larger, abstract idea.

Man-made disasters like oil spills, toxic clouds (Don DeLillo, *White Noise*), and nuclear meltdowns can point to theme. I take up a different kind of man-made threat in my satirical novel *Hog to Hog*, where a humongous hog confinement operation, a mega-ATV event, and a newly constructed prison represent economic and capitalist development run amok, as well as despoliation of the environment.

PLOT AND THEME

The theme of a work is one abstract level higher than the plot—the plot itself points to the theme. Many stories with different plots can have the same basic theme. The plot of Hawthorne's *The Scarlet Letter* deals with the Puritan theocracy's punishment of sin. One theme that comes out of this plot has to do with the question of mercy over justice—or legalism. A quite different novel that takes up this same theme is Victor Hugo's *Les Misérables*.

As you look closely at your manuscript, be sure to think about what the larger implications of your plot are. What ideas and themes does the work suggest over and above the plot? What if the plot could be different, with a different causal relationship overall? Would it suggest ideas that might be worth developing more? The danger in thinking this way is manipulating the plot so that the story "says" something you want it to say. But if your imagination seizes the possibility and it follows quite naturally and smoothly, producing as good a story line as before, or better, then why not?

TITLES AND THEME

The title of a work of fiction should in some way capture the energy of the work. But it can also point in some way toward the theme—directly or indirectly:

- **REPEAT A KEY LINE IN THE WORK:** *The Catcher in the Rye, To Kill a Mockingbird, Gone With the Wind*
- **REFER TO THE SETTING:** *The Magic Mountain, All Quiet on the Western Front, Main Street*
- **REFER TO THE KEY CONFLICT OR THEME:** *Crime and Punishment, A Farewell to Arms, Deliverance*
- **REFER TO A MAJOR CHARACTER:** *Adventures of Huckleberry Finn, The Great Gatsby, Dolores Claiborne*

STYLE AND THEME

There are at least two connections between style and theme:

- **A CONCRETE STYLE CAN HELP DEVELOP THEME:** If a short story is written in a heavily concrete style, descriptive passages of character and setting might serve a second function: to suggest theme. This can certainly be true of a novel also if it is written in a style rich with simile and metaphor.
- **STYLE WORKS IN TANDEM WITH THEME:** If, for instance, you write a postapocalyptic novel, intending it to be as grim in plot and characters as *The Road*, would a formal, detailed style be congruent with your theme? Will it come off as *grim*? If it's grim, it may be grim in a different way. Its formal property could possibly suggest order in the midst of disorder. So you would need to decide if this is the message you want to send.

PROCESS SHEET #14

1. Do you see any characters who represent thematic ideas in your work? Do you see where you could make characters more universal?

2. Do you find character statements that point to the themes or ideas in your work? What kinds of statements are these—direct or figurative? Do you see places where characters might make statements that suggest theme without forcing it?

3. Do any of your characters, or you as author, make use of literary allusions? Do you see any possibilities without forcing it?

4. Do you find places where characters' actions suggest theme? Can you see places where you might make certain actions more suggestive of theme— without forcing it?

5. Do any man-made or natural occurrences point to theme? Would it be possible to include any without forcing it?

6. In what ways does your plot suggest theme? Can you see ways to shape your plot more to develop the theme you have in mind—without forcing it?

7. How does your title function to suggest theme? Can you think of a better title, one that would better capture what you want to "say"?

8. Is your style heavily metaphorical? Do you find that metaphors and similes often point to theme? Do you see more ways to make metaphorical language do this without forcing it?

9. Is your style congruent with your theme? If it's not, will you change style or rethink theme?

EXERCISE 1

Write a scene of about 300 words, putting two characters into conflict with each other. Have either character make a statement that suggests an idea larger, or more general, than the specific conflict they are now embroiled in. (In other words, an abstract idea that many different story conflicts could, in some way, point to.) Rewrite, finding a more indirect way of suggesting the same idea. Which version do you prefer?

EXERCISE 2

Write a scene of about 300 words, putting two characters into conflict with each other—if Exercise 1 works, go with that. Find a way to make actions themselves symbolic of ideas larger than the literal. Then do a second version where you change some or all of the actions so that they suggest a different idea or theme than the first version.

EXERCISE 3

Write a piece of about 300 words including either a natural or man-made occurrence—or disaster, if you want. Bring in at least one character's response to it. Raise this to the level of idea or theme so that the reader can see that you are dealing not only with the literal event but also a more universal idea (perhaps something about technology or about humans when they encounter disasters). Do a second version where a different idea or theme is suggested or expressed.

CHAPTER FIFTEEN

FINE-TUNING

Some writers revise and even fine-tune as they write first drafts. This might work for some, but for others it can be discouraging and even counterproductive. If you work better this way—getting it all right as you go along—then by all means stick to this process. But the approach of this book is to liberate the imagination first, generate a draft while the imaginative fires are raging, and then set about revising. Once the revisions are completed, the work shaped up, it's time to give your book a final polish. You're in the final polishing stage now.

When you fine-tune your story or novel, you deal with the following issues: wordiness; effective wording; effective sentence patterns, grammar, punctuation, and spelling; and accuracy of dates and other real-world things, if you are writing realistic fiction.

I do want to emphasize that everything I've just mentioned must be handled in the context of character, narrative voice, and everything else in the story, including tone. We certainly wouldn't want to apply grammar handbook standards to first-person narrators like Huck Finn, Holden Caulfield, or Russell Banks's Bone. And, depending on the third-person narrative voice desired, we might certainly break with handbook rules and standards. Wordiness, vague word choices, even awkward sentence structures clearly work well if used to create certain kinds of characters or create certain moods. So, as with style, there are no hard-and-fast rules in this chapter. I'll cover the fine-tuning issues, but I will ask you to think context—always context.

I also want to point out that as you fine-tune, changes you make can affect style, and if they do very much, you're back to revision. For instance, if you create a staccato set of sentences, this will affect mood and could even affect character. If you choose a word with a different connotative value, or switch from an informal to a formal word, this may make the reader see your character a little differently. Having said this, I don't mean to suggest that you should leave well enough alone for fear of disturbing things. But do realize that some changes, though they appear to be surface-level changes initially, might be more substantive than you realized.

WORDINESS OR BLOAT

Don't confuse a detailed, fully textured style with one that is weighted down with unnecessary words—*unnecessary*, as I've suggested above, being a relative term. Think of it this way: Pruning unnecessary wordiness makes the writing much stronger by creating a character that works well in a fictional world that works well.

Redundancy

What about "a difficult Gordian knot"? A "large mansion"? "A round circle"? Two principles to consider:

- **IS THE REDUNDANCY USED FOR EMPHASIS?** Life's full of Gordian knots, but this one is especially difficult.
- **IS THE REDUNDANCY USED FOR COMPARISON?** There are many mansions, but this one is much larger than the mansions most of us have in mind. This one takes up two city blocks.

So, even if you're writing straight prose, intending no irony, no wit, you might find a redundancy useful. But, as you fine-tune your story, there is a more important issue at hand: Does a redundancy now and then seem fitting to your character? Can you use redundancies for wit, for humor? Would the use of redundancies suggest something about your character's redundant thinking? If this is true, redundancies might actually work well in character thought as well as in scenes.

Before you prune redundancies, decide on the language needed to create your character, to flesh this character out in all of his complexities. If redundancies—or at least some redundancies—are useful, keep them. Otherwise, prune.

Excess Verbiage or Baggage

1. "THERE WERE A LOT OF THINGS THAT DISTURBED HIM." 2. "A LOT OF THINGS DISTURBED HIM." The first version is certainly, no question, a handbook candidate for reworking—into the second. But it depends, doesn't it? If you want to slow down the sentence, making it less direct, then the first is a better choice. It has a sluggishness to it that might be useful in depicting your character's sluggish feelings. Decide, then, on the basis of character and mood. Don't automatically go for the handbook version.

1. "THERE WERE A LOT OF PEOPLE IN ATTENDANCE." 2. "A LOT OF PEOPLE ATTENDED." The first is, of course, bad writing, certainly on the face of it. But if an I-narrator stated it this way, or if a character, in dialogue, came out with it, we might conclude: stilted, pretentious. And if that's your aim—to reveal a pretentious character—keep it, of course. If not, prune. But what about a third-person narrator dealing with formally educated characters? Why would this third-person narrator ever say: "There were a lot of people in attendance"? Unless it's an embedded voice, an ironic nod at those who might speak this way, there's really no reason not to prune, is there?

Repetition

This is related to excessive baggage, but here I'm speaking of repetition of ideas in a paragraph. I don't mean repetition as a stylistic device. Oftentimes as we're writing, and even revising, we miss places where we've said the same thing twice, though a little differently. This can happen especially with exposition. Imagine in your fast first draft you penned this:

> Max thought that people were generally good-natured. Most people weren't bad. They tended to be good at heart. They might have their problems, but they were generally okay. He knew his share of good-hearted people. He knew very few people he would call bad.

Well, this could be said in about a sentence, right? Unless we want to show Max as working this matter over in his mind—but it would present a challenge to make the writing good, now wouldn't it? If this sounds like Max, from everything else we know about Max—okay, it might work. Otherwise, I'd recommend pruning and going at it differently, wouldn't you?

EFFECTIVE WORD CHOICE

First, I wouldn't depend on a thesaurus. Too often writers will plug in a synonym that just doesn't work well in context. Or, the word just isn't used the way they want to use it. I once read a good distinction: You eradicate *crime*, not criminals. The word *eradicate* isn't used, normally, to speak of people—and if it were, it would sound pretty heartless. My recommendation: Go ahead and use a thesaurus, but depend more on a dictionary. Depend even more on words in action—watching how professional authors use the language.

Diction

Depend ultimately on how the word functions in the sentence, whether in prose or scene. This is cleanup work. You've developed a style for your manuscript by now, but you're working on honing it. The right word depends on being attentive to different issues—four of which are:

Precision in Language

This has to do with those so-called words of power (think *Six Weeks to Words of Power* by Wilfred Funk) that help us to avoid vagueness. They narrow the meaning; they make fine distinctions. For instance, instead of "good," meaning "skilled," you might choose "adept"—*if* your character or narrator is educated. As another example, note how the opening passage of Vladimir Nabokov's *Pnin* establishes the narrator's level of education in his use of precise diction: "The elderly passenger sitting on the north-window side of that *inexorably* moving railway coach..." (italics mine). But it's important to note that Nabokov's narrator doesn't always use such a word as *inexorably*: "Some people—and I am one of them—hate happy ends. We feel cheated." Ordinary diction here: Continual use of more elevated language would seem overdone. Regardless of the narrator's or character's level of education, a vague word choice might even work better at times. In an effort to capture the visceral feelings of his characters, Hemingway makes an art of this. Note the repetitive use of "good" in the following dialogue from *The Sun Also Rises*:

> "Well, how did you like the bulls?" he asked
>
> "Good. They were nice bulls."
>
> "They're all right"—Montonya shook his head—"but they're not too good."
>
> "What didn't you like about them?"
>
> "I don't know. They just didn't give me the feeling that they were so good."

Degree of Formality/Informality

This is related to the issue of precision. Formal word choices like *inexorably* tend to be more precise. Being "adept" at a particular skill is much more precise than being "good" at it. The question is, how formal or informal should your story or novel be? Go over your manuscript to make sure you haven't chosen words that seem out of sync with your character or style. If you have, choose the right word now—or make a note and come back to it later. Granted, you can have a blend of the formal and the informal—Nabokov's novel certainly does, as I've shown. Again, think context. Perhaps you've written in an informal style, but a formal word somehow adds an air of sophistication that seems appropriate to the character's present aims or thinking. Or perhaps you've written in a formal style, and you want to show the character's present laid-back feeling. Choice of formal or informal always relates to character or to narrator—and possibly to circumstance. For instance, one character might order a "pilsner," another a "brewski."

Connotation

Language isn't just denotative; it's also connotative. Often, in early drafts of work, writers don't catch words that might suggest attitudes, values, and so forth that run counter to their character's attitudes and values. Certain words or phrases have distinctly negative connotations. For example, which expression has greater negative connotation: "failing," "missing the mark," or "going down the tubes"? The answer might well depend on the context—probably does—but I'd say, offhand, that "going down the tubes" probably does. This can change; the language is always changing as words take on different connotative values as they're used in new contexts. At any rate, be sensitive to connotation as it relates to your character. If your third-person narrator says your character's business is "in the red," the wording will sound less negative than "going down the tubes." Of course, you may want to choose the more negative connotative expression if the character himself feels this way. My only point is to be aware of the connotative value of words and expressions and to make choices that work well with your character. You may find that you have a lot of fine-tuning to do in terms of connotation. The language is alive with connotation. It's easy to forget this. We often become abruptly aware of it when we unwisely choose a word or expression that offends other people.

Use of Jargon

This is a special diction question. If you've used a lot of jargon, you'll need to decide if you should make the language more accessible to your reader. Otherwise, you will limit your readership. If your writing is energetic enough, readers might be willing to look up the words—or wait for the meaning to reveal itself through the dramatic movement of the story.

Using Effective Language to Hone Description

"He was thin, strong, and tanned, and had unusual blond hair—the kind girls went for." Is this descriptive? Pretty general, isn't it? Can you see this character? If you can, you've filled in the details on your own. It might be okay for a general sense—and perhaps the author will draw you in more indirectly, through dramatic means, as I describe in Chapter Thirteen. But don't mistake this passage for concrete description. It's based on four adjectives that don't place us in a world of the five senses.

The following description of Russell "Curly" Norrys in Geoffrey Clark's *Two, Two, Lily-White Boys* does a much better job—I've underlined the adjectives:

> He was lean and wiry and easily three or four inches taller than me and his skin looked like butterscotch— he'd likely spent a lot of time in the sun. Everything about him seemed finely and delicately made: his thin nose with flaring nostrils, his long limbs—even his hands and fingers—covered with fine blond hair,

his eyes <u>brown</u>; but what you focused on most was his hair: a <u>dark golden</u> mass of <u>corkscrew blond</u> curls, the kind some girls would kill to have. But what really struck me were his hands, for his fingers were very <u>thin</u> and extremely <u>long</u>.

The adjectives here work with the specific details to create a visual, memorable picture of Curly: his physical build, his facial features, his eyes, hair, fingers. How thorough this is! And how nicely compressed. If you've worked with direct (versus indirect) description in this manner, and you are in the fine-tuning stage, your job now is to be sure your writing is this concrete—unless, as I said before, you want to create a general impression. But don't mistake a general impression for concrete description.

SENTENCE ISSUES

Fine-tuning includes all levels of language, from word to sentence, from sentence to paragraph. If you've worked to rid your draft of wordiness, you've already addressed the individual sentence. But another sentence issue awaits your attention, a key issue which has to do with construction: active versus passive.

Active Versus Passive Construction

Active verb constructions like, "The dog bit him," instead of, "He was bitten by the dog," give your writing verve and energy. And yet, once again, no hard-and-fast rules. Let's say you want to show a character's passivity. Instead of the active construction—"Susan packaged up the materials, one by one"—you go with: "The materials were packaged up one by one, by Susan." Not a good sentence if one goes by the handbooks, but in the right context, if Susan is utterly exhausted, just going through the motions, this might work better than the active construction. It's important to know the difference between the active and the passive construction so that you can make the best choice based on the needs of character and circumstance. My recommendation is to go with the active, generally, and be open to the passive as the specific need arises.

Making the Writing Move: Sentence to Sentence

Certainly much of fine-tuning consists of attending to the way the writing is moving—or not moving—from one sentence to another. If every sentence is a simple one, then your language might sound pretty clunky unless the prose style somehow reflects your characters, events, and setting. Everything, as I've said all along, depends on context. Sometimes a series of fragments works well. Sometimes a periodic sentence (where the main idea is suspended until the end) works well; sometimes a loose one (where the main idea comes first, followed by phrases/clauses) works better. Sometimes long sentences are needed, sometimes short ones. You've been making judgments about these issues since you started working on style. You've tried to generate a style that creates the right voice for your work, and in places the style has probably varied. Now, it's time to fine-tune your prose to make sure it's really working. Here's a process to follow:

1. Study the four sentence types: simple, compound, complex, and compound-complex. You can find these in any grammar handbook and certainly on the Internet. Get a good working sense of these sentence types. As you read fiction, notice how sentence types are varied. Try varying sentence types in your own work. Judge the effects of doing so.

2. Find places in your manuscript where the prose sounds like it's working. Pick a half dozen paragraphs of different kinds—exposition, description, and narrative summary—and study these places for the way the sentences are working. Why is the prose working? Did you vary sentence types? Is it the amount of detail you've used? The word

choice? The pacing? Is it certain stylistic devices you've used like alliteration and repetition?

3. Find places in your manuscript where the prose isn't working. What have you done differently here? Why don't these passages sound as good as the ones you've marked as good?

4. Once you've isolated the problems, apply what you've learned from the previous steps and search through your manuscript once more. This might mean combining sentences, eliminating some sentences, and rearranging sentences to give the writing more polish. It might also mean changing style to one that works better—one that has more force. When you're fine-tuning, the more you look, the more you find.

BASIC GRAMMAR AND MECHANICS

Basic grammar covers a number of issues: subject-verb agreement, pronoun-antecedent agreement, misplaced modifiers, and tense issues. Under the heading of mechanics, I'll throw in spelling and some basic punctuation issues.

First, let me say that with creative writing, you can certainly take liberties with basic grammar as well as mechanics. The most obvious example is the uneducated I-narrator, or even the third-person narrator whose voice is adapted to the character—embedding a voice to go with this character. If it works, you can certainly break all the rules of grammar and mechanics. As I said before, no one in his right mind who knows anything about writing wants to fix Huck's grammar. On the other hand, if you're writing in a formal or even neutral style about fairly educated people—doctors, lawyers, teachers—then grammar and mechanics errors will appear to be just that: errors.

Let's think of everything—including grammar and mechanics—as purpose driven. If dialogue works better without quotation marks around it—as we see in *The Road*—then go for it.

Comma splices are sometimes used to move readers more quickly from one sentence to another. Apostrophes are left out in contractions. These kinds of things are open to creative judgment.

If you're unsure of grammatical rules and conventions, search the Internet or buy a college-level grammar handbook. But be ready to break from the conventions in the interests of creativity. It's knowing when to break the conventions that matters. Nothing is "wrong" unless it's out of sync with your characters and their world. If it's in sync, anything goes.

ACCURACY OF REAL-WORLD DETAILS

Naturally, if you are writing realistic fiction, you need to get certain facts straight. If you're taking liberties with reality and everything else about your story or novel seems to be off-center a little, then no, you don't have to worry about this. Otherwise, you don't want to get the wrong date for when a celebrity died, the wrong assassin of a notable historical figure, or the wrong details about a particular kind of business operation, medical procedure, or governmental policy, past or present. Do the necessary research. Factual errors will jerk your reader out of the story.

SUMMING UP

When you fine-tune, you are often dealing with surface-level changes, but sometimes these can lead to changes that go deeper into character and even plot, and certainly tone. One thing to polish is your prose style. Even if you thought you had taken care of stylistic matters after you revised for style, you will probably find places in your manuscript that need some attending to. It's a good idea to read straight through your story or novel as quickly as you can to make sure it reads the way you want it to, that it sounds the way you want it to. If it's clunky in places, give those places the attention they need.

PROCESS SHEET #15

1. Do you see evidence of redundancy in your manuscript? Do you plan to eliminate all cases, or do some cases help create character?

2. Do you see evidence of excess baggage in your manuscript? Do you plan to eliminate most of this, or will some places help create character?

3. Do you find evidence of repetition of thoughts and ideas in your manuscript? Will you eliminate this, or does some of it seem useful to show a character working an idea over in her mind?

4. Are there places in your manuscript where the language seems inappropriately formal or informal?

5. Are there places in your manuscript where some words need to be replaced because of their particular connotative value—that is, they don't seem fitting to your character? Or do you see how these words might work anyway?

6. Have you used any jargon in this work? If so, will you find ways to make the meaning of this jargon clear, or will you leave this matter up to your reader?

7. Do you see descriptions of characters in your manuscript that are more general than concrete? Do you intend to rewrite these descriptive passages to make them more concrete, or will you keep the description general and depend more on dramatic methods of speech and action?

8. Do you find passive constructions in your manuscript? Will you change to active, or do some passive constructions seem useful in revealing things about your character?

9. Are you pleased with the way your sentences flow in a paragraph? If not, do you intend to follow the process I spelled out above? Are there any steps you might leave out?

10. Does your manuscript stick to the basic standards of grammar and mechanics, or do you find creative ways of bending the rules? Do you see any grammatical or mechanical changes to make?

11. Assuming you are writing realism, do you see places in your manuscript that need checking to be sure the details are correct?

EXERCISE 1

Write a 300-word narrative scene using some exposition and description. Write it from the third-person limited omniscient POV. Read it over. Look for any of the following wordiness: redundancies, excess verbiage, or repetition of ideas. If you find such things, eliminate them. Then redo the original draft, keeping the instances of wordiness, but making them suitable to a particular character. Which version do you like better?

EXERCISE 2

Rewrite the piece from Exercise 1 (without the wordiness), but this time change the diction. If you used mostly informal words, now use mostly formal. If you used mostly formal words before, now use informal. How does the character change? Which version do you like better?

EXERCISE 3

Write a 300-word scene that mixes active and passive verb constructions. Then rewrite the scene using only active verb constructions. Which scene do you like better? Which has more impact?

EXERCISE 4

Write a narrative summary of about 200 words using only simple sentences. Then rewrite the narrative summary using all four sentence types: simple, compound, complex, and compound-complex. Which version do you prefer?

CHAPTER SIXTEEN

MARKETING YOUR WORK

Once you have revised and fine-tuned your short story or novel, you are finally ready to submit. For fiction, the premier market guide is *Novel & Short Story Writer's Market*, published by Writer's Digest Books. Not every magazine, journal, or book publisher is listed in this guide, but if you can't find what you need here, you can go online and find more markets for your work. Submitting your work requires a careful process, and it takes patience and endurance. For both short fiction and the novel, be prepared to do further revision if an editor or agent asks for it. Be sure to keep track of manuscripts sent to various magazines, agents, and small press publishers, and the dates you sent them.

SUBMITTING SHORT FICTION

First, you need to study the market. Which magazines and journals are out there, and how many are a good fit for your work? Don't send your work just anywhere. Second, be flexible on the method of submission: regular print or online. And third, prepare for rejection. Be thankful for editors' responses, especially when they are encouraging.

Study the Market

It's important to study the market; i.e., to give your full attention to the kinds of work different magazines and journals are publishing. There are two ways to do this: Study the blurbs in *Novel & Short Story Writer's Market* and read sample copies of the magazine.

Study the Blurbs

Start with *Novel & Short Story Writer's Market*. You will find blurbs that cover literary magazines, small circulation magazines, online markets, and consumer magazines. Blurbs tell you the literary standards editors set for published work. One useful feature is the names of authors the magazine or journal has recently published. You can watch for these authors in other magazines and find out what they are doing to be successful. Pay special attention to what's written under the "Needs" heading. Is this the kind of fiction you write? Also, heed notations stating that only regional writers will be considered, or if it's a Canadian magazine, only Canadian writers. Don't bother sending work after the stated reading period; it won't get read. Some magazines, as you will note, read year round. One last thing: Find out if the magazine accepts simultaneous submissions (work sent to more than one place) and multiple submissions (more than one story to the magazine you are submitting to).

Read Sample Copies

You can get a greater sense of the magazine by reading published stories than you can from simply reading an informational blurb. You will probably be able to read sample copies of a number of magazines and journals at a university or college library and possibly find some at your local library. Many magazines and journals also archive sample stories on their websites. The kinds of fiction the magazine takes should become apparent. If it takes experimental fiction, is this the kind of experimental fiction you write? What sensibility do you gather from reading the work in this magazine? Does it seem urban or rural? Does it seem off-beat or sober?

Submission: Regular Print or Online

Submitting hardcopy stories takes time and is costly, but a number of regular print magazines still demand it. If you submit your work via regular mail, send a cover letter, the story, and either a self-addressed, stamped envelope (SASE) or a return envelope with return postage. Don't send photos, your resume, or anything else. Doing so makes you look unprofessional.

A cover letter is important. Check the Internet for sample cover letters. Some things you should know about writing a cover letter: Don't sum up your story unless the market blurb calls for a summary. Provide a little background about yourself—include anything that relates to the story itself. List any publications your work appears in, plus any writing awards you've won. Make sure you follow standard letter format: your address and date (supply e-mail address), the editor's name (unless it's just "Fiction Editor"), the magazine's address, the salutation, body of letter, and notation about SASE. Many writers today choose to supply a SASE only and let the editor recycle the story if rejected.

More and more regular print magazines are now allowing e-mail submissions or online submissions through a submissions manager, a software program that allows the writer to check the status of submissions at any time. Online magazines, of course, are much more likely to take online submissions. Online submissions are a click away and very cost-effective.

Prepare for Rejection

In a market where many magazines receive hundreds of submissions for any one issue, you need to send your best work. Choose your best stories from the revision stage. Study the market and get your stories circulating. But do prepare for rejection because even if your stories are good, they may not beat out other stories the editors simply prefer for whatever reason. It's undeniable that subjective considerations enter into judgments of editors—they're human, so why wouldn't they? But one thing I do believe is that really good fiction—well-crafted fiction, I mean—will eventually find a home, *if* there's a market for it. If there's not now, there may be later. Save rejected stories. Don't give up on them. Think of the submitting process, then, as: 1) sending your best work, and 2) finding a suitable market for it. However long this takes.

SUBMITTING NOVELS

When you submit a novel you are submitting work written over several months—if you followed this book's process, that's six months of pretty hard work. What you want to do is find the market best suited to this work—commercial or small press.

To get the most out of your search, follow this process:

1. Check *Novel & Short Story Writer's Market* market blurbs for both agents and small-press publishers.
2. Read descriptions and reviews of recently published novels by authors represented by agents (or, in other words, at commercial presses) and by small-press publishers.
3. Work up a strong query letter suited to an agent or small press publisher.
4. Send a portion of your novel—or the whole novel, if requested.

Check Market Blurbs/
Scope Out Sample Novels

Check the listings in *Novel & Short Story Writer's Market* for both agents and small-press publishers. You will need an agent in order to market your work to commercial presses. Check agent blurbs to see which kinds of novels they represent and if they mention specific novels they've represented. Then check the Web for blurbs and reviews. Does your work fit here?

Look for small-press publishers as well. Check blurbs and reviews of novels they've published. If you think your work is more suited to small-press publication, you won't need an agent.

Develop a Strong Query Letter

A query letter is extremely important in novel submissions. Many books address the topic of writing a strong query letter. You also should be able to obtain samples of effective query letters from the Internet. In a query letter for a novel, you must state concisely what the novel is about, though you don't necessarily have to reveal the ending in your query letter—some agents and editors don't want to know. (You do need to reveal the ending in a synopsis of your book, however.) For the query, you also need a one-sentence statement of the premise of the book and then a brief statement of character and plot that runs no longer than a paragraph. The query letter must not run more than one page. Agents and editors want to be able to skim the letter and see if they are interested in a book with a premise like this. Is the premise tightly written? Does it suggest a marketing angle? More and more agents and small press publishers are accepting—and in some cases requiring—e-mail queries. Besides the standard query letter, you may also be asked to send any or all of the following: outline, synopsis, and sample chapter(s).

Send Work Out

When you submit your work, you must follow protocol. Send the agent or editor only what is requested in the blurb. Don't send work by e-mail if doing so isn't the stated policy. If work is to be sent by regular mail, be sure to include a SASE for a response. Don't expect to get a quick reply.

One thing to note: In both cases—commercial and small-press publisher—be prepared to say how you will help promote your novel. Publishers today, especially small-press publishers, expect authors to get involved in promoting their books. You should be ready to develop a website if you don't have one already and to participate in social media as much as possible.

Prepare for Rejection

With all the work that goes into writing a novel, naturally it's easy to get discouraged when your work gets rejected. It's hard not to take it personally, but you have to see rejection as part of the process. If the agent or small-press publisher gave you some feedback, give it serious consideration (it's a good sign that they bothered to make a comment!). Often it's tempting to reject the feedback out of hand, but there may be some truth to it—which sometimes dawns on one after pitching that rejection letter. For this reason, it's best to keep rejection letters that make comments about your work—if you're lucky enough to get one instead of the standard form letter.

One last thing: Whether you are writing short fiction or long, you may have to wait for your work to be published—even your best work. It's best to move on to other projects. Don't obsess over work not yet published. If your first novel isn't picked up by a publisher, maybe your second will be. And then, you might find there's interest in your first. Don't give up, and keep writing!

PROCESS SHEET #16

1. If you're submitting short fiction, what will your process be? Identify each step you will take.
2. If you're submitting a novel, what will your process be? Identify each step you will take.

EXERCISE 1

Find one market blurb for a magazine that publishes short fiction you admire. Read some sample stories from this magazine. Did reading the stories help you better understand what the magazine wants?

EXERCISE 2

Read blurbs for small-press publishers or agents. Choose one publisher or agent that sounds like a good fit for your novel. Read several descriptions and blurbs of novels published by this press or placed by this agent. Having read these, do you still think this publisher/agent is a good fit for your novel?

NOTES ON THE CHAPTERS

CHAPTER ONE

BURROWAY, JANET. *WRITING FICTION: A GUIDE TO NARRATIVE CRAFT*, 3RD ED. (New York: HarperColllins Publishers, 1992), 211.

CONRAD, JOSEPH. *LORD JIM* (New York: The Modern Library, 1931), 70, 214.

FORSTER, E.M. *ASPECTS OF THE NOVEL* (New York: Harcourt, 1955), 67, 78, 86.

HILLS, RUST. *WRITING IN GENERAL AND THE SHORT STORY IN PARTICULAR: AN INFORMAL TEXTBOOK*, REV.ED. (New York: Mariner Books, 2000), 2.

MANSFIELD, KATHERINE. "MISS BRILL." IN *THE SHORT STORIES OF KATHERINE MANSFIELD* (New York: Knopf, 1965), 553.

MCCARTHY, CORMAC. *NO COUNTRY FOR OLD MEN* (New York: Vintage Books, 2006), 71.

UPDIKE, JOHN. "A&P." IN *THE EARLY STORIES: 1953-1975* (New York: Ballantine Books, 2003), 601.

CHAPTER FIVE

BELLOW, SAUL. "ZETLAND: BY A CHARACTER WITNESS." IN *COL-LECTED STORIES*, edited by Janis Bellow (New York: Penguin Books, 2002), 243.

JOHNSTON, TIM. "IRISH GIRL." IN *IRISH GIRL* (Denton, TX: University of North Texas Press, 2009), 137.

MCCARTHY, CORMAC. *THE ROAD* (New York: Vintage Books, 2006), 5.

NABOKOV, VLADIMIR. *PNIN* (New York: Vintage Books, 1989), 7.

CHAPTER SIX

GARDNER, LEONARD. *FAT CITY* (New York: Vintage Books, 1986), 128.

HARUF, KENT. *PLAINSONG* (New York: Alfred A. Knopf, 1999), 31.

MCBREARTY, ROBERT GARNER. "THE BIKE." IN *EPISODE* (Clifton, VA: Pocol Press, 2009), 71.

MCINERNEY, JAY. *BRIGHT LIGHTS, BIG CITY* (New York: Vintage Books, 1984), 1.

MUST, DENNIS. "QUEEN ESTHER." IN *OH, DON'T ASK WHY* (Los Angeles: Red Hen Press, 2007), 22, 23, 28.

SALINGER, J.D. *THE CATCHER IN THE RYE* (New York: Little, Brown, 1991), 1.

CHAPTER SEVEN

MARTIN, MAN. *DAYS OF THE ENDLESS CORVETTE* (New York: Carroll & Graf Publishers, 2007), 113.

CHAPTER EIGHT

JACKSON, SHIRLEY. "THE LOTTERY." IN *NOVELS AND STORIES: THE LOTTERY, THE HAUNTING OF HILL HOUSE, WE HAVE ALWAYS LIVED IN THE CASTLE, OTHER STORIES AND SKETCHES* (New York: Library of America, 2010), 232, 235.

CHAPTER NINE

BANKS, RUSSELL. *RULE OF THE BONE* (New York: HarperCollins Publishers, 1995), 126.

BAUSCH, RICHARD. *REBEL POWERS* (New York: Vintage Books, 1993), 227.

CLARK, GEOFFREY. "A PLACE FOR YOUR GUESTS." IN *RABBIT FEVER: TWELVE STORIES AND A MEMOIR* (Greensboro, N.C.: Avisson Press, 2000), 31.

DELILLO, DON. *WHITE NOISE* (New York: Viking, 2001), 9.

GARDNER, LEONARD. *FAT CITY* (New York: Vintage Books, 1986), 14, 15, 23.

HANSEN, RON. *A WILD SURGE OF GUILTY PASSION* (New York: Scribner, 2011), 52-53.

HENRY, DEWITT. *THE MARRIAGE OF ANNA MAYE POTTS* (Knoxville, TN: University of Tennessee Press, 2001), 3-4.

MADONIA, KRISTEN-PAIGE. *FINGERPRINTS OF YOU* (New York: Simon & Schuster, 2012), 19-20.

MCBREARTY, ROBERT GARNER. "THE EDGE HE CARRIES." IN *LET THE BIRDS DRINK IN PEACE* (Denver, CO: Conundrum Press, 2011), 125.

MCDERMOTT, ALICE. *AT WEDDINGS AND WAKES* (New York: Farrar, Straus and Giroux, 2009), 107-108, 159.

MCINERNEY, JAY. *BRIGHT LIGHTS, BIG CITY* (New York: Vintage Books, 1984), 40.

MUST, DENNIS. "TYPEWRITER." IN *OH, DON'T ASK WHY* (Los Angeles: Red Hen Press, 2007), 1.

SALINGER, J.D. *THE CATCHER IN THE RYE* (New York: Little, Brown, 1991), 117.

SUSSMAN, ELLEN. *ON A NIGHT LIKE THIS* (New York: Warner Books, 2004), 15, 53.

WISNIEWSKI, MARK. *SHOW UP, LOOK GOOD* (Arlington, VA: Gival Press, 2011), 10.

WOODRELL, DANIEL. *WINTER'S BONE* (New York: Bay Back Books, 2006), 129-130.

CHAPTER TEN

BAUSCH, RICHARD. *IN THE NIGHT SEASON* (New York: HarperCollins, 1998), 325-326.

CARVER, RAYMOND. "WHY DON'T YOU DANCE?" IN *WHERE I'M CALLING FROM* (New York: Vintage Books, 1989), 160.

GAINES, ERNEST J. "THE SKY IS GRAY." IN *BLOODLINE* (New York: Dial Press, 1968), 97.

MARTIN, MAN. *PARADISE DOGS* (New York: St. Martin's Press, 2011), 9, 54.

MCCARTHY, CORMAC. *THE ROAD* (New York: Vintage Books, 2006), 184-185.

O'CONNOR, FLANNERY. "A GOOD MAN IS HARD TO FIND." IN *A GOOD MAN IS HARD TO FIND AND OTHER STORIES* (Orlando, FL: Harcourt Brace Jovanovich, 1977), 4.

SUSSMAN, ELLEN. *FRENCH LESSONS* (New York: Ballantine Books, 2011), 9.

CHAPTER ELEVEN

BOYLE, T.C. *THE ROAD TO WELLVILLE* (New York: Penguin Books, 1993), 6-7.

CLARK, GEOFFREY. "ICE FISHING." IN *SCHOOLING THE SPIRIT* (Santa Maria, CA: Asylum Arts, 1993), 37.

CRANE, STEPHEN. *THE RED BADGE OF COURAGE* (New York: Washington Square Press, 1964), 1.

DAVIS, REBECCA HARDING. *LIFE IN THE IRON MILLS, AND OTHER STORIES* (Old Westbury, NY: Feminist Press, 1985), 11-12.

DICKEY, JAMES. *DELIVERANCE* (New York: Dell Publishing, 1994), 70, 82, 83, 87.

DREISER, THEODORE. *SISTER CARRIE* (New York: Holt, Reinhart, and Winston, 1957), 16-17

FITZGERALD, F. SCOTT. *THE GREAT GATSBY* (New York: Scribner, 2004), 120.

GILMAN, CHARLOTTE PERKINS. *THE YELLOW WALLPAPER AND OTHER WRITINGS* (New York: Bantam Books, 1989), 4.

HEMINGWAY, ERNEST. "A CLEAN, WELL-LIGHTED PLACE." IN *THE SNOWS OF KILIMANJARO AND OTHER STORIES* (New York: Charles Scribner's Sons, 1964), 32, 33.

MANN, THOMAS. *THE MAGIC MOUNTAIN,* translated by John E. Woods (New York: Vintage Books, 1996), 5.

O'BRIEN, TIM. *NORTHERN LIGHTS* (New York: Broadway Books, 1999), 170, 182.

POE, EDGAR ALLAN. "THE FALL OF THE HOUSE OF USHER." IN *EDGAR ALLAN POE: SELECTED PROSE AND POETRY* (New York: Holt, Reinhart, and Winston, 1950), 1.

REMARQUE, ERICH MARIA. *ALL QUIET ON THE WESTERN FRONT* (New York: Ballantine Books, 1982), 9.

SOLZHENITSYN, ALEXANDER. *ONE DAY IN THE LIFE OF IVAN DEN-ISOVICH* (New York: New American Library, 2008), 19-20.

TWAIN, MARK. *ADVENTURES OF HUCKLEBERRY FINN* (Boston: Houghton Mifflin Company, 1958), 69.

WHITECLOUD, THOMAS S. "BLUE WIND DANCING." WIKIPEDIA: THE FREE ENCYCLOPEDIA (http://en.wikipedia.org/wiki/Blue_Winds_Dancing)

CHAPTER TWELVE

BANKS, RUSSELL. *RULE OF THE BONE* (New York: Harper Perennial, 1996), 1.

BERGMAN, MEGAN MAYHEW. "HOUSEWIFELY ARTS." IN *BEST AMERICAN SHORT STORIES 2011* (Boston: Houghton Mifflin Harcourt, 2011), 14.

BURROWAY, JANET. *WRITING FICTION: A GUIDE TO NARRATIVE CRAFT, 3RD ED.* (New York: HarperColllins Publishers, 1992), 176.

CATES, DAVID. *X OUT OF WONDERLAND* (Hanover, NH: Zoland Books, 2005), 1-2.

DOCTOROW, E.L. *THE MARCH* (New York: Random House, 2006), 363.

FITZGERALD, F. SCOTT. *THE GREAT GATSBY* (New York: Scribner, 2004), 180.

FORD, RICHARD. "ROCK SPRINGS." IN *ROCK SPRINGS* (New York: Vintage Books, 1988), 27.

GROFF, LAUREN. "EYEWALL." IN *THE PEN/O. HENRY PRIZE STORIES 2012* (New York: Anchor Books, 2012), 324.

HEMINGWAY, ERNEST. *A FAREWELL TO ARMS* (New York: Charles Scribner's Son, 1957), 3, 343.

_____. "IN ANOTHER COUNTRY." IN *THE SNOWS OF KILIMANJARO AND OTHER STORIES* (New York: Charles Scribner's Son, 1964), 65.

HORNBY, NICK. *HIGH FIDELITY* (New York: Riverhead Books, 1996), 3-4.

HORROCKS, CAITLIN. "THE SLEEP." IN *BEST AMERICAN SHORT STORIES 2011* (Boston: Houghton Mifflin Harcourt, 2011), 118.

KAFKA, FRANZ. "THE METAMORPHOSIS." IN *SELECTED SHORT STORIES OF FRANZ KAFKA* (New York: Random House, 1952), 19.

MCCARTHY, CORMAC. *THE ROAD* (New York: Vintage Books, 2006), 286-287.

MCEWAN, IAN. *AMSTERDAM* (Toronto: Vintage Canada, 1999), 3.

MOODY, RICK. *THE ICE STORM* (New York: Warner Books, 1997), 3.

NABOKOV, VLADIMIR. *THE ANNOTATED LOLITA* (New York: Vintage Books, 1991), 9.

SOLZHENITSYN, ALEXANDER. *ONE DAY IN THE LIFE OF IVAN DENISOVICH* (New York: New American Library, 2008), 139.

THURBER, JAMES. "THE SECRET LIFE OF WALTER MITTY." IN *THE THURBER CARNIVAL* (New York: HarperPerennial, 1999), 60.

TWAIN, MARK. "THE WAR PRAYER." IN *MARK TWAIN: SELECTED WRITINGS OF AN AMERICAN SKEPTIC*, EDITED BY VICTOR DOYNO (Buffalo, NY: Prometheus Books, 1983), 424, 425.

UPDIKE, JOHN. *RABBIT, RUN* (New York: Ballantine Books, 1996), 264.

WEST, NATHANIEL. *THE DAY OF THE LOCUST.* IN *MISS LONELY-HEARTS & THE DAY OF THE LOCUST* (New York: New Directions Publishing Corporation, 1969), 59.

WILLIAMSON, ERIC MILES. *TWO-UP.* (Huntsville, TX: Texas Review Press, 2006), 1, 274-275.

CHAPTER THIRTEEN

BANKS, RUSSELL. *RULE OF THE BONE* (New York: Harper Perennial, 1996), 23.

BAUSCH, RICHARD. *HELLO TO THE CANNIBALS* (New York: HarperCollins Publishers, 2002), 497.

BOYLE, T. CORAGHESSAN. "BIG GAME." IN *WITHOUT A HERO* (New York: Penguin Books, 1995), 1-2.

_____. *THE INNER CIRCLE* (New York: Penguin Books, 2005), 117.

CARVER, RAYMOND. "THEY'RE NOT YOUR HUSBAND." IN *WHERE I'M CALLING FROM* (New York: Vintage Books, 1989), 45.

CLARK, GEOFFREY. *TWO, TWO, LILY-WHITE BOYS* (Pasadena, CA: Red Hen Press, 2012), 1.

CLEAVE, CHRIS. *INCENDIARY* (New York: Simon & Schuster, 2005), 12-13.

DELILLO, DON. *WHITE NOISE* (New York: Viking, 2001), 3, 22.

DICKEY, JAMES. *DELIVERANCE* (New York: Dell Publishing, 1994), 111.

DOCTOROW, E.L. *THE MARCH* (New York: Random House, 2006), 8.

ERIAN, ALICIA. *TOWELHEAD* (New York: Simon & Schuster, 2005), 2, 102-103.

FAULKNER, WILLIAM. *ABSALOM, ABSALOM!* (New York: Vintage Books, 1990), 3.

GREENFELD, KARL TARO. "MICKEY MOUSE." IN *THE PEN/O. HENRY PRIZE STORIES 2012* (New York: Anchor Books, 2012), 119, 130.

HEMINGWAY, ERNEST. *THE SUN ALSO RISES* (New York: Charles Scribner's Sons, 1954), 3.

HEMPEL, AMY. "TONIGHT IS A FAVOR TO HOLLY." IN *THE COLLECTED STORIES OF AMY HEMPEL* (New York: Scribner, 2006), 5.

HENRY, DEWITT. *THE MARRIAGE OF ANNA MAYE POTTS* (Knoxville, TN: University of Tennessee Press, 2001), 19, 49, 54.

KUNDERA, MILAN. *IGNORANCE,* translated by Linda Asher (New York: HarperCollins Publishers, 2002), 45-46.

MCBREARTY, ROBERT GARNER. "THE COMEBACK." IN *EPISODE* (Clifton, VA: Pocol Press, 2009), 80.

_____. "THE HELMETED MAN." IN *LET THE BIRDS DRINK IN PEACE* (Denver, CO: Conundrum Press, 2011), 11.

MCDERMOTT, ALICE. *AT WEDDINGS AND WAKES* (New York: Farrar, Straus and Giroux, 2009), 98.

MCEWAN, IAN. *ATONEMENT* (New York: Anchor Books, 2003), 3, 179, 181.

MOODY, RICK. *THE ICE STORM* (New York: Warner Books, 1997), 40-41.

NABOKOV, VLADIMIR. *PNIN* (New York: Vintage Books, 1989), 61.

O'NAN, STEWART. *SONGS FOR THE MISSING* (New York: Penguin Books, 2008), 1, 15.

PROULX, E. ANNIE. "ON THE ANTLER." IN *HEART SONGS* (New York: Simon & Schuster, 1995), 13.

ROBINSON, MARILYNNE. *GILEAD* (New York: Farrar, Straus and Giroux, 2004), 179.

WISNIEWSKI, MARK. *CONFESSIONS OF A POLISH USED CAR SALESMAN* (Davis, CA: Hi Jinx Press, 1997), 50.

_____. "3 X 5 STEVE." IN *ALL WEEKEND WITH THE LIGHTS ON* (Chantilly, VA: Leaping Dog Press, 2001), 45,48.

_____. *SHOW UP, LOOK GOOD* (Arlington, VA: Gival Press, 2011), 7, 170.

WOODRELL, DANIEL. *WINTER'S BONE* (New York: Bay Back Books, 2006), 8.

CHAPTER FOURTEEN

BISSELL, TOM. "A BRIDGE UNDER WATER." IN *BEST AMERICAN SHORT STORIES 2011* (Boston: Houghton Mifflin Harcourt, 2011), 41.

DICKEY, JAMES. *DELIVERANCE* (New York: Dell Publishing, 1994), 160.

FITZGERALD, F. SCOTT. "THE RICH BOY." IN *BABYLON REVISED AND OTHER STORIES* (New York: Charles Scribner's Sons, 1960), 152.

MCBREARTY, ROBERT GARNER. "FIRST DAY." IN *LET THE BIRDS DRINK IN PEACE* (Denver, CO: Conundrum Press, 2011), 57, 60.

MCCARTHY, CORMAC. *THE ROAD* (New York: Vintage Books, 2006), 184.

SALINGER, J.D. *THE CATCHER IN THE RYE* (New York: Little, Brown, 1991), 173.

SOLZHENITSYN, ALEXANDER. *ONE DAY IN THE LIFE OF IVAN DENISOVICH* (New York: New American Library, 2008), 68.

CHAPTER FIFTEEN

CLARK, GEOFFREY. *TWO, TWO, LILY-WHITE BOYS* (Pasadena, CA: Red Hen Press, 2012), 5.

HEMINGWAY, ERNEST. *THE SUN ALSO RISES* (New York: Charles Scribner's Sons, 1954), 144.

NABOKOV, VLADIMIR. *PNIN* (New York: Vintage Books, 1989), 7, 25.

INDEX